D1447441

MARXIST GOVERNMENTS

A World Survey

Volume 2   Cuba – Mongolia

Also edited by Bogdan Szajkowski

MARXIST GOVERNMENTS

MARXIST GOVERNMENTS

A World Survey

Volume 2   Cuba – Mongolia

Edited by

BOGDAN SZAJKOWSKI
Lecturer in Politics and Comparative Communism
University College, Cardiff

St. Martin's Press   New York

Printed in Hong Kong
First published in the United States of America in 1981

Volume 1   Albania – The Congo   ISBN 0–312–51857–9
Volume 2   Cuba – Mongolia   ISBN 0–312–51858–7
Volume 3   Mozambique – Yugoslavia   ISBN 0–312–51859–5

Library of Congress Cataloging in Publication Data

Main entry under title:

Marxist governments.

    Includes indexes.
    CONTENTS: v. 1.   Albania – The Congo.
– v. 2.   Cuba – Mongolia. – v. 3.   Mozambique – Yugoslavia.
    1. Communist state. 2.   Communist countries –
Politics and government. I.   Szajkowski, Bogdan.
JC474.M3512   1980   320.9′171′7   79–25471

088039

FOR VARA

Contents

List of Maps

List of Figures

List of Tables

Preface

The growth in the number, global significance and ideological and political impact of countries ruled by parties which subscribe to the principles of Marxism-Leninism has presented students of politics with an increasing challenge. In meeting this challenge, Western commentators have put forward a dazzling profusion of terms, models, programmes and varieties of interpretation. It is against the background of this profusion that the present comprehensive survey of the Marxist-Leninist regimes is offered.

This collection, in three volumes, is envisaged as a textbook and to some extent reference book on the governments and politics of these states. Each of the monographs in these volumes was prepared by a specialist on the country concerned. Thus, twenty-five scholars from all over the world have contributed monographs which are based on first-hand knowledge. The geographical diversity of the authors, combined with the fact that as a group they represent many disciplines of social science, gives their individual analyses, and the collection as a whole, an additional and unique dimension. Each volume contains short biographical notes on the relevant authors.

The collection, which is organised alphabetically by country, is preceded by two theoretical chapters. The first, 'The Communist Movement: from Monolith to Polymorph', by outlining the history and development of the study of the Marxist-Leninist regimes, suggests that a radically new approach be taken to the study of the politics of communism. The second chapter, on the meaning of a Marxist regime, examines the theoretical parameters of the collection.

Three regimes have had to be omitted. In the case of the Democratic Republic of Afghanistan and the Democratic Republic of Madagascar, this was more for reasons of insufficient data than because their Marxist-Leninist orthodoxy was in dispute. Also excluded from the analysis is the communist government of San Marino, which was voted into office when the preparation of this collection was in its final stages.

It is hoped in subsequent editions to include chapters on the communist-led state governments in India, the communist parties' experiences in post-war West European governments, and the communist-led local councils in Italy, France, the Federal Republic of Germany and Portugal.

Each of the twenty-five scholars who contributed to this collection was asked to analyse such topics as the governmental structure, including the constitutional framework, the system of elections, the ruling party – variously called communist, labour, socialist or workers' – other mass organisations, party state relations, the economy, domestic policies and foreign relations, as well as any features peculiar to the country and/or party under discussion. The exceptions to the pattern are the chapters on the USSR and China, where the wealth of material available could not be satisfactorily presented within the available space, and the article on Ethiopia, where the Marxist-Leninist experiment is still very new and does not yet permit extensive analysis.

Every effort has been made by the contributors to compile and present data on party and mass-organisation membership, electoral returns and multiple office-holding, except in the few cases where no such data exist.

In the preparation of this collection I have been given help by many people, some of whom should be singled out for special acknowledgement.

I am most grateful for the help afforded me by the Hon. Dr Abdulai Conteh, Minister for Foreign Affairs, Sierra Leone; Dr Thomas G. Hart of the Swedish Institute of International Affairs; Dr Tom Keenoy of University College, Cardiff; Dr Gary Troeller of the United Nations High Commission for Refugees; and Mr Richard Hodder-Williams of the University of Bristol.

I am grateful to all the contributors. Special thanks are due to Mr Michael Waller, Dr Ronald Hill, Ms Laura Summers, Professor Peter Schwab, Mr Fred Singleton and Dr Leslie Holmes.

Very special thanks are also due to Mrs Val Dobie for her help with the manuscripts, to Mr Tom Dawkes for his help in compiling the indexes, and to Mr Michael Breaks, the Social Science Librarian at University College, Cardiff, for his advice. I would also like to thank Miss Valery Brooks and her colleagues at Macmillan for their help in seeing these books through the press.

I am also very grateful to Mrs Jeanne Moorsom, whose house, The Coppice, proved to be the perfect place in which to write and was a most welcome refuge from the noise of my otherwise lovable children.

All the maps in this collection have been superbly drawn by Mrs Margaret Millen of the Department of Geology of University College,

Cardiff; her patience and endeavour were very much appreciated.

Above all, my very special gratitude goes to my wife, Martha, whose encouragement and help have been invaluable throughout the many months of work on these volumes.

4 January 1979   Bogdan Szajkowski
Dinas Powis

List of Abbreviations

Note: Owing to their great familiarity, abbreviations such as km., vol., EEC, US and USSR are omitted from this list.

AEPA	All-Ethiopian Peasant Association
ANAP	National Association of Small Farmers (Cuba)
CC	Central Committee
CCP	Czechoslovak Communist Party
CDR	Committee for the Defence of the Revolution (Cuba)
CDU	Christian Democratic Union [Federal Republic of Germany]
CELU	Confederation of Ethiopian Labour Unions
CIA	Central Intelligence Agency (USA)
Comecon	Council for Mutual Economic Assistance
Comintern	Communist International
CPH	Communist Party of Hungary
CPK	Communist Party of Kampuchea
CPSU	Communist Party of the Soviet Union
ČSSR	Československa Socialistika Republica [Czechoslovak Socialist Republic]
CTC	Confederation of Cuban Workers
DDR	Deutsche Demokratische Republik [German Democratic Republic]
DPRK	Democratic People's Republic of Korea
DR	Directorio Revolucionario [Revolutionary Directorate] (Cuba)
DSF	Association for German-Soviet Friendship [German Democratic Republic]
EDU	Ethiopian Democratic Union
ELF	Eritrean Liberation Front (Ethiopia)
ENDRP	Ethiopian National Democratic Revolution Programme
EPLF	Eritrean People's Liberation Front (Ethiopia)

EPRP	Ethiopian People's Revolutionary Party
FDGB	[Trade Union Collective Organisation] (GDR)
FDJ	Freie Deutsche Jugend [Free German Youth] (GDR)
FMC	[Federation of Cuban Women]
FRG	Federal Republic of Germany
GDR	German Democratic Republic
HSWP	Hungarian Socialist Workers' Party
ICP	Indochinese Communist Party
KCP	Korean Communist Party [southern branch]
KISz	Kommunista Ifjùsàgi Szöversèg [Communist Youth Movement] (Hungary)
KJVD	Young Communist League of Germany
KPD	Kommunistische Partei Deutschlands [German Communist Party]
KSČ	Komunisticka Strana Československa [Czechoslovak Communist Party]
KWP	Korean Workers' Party
LPDR	Lao People's Democratic Republic
LPRP	Lao People's Revolutionary Party
M 26/7	Movimiento de 26 de julio [26 July Movement] (Cuba)
MPR	Mongolian People's Republic
MPRP	Mongolian People's Revolutionary Party
MSzM	Magyar Szocialista Munkáspárt [Hungarian Socialist Workers' Party]
NKCP	Korean Communist Party [northern branch]
NLH	Neo Lao Haksat [Lao Patriotic Front]
NPCC	National Political Consultative Council (Laos)
NUFSK	National United Front for the Salvation of Kampuchea
OAU	Organisation of African Unity
OPEC	Organisation of Petroleum Exporting Countries
OPP	Organ of People's Power (Cuba)
ORI	Organizaciones Revolucionarias Integradas [Integrated Revolutionary Organisations] (Cuba)
PAIGC	Partito Africano de Independência de Guiné e Cabo Verde [African Independence Party of Guinea and Cape Verde]
PCC	Partido Comunista de Cuba [Cuban Communist Party]

PMAC	Provisional Military Administrative Committee (Ethiopia)
POMOA	Provisional Office for Mass Organisational Affairs (Ethiopia)
PPF	People's Patriotic Front (Hungary)
PSP	Partido Socialista Popular [Popular Socialist Party] (Cuba)
PURS	Partido Unido de la Revolución Socialista [United Party of the Socialist Revolution] (Cuba)
RLG	Royal Lao Government
ROK	Republic of Korea
RSFSR	Russian Soviet Federative Socialist Republic
SED	Sozialistische Einheitspartei Deutschlands [Socialist Unity Party of Germany] (GDR)
SPD	Sozialdemokratische Partei Deutschlands [German Social Democratic Party]
SR	Socialist Republic
TLM	Tigre Liberation Movement (Ethiopia)
UJC	[Union of Young Communists] (Cuba)
URC	Union Revolucionaria Comunista [Revolutionary Communist Union] (Cuba)
WSLF	Western Somali Liberation Front
WTO	Warsaw Treaty Organisation

Notes on the Editor
and Contributors

BOGDAN SZAJKOWSKI was educated in Eastern Europe and at the Centre for Russian and East European Studies at Birmingham University. He conducted his postgraduate research at King's College, Cambridge, and St Antony's College, Oxford. Subsequently he was appointed to a lectureship in Comparative Communism at the Australian National University in Canberra. He has also taught at University College, Dublin, and is now Lecturer in Politics and Comparative Communism at University College, Cardiff. His writings on contemporary communist affairs have appeared in professional journals and the press, and he has extensive broadcasting experience. He is the editor of the annual volume *Documents in Communist Affairs*.

BRUCE CUMINGS was educated at the Universities of Denison, Indiana and Columbia, where he received his Ph.D in 1975. He has received several academic awards and fellowships and has been conducting research on Korea since 1968. Dr Cumings has taught at several universities in the United States, including the University of Indiana and the University of Washington, where he is now Assistant Professor. He has published extensively on Korea and is at present working on a book on the origins of the Korean War.

BASIL DAVIDSON is a writer, historian and student of Africa; sometime Visiting Professor at the Universities of Ghana, California at Los Angeles, and Edinburgh; Hon. Research Fellow, University of Birmingham (Centre of West African Studies); Simon Senior Research Fellow, University of Manchester, 1975–6; Hon. D Litt., University of Ibadan; Associate Member, Academie des Sciences d'Outre-Mer, Paris. Published books immediately relevant to his contribution to this book include *The Liberation of Guiné: Aspects of an African Revolution* (London and Baltimore: Penguin African Library, 1969; also in other languages); *In the Eye of the Storm: Angola's People* (London: Longman, 1972; New York: Doubleday, 1972; also in other languages);

Africa in Modern History: The Search for a New Society (London: Allen Lane, 1978; [under the title *Let Freedom Come*] Boston, Mass.: Atlantic–Little, Brown, 1978; also in other languages).

WILLIAM LEOGRANDE is Assistant Professor of Government at American University, Washington, D.C. He is the author of several articles and essays on Cuban politics. He received his MA and Ph.D in political science from the Maxwell School, Syracuse University. Among his recent works are 'Continuity and Change in the Cuban Political Elite', *Cuban Studies*, VIII, no. 2 (July 1978); 'Mass Participation in Socialist Cuba', in John A. Booth and Mitchell Seligson (eds), *Political Participation in Latin America: Citizen and the State* (New York: Holmes and Meier, 1978); and 'A Bureaucratic Approach to Civil–Military Relations in Communist Systems: The Case of Cuba', in Dale Herspring and Ivan Volgyes (eds), *Civil–Military Relations in Communist Systems* (Boulder, Col.: Westview Press, 1978).

URGUNGE ONON was born in 1919 in Inner Mongolia and was educated in Manchuria and at Toyo University in Tokyo, where he obtained his diploma in political science. In 1948 he joined the Walter Hines Page School of International Relations at the Johns Hopkins University, Baltimore, where he worked with Professor Owen Lattimore. Subsequently he worked at Georgetown University, Washington, D.C., and since 1963 he has been a lecturer at the University of Leeds and now heads the Mongolian Studies Programme. He has published extensively on Mongolia and translated and annotated (together with W. A. Brown) the official *History of the Mongolian People's Republic 1917–1966* (Cambridge, Mass., and London: Harvard University Press, 1976). Other publications include *My Childhood in Mongolia* (London: Oxford University Press, 1972); (with Owen Lattimore), *Nationalism and Revolution in Mongolia* (Leiden: Brill, 1955); *Mongolian Heroes of the Twentieth Century* (New York: AMS Press, 1976); and *Manchu-Chinese Colonial Rule in Northern Mongolia* (London: C. Hurst, forthcoming).

ALEX PRAVDA was born in Prague in 1947 but left Czechoslovakia with his family in 1948 and was educated in England. Having read history at Balliol College, Oxford, he went on to complete a doctoral dissertation on the Czechoslovak Reform Movement in 1968 at St Antony's College, Oxford, in 1972. His publications include (as co-editor) *Czechoslovakia: the Party and the People* (London: Allen Lane, 1973); and *Reform and Change in the Czechoslovak Political System: January–August 1968*, Sage Research Papers in the Social Sciences,

Contemporary European Studies, vol. III (London and Beverley Hills, 1975). Dr Pravda is at present engaged in writing a comparative study on workers and politics in communist states. He lectures in politics at the University of Reading.

GEORGE SCHÖPFLIN is a joint lecturer in the Political Institutions of Eastern Europe at the London School of Economics and the School of Slavonic and Eastern European Studies, University of London. Formerly on the staff of the BBC, he has travelled extensively in Eastern Europe and is a regular visitor there. He has published widely on contemporary political problems involving the area, notably on nationalism and national minorities. He edited *The Soviet Union and Eastern Europe: A Handbook* (London: Anthony Blond, 1970) and wrote *The Hungarians of Rumania* (Minority Rights Group, 1978), as well as contributed chapters on Hungary to the following symposia: A. H. Brown and J. Gray (eds), *Political Culture and Political Change in Communist States* (London: Macmillan, 1977); M. McCauley (ed.), *Communist Power in Europe 1944–49* (London: Macmillan, 1977); B. Vágó (ed.), *Jewish Assimilation in Modern Times* (forthcoming); and R. Tőkés (ed.), *Opposition in Eastern Europe* (forthcoming). Articles by him on Croatian and Romanian nationalism have been published in *Survey* (1973 and 1974). In addition, he has written numerous articles in the daily and weekly press on Eastern Europe, and broadcasts regularly.

PETER SCHWAB is Associate Professor of Political Science at the State University of New York, College at Purchase. He received his Ph.D in political science from the New School for Social Research in 1969. Dr Schwab has published widely on the area of Ethiopia and the Horn of Africa. Among his major works are *Decision Making in Ethiopia* (London: Fairleigh Dickenson University Press, 1972) and *Human Rights: Cultural and Ideological Perspectives* (New York: Praeger, 1978). He has also written a critical analysis of the US government, *Is America Necessary?* (St Paul, Minn., 1976). Soon to be published is his most recent work, *Haile Selassie: Ethiopia's Lion of Judah*. His articles on Ethiopia have appeared in *African Affairs*, the *Journal of Modern African Studies*, *Plural Societies*, *Genève-Afrique*, *East Africa Journal*, and others. Dr Schwab is a consultant on Ethiopia to the *Encyclopaedia Americana*. He lives in New York.

LAURA J. SUMMERS is Lecturer in Politics at the University of Lancaster. Born in the United States in 1945, she holds degrees from Hamline University (St Paul, Minn.) and Cornell University (Ithaca,

NY) and studied South-east Asian languages at the University of Hawaii, Yale University and the University of Paris. Before leaving the United States, she was Chairman of the Minnesota Young Democratic Farmer-Labor Party and active in the American anti-war movement. In 1973 she testified before the US Senate Foreign Relations Committee in opposition to the Nixon administration's saturation bombing of Cambodia. She has translated Dr Khieu Samphan's *Cambodia's Economy and Industrial Development* (Cornell University South-East Asia Program, 1978) and published articles on Lao, Kampuchean and French politics in *Current History, Indochina Chronicle, Bulletin of Concerned Asian Scholars, Journal of the Siam Society, Canadian Journal of Political Science* and *Collier's Encyclopedia Yearbook 1971.* She is a member of the Committee of Concerned Asian Scholars.

H ANS W ASSMUND studied at the Universities of Hamburg, Berlin and Paris and conducted his postgraduate work at the Universities of Indiana and Columbia. He received his doctorate from the Free University of Berlin in 1971. Since 1972 he has been teaching political science at the University of the Saarland in Saarbrücken, where he is at present a reader. He has been Visiting Professor at the University of Missouri and Kennedy Fellow at the Centre for European Studies at Harvard University. His publications include *Kontinuität im Wandel – Bestimmungsfaktoren der sowjetischen Deutschlandpolitik in der Nach-Stalin-Zeit* ('Continuity in Change – Determining Factors of Soviet Policy toward Germany in the Post-Stalin Period') (Cologne and Vienna, 1974); *Revolutionstheorien – Eine Einführung* ('Theories of Revolution – An Introduction') (Munich: C. H. Beck, 1978); and several articles on international affairs.

9 Republic of Cuba

WILLIAM LEOGRANDE

Cuba, the largest island of the Greater Antilles chain, lies less than 100 miles off the southern tip of Florida. The island has long been of prime strategic interest to the United States, both because of its proximity and because it commands the approaches to the Panama Canal.

Cuba's tropical location is ideally suited for agriculture. Its excellent climate and soil conditions favour the cultivation of cane sugar, a commodity which has been the mainstay of the Cuban economy since the colonial era.

Cuba's indigenous population was exterminated during the Spanish conquest, and African slaves were imported during the colonial period to work the sugar plantations. By 1820, 40 per cent of the population were slaves, and an additional 20 per cent were former slaves. Fearing a repetition of the Haitian slave revolt, Cuba failed to take up arms against Spain in the 1820s, when the rest of Latin America became independent. A ten-year war of independence, from 1868 to 1878, ended in failure, and it was not until 1898 that Cuba succeeded in gaining independence.[1]

Even then, Cuban nationalism was frustrated by the intervention of the United States. After assisting Cuban insurrectionists to put an end to Spanish rule in 1898, the United States reduced Cuba to *de facto* protectorate status.[2] Though the island was granted nominal sovereignty, the imposition of the Platt amendment to the Cuban Constitution granted the United States the right of intervention to maintain order and safeguard US interests. Those interests were primarily economic. At the turn of the century, US investment in the Cuban economy was massive, second only to that in Mexico. Subsequent US military interventions and political manipulations were common, rendering Cuba's post-independence governments impotent, and giving Cuban nationalism its distinctly anti-US character.[3] Political

237

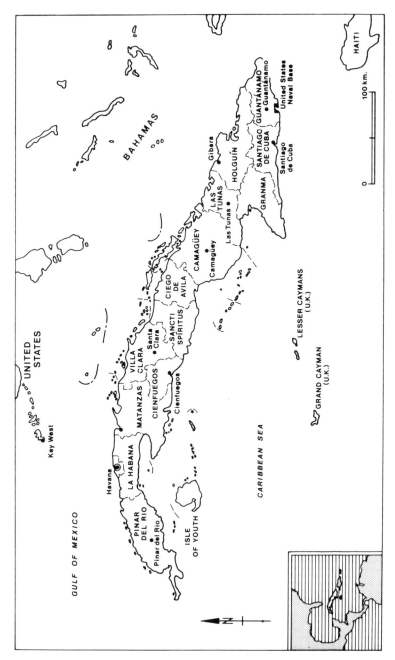

Cuba: provincial boundaries

corruption and political violence were endemic in the first half of the twentieth century.

THE CUBAN COMMUNIST MOVEMENT PRIOR TO 1959

Since the Cuban economy depended almost totally on the production and export of sugar, the collapse of international trade during the world depression of the 1930s demolished the Cuban economy and provoked an upsurge in social turmoil. Founded in 1925, the Cuban Communist Party (Partido Comunista de Cuba, PCC) grew rapidly into one of the largest and most influential Marxist-Leninist parties in Latin America.[4] By 1930 the PCC had become the dominant political force in the Cuban labour movement, a position it retained until the unions were purged by the government in 1947.

The Party's most militant period came in the 1930s, when it was an important element in the revolutionary opposition that overthrew the Machado dictatorship in 1933. But, rather than support the reformist administration of Grau San Martín, the PCC remained in opposition, calling for a worker's government and forming soviets among sugar workers in the countryside. This proved to be a tactical error, as Grau's government was soon overthrown from the Right, at US instigation, by a military coup.

During the Popular Front period of the Communist International, the PCC reached a *modus vivendi* with the government of Fulgencio Batista. The Party was legalised in 1939, changing its name to the Revolutionary Communist Union (Unión Revolucionaria Communista, URC). It participated in drafting the socially activist constitution of 1940 and joined with Batista in an electoral coalition which won the subsequent elections. During the Second World War the Cuban communists became the first in Latin America to receive ministerial posts in the government. Shortly thereafter, the URC changed names once again, to become the Popular Socialist Party (Partido Socialista Popular, PSP), and by 1946 could claim 10 per cent of the voter registration.

The PSP's decline began in the mid 1940s. The Autenticos Party, founded by Grau San Martín after his ousting in 1933, won the 1944 election. In 1947, coincident with the outbreak of the cold war internationally, the Autenticos launched a campaign of repression against the PSP, driving it underground once again, and there it remained until 1959. When Batista returned to power by military coup in 1952, the PSP opposed his suspension of the Constitution, but, having lost much of their influence in the labour movement, could mount no significant resistance. The PSP's prestige suffered during the 1950s because its role in the struggle against Batista was marginal. The Party regarded Fidel Castro's 26 July Movement (Movimiento de 26 de julio, M 26/7) as adventurist, and did not even publicly endorse the guerrilla war until 1958.

THE TRANSITION TO SOCIALISM, 1959–61

The revolutionary coalition which took power when Batista fled on 1 January 1959 was held together solely by its opposition to the dictatorship. When faced with issues of how Cuba ought to be governed, the coalition disintegrated rapidly. Three issues polarised the victorious revolutionaries into opposing camps: (1) how much social reform the new government ought to promote; (2) what Cuba's future political and social relations with the United States ought to be; and (3) whether the communists, the PSP, ought to be allowed into the government. On the Left stood the student Revolutionary Directorate (Directorio Revolucionario, DR) and much of the rebel army, under guerrilla commanders Che Guevara and Raúl Castro. On the Right stood the politicians of the old political parties and the leaders of the Civic Resistance (the urban wing of the M 26/7). Between these increasingly hostile groups was the *líder máximo* of the revolution, Fidel Castro.[5]

As it became clear that the Right opposed even marginal social reforms, and, as US hostility became manifest, Castro moved closer to the Left. His immense personal authority and prestige assured the eventual triumph of socialism in Cuba. Nationalisations of both foreign and domestic enterprises proceeded apace in late 1960 and early 1961 until finally, at the time of the ill fated US-sponsored Bay of Pigs invasion, Castro declared that the Cuban revolution was a socialist revolution. Only then was the PSP acknowledged as an equal partner in the new coalition of the DR and the left wing of the M 26/7.

LAYING THE FOUNDATIONS OF SOCIALISM IN CUBA, 1961–5

Once the struggle over Cuba's future had been resolved in favour of a socialist path of development, the leaders of the revolution faced two central problems: the creation of a planned economy, and the creation of a new socialist polity.

The economic problem was met with great enthusiasm. Early policies aimed at boosting production by increasing demand had been highly successful, since the pre-revolutionary economy had substantial unused capacity that could be drawn into production. The euphoria of early successes led to the adoption of an ambitious development plan.[6] Cuba would diversify agriculture to overcome its dependence on sugar, while at the same time pursuing a heavy industrialisation programme. All this would be accomplished while the standard of living continued to rise. Any minor balance-of-payments problem that might result would be short-term, and would be covered by credits from Cuba's new found friends in the socialist bloc, especially the Soviet Union.

The strategy of balanced growth, however, proved to be unworkable. Agriculture diversification away from sugar caused serious declines in foreign-exchange earnings. Combined with the costs of rapid industrialisation, this generated an intolerably severe and persistent trade deficit. Domestically, the rapidity of nationalisation and the inexperience of Cuba's new administrators generated chaos rather than a planned economy. Production fell, and with it the standard of living. Finally, in 1963, the revolutionary leadership abandoned hopes for rapid industrialisation, replacing the balanced growth strategy with an unbalanced strategy based upon expanding rather than reducing sugar production.

Building a new set of political institutions proved to be as difficult as building a planned economy. Initially, the revolutionaries dismantled the administrative apparatus of the old regime and replaced it with the embryonic administrative structure developed by the rebel army during the guerrilla war. The result was a thorough lack of co-ordination and control when the rebels began to administer the entire country – a malady the Cubans dubbed 'guerrilla administration'. To alleviate these deficiencies, strict regulations were imposed on local administrators, an over-compensation which led, in turn, to a loss of local initiative and 'bureaucratism'. Despite numerous institutional reorganisations aimed at overcoming administrative red tape and inefficiency, the problem of bureaucratism persisted into the late 1960s.[7]

But nowhere were the difficulties of creating a new polity clearer than in the attempts to build a new communist party.[8] In 1961, the PSP, DR and M 26/7 merged to form the Integrated Revolutionary Organisations (Organizaciones Revolucionarias Integradas, ORI). Initially the leadership of the ORI was dominated by former PSP members, since only the

Marxist Governments

PSP had the apparatus and expertise to build a new party. As the construction of the ORI proceeded, however, it became clear that these officials, led by Aníbal Escalante, were packing the new apparatus with former PSP members to the virtual exclusion of other revolutionary veterans. In March 1962, after several months of personal investigation, Castro publicly denounced Escalante's attempt to dominate the new party through bureaucratic manipulation, and the ORI was dismantled.[9]

The second attempt to build a new party began immediately, but this time it was constructed from the ground up. Members were chosen by the 'mass method', by which workers nominate outstanding co-workers as candidates for membership and then ratify the Party's final recruitment decisions. This recruitment method is still used today.[10]

The new party was initially called the United Party of the Socialist Revolution (Partido Unido de la Revolución Socialista, PURS). By 1965 the basic apparatus had been built; the Party was then formally inaugurated and its name was changed to the Communist Party of Cuba (Partido Comunista de Cuba, PCC).

The Cubans' initial negative experiences with new political institutions left a legacy which persisted throughout the 1960s. Fidel Castro's charismatic authority was the revolution's most valuable political resource.[11] It eased the transition to socialism and allowed the regime to survive even serious errors of economic policy with its base of popular support largely intact. Thus, the revolutionary leadership was hesitant to routinise Castro's appeal by institutionalising the political process, especially when the early experiments at institution-building turned out so badly. As a result, Cuban political institutions remained 'provisional' throughout the first decade of revolutionary government, built not to provide an enduring structure for politics, but rather to serve the immediate needs of the leadership.[12] When circumstances changed, the leadership reorganised the polity's institutions.

For example, the PCC remained extremely weak throughout the 1960s, operating without either programme or statutes. By 1969 its membership numbered only 55,000 (0·7 per cent of the population), and it had yet to hold a Party congress. Only the very largest work centres had Party organisations, and even these were disorganised and poorly co-ordinated.[13] Rather than directing the political process, the PCC was essentially an organisational extension of Fidel Castro's personal authority.

Only the military was institutionalised, as it had to be in order to defend the island in the face of US hostility. Consequently, the military came to be an extremely important participant in politics, especially in the latter half of the decade.[14]

BUILDING SOCIALISM AND COMMUNISM SIMULTANEOUSLY, 1966–70

By 1966, the economy had largely recovered the ground lost by planning difficulties in 1961–3, but its severe balance of payments deficit persisted. Eliminating the deficit became the focus of development policy. The unbalanced growth strategy called for an expansion of sugar exports as the means to this end, and the revolutionary leadership established an economic goal that was to be the symbolic measuring rod of the revolution's progress: Cuba would produce a record 10 million tons of sugar in 1970. Meeting this target required vast investments to expand the capacity of the sugar sector, and every other economic sector, including consumer goods, was relegated to second place. The period 1966–70 was one of extreme austerity, with investment reaching 35 per cent of the gross material product.[15]

Politically, such austerity was to be made possible by the rapid creation of the 'new socialist man', whose hard work and self-sacrifice would be motivated by moral rather than material incentives – by revolutionary *consciencia*. With their strength of revolutionary will, Cubans would overcome the objective economic conditions of underdevelopment and build both socialism and communism simultaneously. In pursuit of this policy, wage differentials were levelled, work norms were abolished, and voluntary labour campaigns were expanded. Though Che Guevara had left the island by 1966, the policies of this period are clearly those he had advocated since 1963.[16]

The system of moral incentives proved to be unworkable. Despite the leadership's best attempts to stir the population's revolutionary fervour, austerity was accompanied by declines in productivity and a frightening rise in work absenteeism. This in turn caused further production losses and greater austerity, as planning targets slipped further and further from realisation. By 1968 the moral incentive programme had clearly failed. In addition, the government bureaucracy's weakness and inefficiency made it incapable of directing the massive economic effort required to produce 10 million tons of sugar in 1970.

The revolutionary leadership turned to the only institution that was sufficiently well organised to direct the economy – the armed forces. From 1968 to 1970, the military essentially took over management of the economy, both to improve administrative efficiency and to instil military discipline into the lagging work force. But even the military was incapable of stemming the rapid collapse of productivity, and in 1970 Cuba was only able to produce 8·5 million tons of sugar.[17]

INSTITUTIONALISATION AND DEMOCRATISATION, 1970–9

The failure to meet the goal on which the revolutionary leadership had staked its prestige and the prestige of the revolution was a devastating blow. Though 8·5 million tons was a record harvest, it was purchased at the expense of the rest of the economy. Production in every other sector declined precipitously, and popular unrest over five years of unrelenting austerity was at its peak.

The revolutionary leadership responded to this crisis with a major shift in economic policy and a thoroughgoing reorganisation of the political system. To bolster production, material incentives – including wage differentials and work norms – were reintroduced. Priority was given to economic recovery in the consumption sector in order to ease the austerity and hence to recover some of the popular support lost over the preceding few years.[18]

While the unbalanced growth strategy emphasising sugar was retained, growth targets were revised downward, and expansion in that sector was no longer to be pursued at the expense of other sectors. These policy revisions, combined with improvements in the planning process, proved to be largely successful. Economic management was returned to the civilian planning apparatus, and by 1974 the economy had regained an equilibrium that allowed for modest but sustained growth through the 1970s.

Politically, the revolution entered a 'new phase' in 1970 marked by a strengthening of all political institutions and an expansion of mass participation in the policy process. After improving its internal co-ordination and control, the PCC finally began to take over direction of the political system. In 1975 it held its First Congress, adopting both statutes and a programme. In 1976 a new constitution was ratified, providing for an extensive reorganisation of the government bureaucracy, including the creation of the Organs of People's Power – the first elected representative assemblies in the revolutionary period. This strengthening of civilian political institutions not only reduced the revolution's dependence on the charismatic authority of Fidel Castro, but also served to reduce the military's extensive influence in non-military matters.[19]

THE COMMUNIST PARTY OF CUBA

Organisation

The organisation of the PCC is closely modelled on that of the Soviet and Eastern European parties. The Party Congress, when it is in session, is the highest Party authority. Between congresses the Central Committee (CC) is the authoritative body, and between CC plenums the Political Bureau acts in the name of the CC as its executive body. Administrative matters are handled by the Secretariat of the CC. In 1978 the CC was composed of 110 full members and twelve alternates (112 full members were elected at the First Congress in 1975, but two have since died). The Political Bureau has thirteen members, and the Secretariat nine.

The hierarchical organisation of the PCC apparatus parallels the administrative division of the island. There are fourteen provincial Party committees, and 169 municipal committees, each headed by an executive committee. The base unit of the PCC is the Party cell, organised at work centres and educational institutions. The basic functions of the cells are to recruit new members, and provide ideological guidance and political education, encourage the improvement of overall educational level of both members and non-members, carry out the directives of higher Party bodies, oversee members' adherence to Party statutes, discipline violations of those statutes, keep the Party in close contact with the working class, oversee factory management, and stimulate production.[20]

The Party has had three distinct leading bodies: from 1961 to 1965, when it was the PURS, the Party was headed by a National Directorate. This body was replaced in 1965 with the first CC, whose membership was appointed by Fidel Castro. A new CC was elected at the First Congress in 1975. An analysis of the institutional affiliations of these three bodies demonstrates the tremendous influence enjoyed by the military during the 1960s and the relative weakness of the Party apparatus (Table 9.1). In the 1975 CC the military's representation had declined substantially, while the number of members drawn from the PCC apparatus had risen noticeably.

TABLE 9.1 Institutional representation (per cent) in the Cuban political elite, 1962–75

	1962 National Directorate (N = 25)	1965 CC (N = 100)	Pre-Congress CC (N = 90)	1975 CC (N = 124)	New members, 1975 CC (N = 47)
Party apparatus	16·0	12·0	24·0	29·0	29·8
Government apparatus	40·0	22·0	33·3	28·2	19·1
Military/ police	32·0	57·0	35·6	29·8	27·7
Mass organisations	4·0	6·0	3·3	7·3	12·8
Cultural/ scientific	8·0	3·0	3·3	4·8	6·4
Other/ unknown	0·0	0·0	0·0	0·8	4·3
Total	100·0	100·0	99·9	99·9	100·1

Source: W. M. LeoGrande, 'Continuity and Change in the Cuban Political Elite', *Cuban Studies,* VIII, no. 2 (July 1978) 1–33.

Membership

Party members are recruited both from the Union of Young Communists (UJC) and directly from the nation's work centres. The 'mass method' of nomination by one's co-workers is still used as the means of direct recruitment into both the PCC and UJC. In 1975, approximately 40 per cent of new members entered the PCC from the UJC.

The weakness of the PCC during the 1960s is reflected in its small size, and its strengthening during the 1970s is likewise reflected in the very rapid expansion of Party membership from 51,000 to over 200,000 in just a few years (Table 9.2).

Data on the social composition of the PCC are very sparse.

Women constitute approximately 15 per cent of PCC membership. This figure is relatively unchanged from the 1960s, but the UJC is 30 per cent female, so the number of women in the PCC will probably rise in the future. Table 9.3 provides a breakdown of the distribution of Party membership by occupation.

Republic of Cuba 247

TABLE 9.2 Party membership in Cuba, 1962–76

	Total members	Cells	Members as % of population
1962	2,109	331	0·03
1963	16,002	2,209	0·2
1964	35,558	4,189	0·4
1965	50,000	n.a.	0·5
1969	55,000	n.a.	0·6
1970	100,000	n.a.	1·2
1971	101,000	n.a.	1·2
1972	122,000	n.a.	1·4
1973	153,000	14,360	1·7
1974	170,000	16,000	1·9
1975	186,995	n.a.	2·0
1976	202,807	n.a.	2·2

Source: W. M. LeoGrande, *The Development of the Party System in Revolutionary Cuba* (1978).

TABLE 9.3 Composition of the PCC, 1975

Occupation	% of PCC membership
Workers in material production and services	35·9
Small farmers	1·8
Administrative workers	4·1
Professional and technical workers	9·2
Administrative leaders	33·4
Political leaders	8·7
Other	6·9

Source: 'Sobre la vida interna del Partido', in *Tesis y Resoluciones: Primer Congreso del Partido Comunista de Cuba* (La Habana: Departamento de Orientación Revolucionaria, 1976).

GOVERNMENT

The Constitution

The institution structure of Cuba's socialist political system was not formalised until 1976, when a new constitution was adopted by popular referendum. Between 1959 and 1976, governmental institutions underwent numerous reorganisations at the direction of the revolutionary leadership acting through the Council of Ministers – the highest governmental body during those years.

The 1976 constitution declares Cuba to be a socialist republic in which 'all power belongs to the working people', and in which the Communist Party of Cuba is 'the highest leading force of the society and of the State'. It guarantees citizens the right to employment, education, health care, and housing, and prohibits discrimination on the basis of race, colour, sex or national origin. Civil liberties, including freedom of religion, are guaranteed with the provision that none may be exercised 'contrary to the existence and objective of the socialist State' – i.e. the construction of socialism and communism.

The Organs of People's Power

The Organs of People's Power (OPP), first created nationwide in 1976, form the backbone of the State apparatus.[21] Organised at the municipal, provincial and national levels, these elected assemblies are the formal sovereign State authority. The Constitution refers to the National Assembly of People's Power as the 'supreme organ of State power'. The OPPs were organised from the base upward. Delegates to the municipal OPP assemblies are popularly elected by secret ballot in multi-candidate elections. Nominations are made by the general populace in neighbourhood meetings convened for that purpose. Delegates to the provincial assemblies and the National Assembly are elected by the municipal delegates from multi-candidate lists compiled by special election commissions. These commissions include representatives of the PCC and of the major mass organisations. Delegates serve for a three-year term, though they may be recalled at any time, and in the 1976 municipal-delegate elections voter turnout was 95 per cent.

The OPPs have authority over the administrative agencies of the State. They set policy, oversee its execution, appoint agency and enterprise administrators, and can remove them. Administrators, however, are also responsible to their administrative superiors and to nationally established policy.

The National Assembly of People's Power is headed by an executive committee, the Council of State, which consists of a President, First Vice-president, five other vice-presidents, and twenty-three other members. The President is both head of State and head of government (i.e. chief executive).

The Council of Ministers

The Council of Ministers, the highest administrative body, is headed by the President and vice-presidents, and is composed of the ministers and heads of various central-government agencies.[22] These are appointed by the National Assembly, to which the Council is constitutionally responsible. In 1976 the Council of Ministers had forty-five members, of which twenty-seven were members of the PCC Central Committee.

Party–State relations

The history of Party–State relations in socialist Cuba has been a volatile one. One of the criticisms levelled at the ORI when it was dismantled in 1961 was that it had become an 'administrative party' interfering with the operations of State agencies. With the inauguration of the PCC in 1965, regulations were promulgated delineating the proper relationship between State and Party organs, but these were often ignored in practice. From 1966 to 1968, a measure of conflict between State and Party was generated by the Party's 'struggle against bureaucratism' in State agencies. Not until 1973 was the relationship between the two institutions fully defined and enforced. The PCC plays the 'leading role' by undertaking policy initiatives, making major policy decisions, overseeing administration and making personnel recommendations.

At the highest levels, Party–State conflict is prevented by substantial overlap in personnel. Table 9.4 summarises the extent of joint membership in the highest State and Party organs. In addition, Fidel and Raúl Castro hold the highest posts not only in both State and Party, but also in the military. Fidel is President of the Republic, First Secretary of the Party, and Commander-in-Chief of the Revolutionary Armed Forces. Raúl is First Vice-president, Second Secretary of the PCC, and Minister of the Revolutionary Armed Forces.

MASS ORGANISATIONS

There are four major mass organisations in Cuba: the Committee for the Defence of the Revolution (CDR); the Confederation of Cuban Workers (CTC); the Federation of Cuban Women (FMC); and the National Association of Small Farmers (ANAP). Organised in the 1960s, these institutions have been the primary mechanism for mobilising mass participation in politics.[23]

TABLE 9.4 Personnel overlap between PCC and government leaderships, 1976

	Political Bureau members (N = 13)	Other CC members (N = 111)	All CC members (N = 124)
Council of State (N = 31)	13 (42%)[a]	17 (55%)	30 (97%)
Executive Officers (N = 7)	7 (100%)	0 (0%)	7 (100%)
Council of Ministers (N = 45)	8 (18%)	19 (42%)	27 (60%)
Executive Officers (N = 10)	6 (60%)	4 (40%)	10 (100%)

[a] Percentage of the government body's members who are also members of the Party body in question.

Source: LeoGrande, in *Cuban Studies*, VII, 2 (July 1978) pp. 1–33.

The basic structure of all four mass organisations is the same, and parallels other administrative divisions in order to facilitate co-operation between them, and between them and other political organs. Since they pursue similar tasks, the horizontal administrative division of the mass organisations along functional lines is also very similar. All, for example, include departments of public health, education, voluntary labour, and so on.

The specific tasks undertaken by the mass organisations have been as diverse as they have been numerous, changing considerably over time as the national policies and goals of the regime have changed.

The CTC (the trade unions) has the dual responsibility of representing the interest of its members in the work place, and of stimulating production. Until the 1970s the latter duty was predominant, but since the Thirteenth Congress of the CTC, in 1973, its representative function has received increasing attention.[24]

The FMC's responsibility is to integrate fully Cuban women both into the revolution and into Cuban society generally. During the 1960s its primary goal was getting women into the work force. In the 1970s it has pressed for more rapid progress in the field of women's equality and has succeeded in making this a prominent issue on the agenda of the Party leadership.

The ANAP has always been closely tied to the State agencies charged with agricultural planning, and has generally acted as a liaison between these agencies and Cuba's remaining private farmers. It is clearly less representative than the other mass organisations, and has tended in the past to act primarily as an arm of the planning apparatus.

The CDR is by far the most important of Cuba's mass organisations. It is open to all adults who support the revolution, and has always been the first place to which the leadership has turned when faced with a task requiring widespread popular mobilisation. Before the creation of the OPPs, the CDR was virtually the only institutional channel for popular input into the policy-making process. It includes over 80 per cent of the adult population, and its goal is eventually to incorporate everyone.

INTERNAL AFFAIRS

Education

Though Cuba was one of the most literate nations in Latin America before the revolution, the 75 per cent literacy rate masked huge inequalities between the urban and rural sectors. Moreover, the public education system was racked by corruption and had been in a state of decline for several decades.

Eradicating illiteracy was one of the earliest goals of the revolutionary leadership, and was largely accomplished by the National Literacy Campaign of 1961. The stress on education has continued, however; the most recent national campaign had the goal of raising everyone to at least a sixth-grade education.

Since 1959, school enrolments have more than tripled, and in 1973 educational expenditures in Cuba were at least four times the Latin American average. Adult-education and technical-training programmes proliferate, and virtually everyone in the country is involved in some sort of study programme. Improving one's educational level is regarded as an essential duty of good citizenship, and is actually a formal requisite for PCC membership. It is fair to say that education is Cuba's highest social priority, and the emphasis placed on education is probably the greatest of any country in the world.[25]

Health

Cuban health was similar to Cuban education prior to 1959. While the formal infrastructure for providing health care was one of the most developed in Latin America, extreme disparities existed between health care in urban and health care in rural areas. In the countryside, health care was largely non-existent, and the population suffered from all the traditional diseases of poverty and underdevelopment. The health sector was especially hard hit by the departure of professionals in the early 1960s; over half of Cuba's physicians emigrated as the revolution moved to the Left.

Improvement in health care has, like education, been a high priority for the revolutionary regime. Health policy combines both post-traumatic and preventative strategies. The main element of the former has been a rapid expansion of available facilities and medical personnel, especially in the rural areas. The preventative strategy has aimed at improving housing, public sanitation and nutrition, and, most importantly, at increasing public awareness of disease and disease prevention.

All Cuba's mass organisations regularly conduct vaccination campaigns, nutrition and public-sanitation classes, and so forth. The success of these efforts are reflected in mortality statistics. Cuba's infant mortality rate is the lowest in Latin America, and the island's leading causes of death are the diseases of development – cancer and arteriocoronary disease.[26]

Economy

The shift away from moral incentives after the failure of the 10 million ton sugar harvest succeeded in improving worker productivity, and from 1972 to 1976 the Cuban economy enjoyed a period of unprecedented economic growth. Decentralisation of economic management and rationalisation of the planning process have combined to improve the efficiency of the economy, but its greatest weakness – the dependence on sugar – remains. In part, the economic expansion of the early 1970s was attributable to the tremendous rise in world sugar prices. When those prices declined, the Cuban economy's expansion declined with them.

The policy decision made in 1970 to ease the austerity of the late 1960s and then, at the very least, to stabilise consumption means that investment levels (and, hence, rates of growth) are almost wholly dependent upon the export sector. This vulnerability to external forces is a continuing characteristic of Cuban political economy and constitutes its greatest weakness.[27]

EXTERNAL AFFAIRS

The rapid deterioration of US–Cuban relations following the collapse of the Batista dictatorship was rooted in the long support Batista had enjoyed from the United States.[28] The key issue on the break between the two countries, however, was the Cuban agrarian reform law of 1959, which nationalised sizable US holdings. Conflict over adequate compensation escalated into an exchange of increasingly hostile accusations between the two governments, and culminated in US cancellation of the Cuban sugar quota. This measure, by cutting off Cuba's major export market, was designed to promote changes in government policy (if not personnel) by weakening the Cuban economy.

Cuba retaliated by nationalising all US-owned enterprises, and, in the following months, most domestically owned enterprises as well. Cuba also began expanding its ties with the Soviet Union, by purchasing arms, by concluding trade agreements, and, finally, by establishing diplomatic relations.

In April 1961 the US Central Intelligence Agency sponsored the ill-fated Bay of Pigs invasion. In the wake of that debacle, the US undertook a policy of forcible containment, aimed at isolating Cuba economically and diplomatically, while striking at the island with small-scale covert military operations. Though this policy was eased somewhat in 1968, no substantial improvement in US–Cuban relations was noticeable until the early 1970s.

Despite some instances of contention (such as Soviet handling of the 1962 missile crisis), Soviet–Cuban relations remained firm throughout the 1960s and into the 1970s. The USSR continues to equip the Cuban armed forces and continues to provide Cuba with substantial economic and technical assistance. In 1966 Cuba openly sided with the Soviets in the Sino-Soviet dispute, and it has since been a strongly pro-Soviet voice in all international forums.[29] Increases in Soviet aid after the Cuban economic crisis of 1970 cemented relations between the two countries, bringing them to an unprecedented level of friendship and co-operation.

Cuban foreign policy has been a militant one since the earliest years of the revolution. During the 1960s policy was directed primarily at providing training, aid and ideological support to guerrilla movements in various Latin American countries. This 'export of revolution' reached its climax when Ernesto 'Che' Guevara, third-ranking leader of the revolution, attempted to initiate a guerrilla war in Bolivia.[30] His capture and execution, along with the consistent failure of similar guerrilla tactics, led the Cubans to reduce substantially their support for this particular strategy of promoting socialism. In the 1970s the emphasis on aiding Latin American guerrillas was replaced by a rapid expansion of Cuban aid to guerrilla movements and friendly governments in Africa.[31] In 1976 Cuba for the first time sent large numbers of regular combat troops to the aid of Agostinho Neto's government during the Angolan civil war; and in 1978 Cuba sent troops to aid the Ethiopian revolutionary government in its war with Somalia over the disputed Ogaden region.

BIOGRAPHIES

Fidel Castro Ruz, President of the Republic, was born on 13 August 1927, the son of a moderately wealthy landowner. His interest in politics was sparked at secondary school, where he first encountered the writings of José Martí, hero of Cuba's struggle for independence. In 1945 Castro entered the University of Havana to study law, and he quickly became involved in student politics. An admirer of Eduardo Chibás, founder of the Ortodoxo Party, Castro stood as an Ortodoxo candidate for Congress in the 1952 elections, which were cancelled after Batista's *coup d'état*.[32]

Castro then organised and led 135 men and women in the famous but unsuccessful attack on the Moncada barracks, 26 July 1953. The assault marked the beginning of the insurrection against Batista and elevated Castro to national prominence. After his release from prison in 1955, Castro founded the 26 July Movement, which became the foremost of the revolutionary organisations. He then spent nearly two years in exile in Mexico organising a guerrilla army to fight against Batista. They returned to Cuba in December 1956, and within two years won control of the island.

Castro was from the beginning the *líder máximo* of the revolution. He was commander of the rebel army during the insurrection, and today retains the position of Commander-in-chief of the Revolutionary Armed Forces. As President of the Republic, he also heads the government, and he has been First Secretary of the PCC since its founding in 1965.

Raúl Castro Ruz, First Vice-president and Fidel's younger brother, participated in the revolutionary struggle from its inception. A veteran of the Moncada attack, Raúl went to Mexico with Fidel and returned with him to begin the guerrilla war. During the insurrection, Raúl commanded a rebel army column of his own in the Sierra Cristal. One of the radical leaders of the 26 July Movement, Raúl was an important influence on the leftward shift of the revolution after 1959. Today, Raúl is indisputably second in command. He is Minister of the Revolutionary Armed Forces, First Vice-president of the Republic, and Second Secretary of the PCC.

BASIC FACTS ABOUT CUBA

Official name: Republic of Cuba (Republica de Cuba).

Area: 114,524 sq. km. (44,050 sq. miles).

Population (1970 census): 8,553,395.

Population density: 74·7 per sq. km.

Population distribution: 60·5 per cent urban, 39·5 per cent rural.

Membership of the CPC (1976): 202,807.

Administrative division: 13 provinces and 1 special administrative area (Isle of Pines).

Population of major towns (1970 est.): Havana (the capital), 1,755,400; Santiago de Cuba, 276,000; Camagüey, 196,900; Santa Clara, 131,500; Holguín, 131,500; Guantánamo, 130,100.

Gross social product by sector (1974): industry, 41·0 per cent; commerce, 32·8 per cent; agriculture and fishing, 10·1 per cent; construction, 9·0 per cent; transport, 6·6 per cent; communications, 0·5 per cent.

Work force (1973): 2,245,700 (agriculture and fishing, 30 per cent; industry, 20 per cent; construction, 8 per cent; transport, 7 per cent; communications, 1 per cent; commerce, 8 per cent; social services, 23 per cent; others, 3 per cent).

Main natural resources: nickel, cobalt and iron ores.

Foreign trade (1974): exports, $2,745,000; imports, $2,650,000; total, $5,395,000. (1 peso = $1·25.)

Main trading partner: USSR.

Rail network: 14,667 km.

Road network: 20,339 km. (8582 km. paved).

Universities: 3 – University of Havana, University of Santa Clara and University Centre in Camagüey, with 76,900 students in 1976.

Foreign relations: member of the UN, Comecon (since 1972) and the Conference of Non-aligned Nations. Diplomatic relations with 94 countries; 74 diplomatic commissions residing in Havana.

NOTES

1. The most comprehensive history of Cuba in English is H. Thomas, *Cuba: The Pursuit of Freedom* (1971).
2. On the US intervention, see P. S. Foner, *The Spanish–Cuban–American War and the Birth of American Imperialism* (1972).
3. R. F. Smith, *The United States and Cuba: Business and Diplomacy* (1960).
4. On the history and influence of communism in pre-revolutionary Cuba, see R. J. Alexander, *Communism in Latin America* (1957) pp. 270–94; and M. Zeitlin, 'Cuba: Revolution Without a Blueprint', in I. L. Horowitz, *Cuban Communism*, 3rd ed. (1978) pp. 199–210.
5. L. Huberman and P. Sweezy, *Cuba: Anatomy of a Revolution* (1960); J. O'Connor, *The Origins of Socialism in Cuba* (1970).
6. E. Boorstein, *The Economic Transformation of Cuba* (1968); A. R. M. Ritter, *The Economic Development of Revolutionary Cuba: Strategy and Performance* (1974); C. Mesa-Lago (ed.), *Revolutionary Change in Cuba* (1971).
7. E. Guevara, *Venceremos: The Speeches and Writings of Che Guevara* (1969) pp. 220–1. Cf. Boorstein, *Economic Transformation*, pp. 162ff.; and Ritter, *Economic Development*, pp. 248–50.
8. W. M. LeoGrande, *The Development of the Party System in Revolutionary Cuba* (1978).
9. Fidel Castro, *Fidel Castro Denounces Sectarianism* (1962); M. Zeitlin, 'Castro and Cuba's Communists', *The Nation*, CXCV, no. 14 (3 Nov 1962) 284–89.
10. The 'mass method' is described in 'La Selección del Trabajador Ejemplar', *Cuba Socialista*, no. 9 (May 1962) 129–32.
11. R. R. Fagen, 'Charismatic Authority and the Leadership of Fidel Castro', *Western Political Quarterly*, XVIII, no. 2 (June 1965) 275–84.
12. L. Huberman and P. Sweezy, *Socialism in Cuba* (1969).
13. LeoGrande, *Development of the Party System*.
14. J. Domínguez, 'The Civic Soldier in Cuba', in C. Kelleher (ed.), *Politico–military Systems* (1974); W. M. LeoGrande, 'The Politics of Revolutionary Development: Civil–Military Relations in Cuba', *Journal of Strategic Studies*, I (December 1978) 260–94; R. Dumont, *Is Cuba Socialist?* (1974).
15. Ritter, *Economic Development*.
16. See especially B. Silverman, *Man and Socialism in Cuba* (1973); and R. M. Bernardo, *The Theory of Moral Incentives in Cuba* (1971).
17. LeoGrande, *Development of the Party System*.
18. On economic policy in the 1970s, see C. Mesa-Lago, *Cuba in the 1970s* (1978); and S. Roca, 'Cuban Economic Policy in the 1970s', in Horowitz, *Cuban Communism*, pp. 265–301.
19. On the OPPs, see Harnecker, *Cuba: ¿ Dictadura o Democracia?* (1975); and W. M. LeoGrande, 'Cuba's Socialist Democracy in Theory and Practice', forthcoming in *Studies in Comparative Communism*. See also H. L. Matthews, *Revolution in Cuba* (1975); and Mesa-Lago, *Cuba in the 1970s*.
20. *Estatutos del Partido Comunista de Cuba* (1976).
21. LeoGrande, *Development of the Party System*; Harnecker, *Cuba*; L. Casals, 'On Popular Power: The Organization of the Cuban State During the Period

of Transition', *Latin American Perspectives*, II, no. 4 (1975) 78–88; *Constitution of the Organs of People's Power* (1976); and *Sobre los Organos del Poder Popular* (1976).
22. For a listing of the members of the Council of Ministers, see 'Council of Ministers', *Granma Weekly Review*, 12 Dec 1976, p. 5.
23. R. R. Fagen, *The Transformation of Political Culture in Cuba* (1969).
24. See Mesa-Lago, *Cuba in the 1970s*; Matthews, *Revolution in Cuba*; and 'Theses of the 13th Workers Congress of the CTC', *Granma Weekly Review*, 2 Sep 1973, pp. 7–12.
25. On educational policy, see S. Bowles, 'Cuban Education and Revolutionary Ideology', *Harvard Education Review*, XLII, no. 4 (Nov 1971) 473–501; *Cuba: The Educational Movement* (1970); Fagen, *Transformation*; Matthews, *Revolution in Cuba*; *Cuba Review* v, no. 2 (June 1975) – special issue on education; M. Leiner, 'Major Developments in Cuban Education', in D. P. Barkin and N. Manitzas (eds), *Cuba: The Logic of the Revolution* (1973); R. Paulston, *Cuban Rural Education* (1973).
26. On health policy, see V. Olsen, 'Confluences in Social Change: Urban Women and Health Care', *Journal of Interamerican Studies*, XVII, no. 4 (Nov 1975) 398–408; M. Roemer, 'Development of Medical Services under Social Security', *International Labour Review*, CVIII, no. 1 (July 1973) 1–24; N. P. Valdés, 'Health and Revolution in Cuba', *Science and Society*, XXXV, no. 3 (1971) 311–35.
27. Roca, in Horowitz, *Cuban Communism*.
28. See especially L. Bender, *The Politics of Hostility* (1975).
29. E. Gonzalez, 'Relationship with the Soviet Union', in Mesa-Lago, *Revolutionary Change*, pp. 81–104; D. B. Jackson, *Castro, the Kremlin, and Communism in Latin America* (1969).
30. Jackson, *Castro, the Kremlin, and Communism in Latin America*; Ernesto F. Betancourt, 'Exporting the Revolution to Latin American', in Mesa-Lago, *Revolutionary Change*, pp. 105–26; Mesa-Lago, *Cuba in the 1970s*.
31. On Cuba's African policy, see J. I. Domínguez, 'Cuban Foreign Policy', *Foreign Affairs*, LVII, no. 1 (1979), and 'The Cuban Operation in Angola', *Cuban Studies*, VIII, no. 1 (Jan 1978) 10–21; G. G. Marguez, 'Cuba en Angola: Operación Carlota', *Proceso*, Jan 1977.
32. H. Matthews, *Fidel Castro* (1969); L. Lockwood, *Castro's Cuba, Cuba's Fidel* (1967); R. Bonachea and N. P. Valdés, Introduction to *Revolutionary Struggle: The Selected Works of Fidel Castro* (1972).

BIBLIOGRAPHY

Alexander, R. J., *Communism in Latin America* (New Brunswick, N.J.: Rutgers University Press, 1957).
Barkin, David P. and Manitzas, Nita R. (eds), *Cuba: The Logic of the Revolution* (Andover, Mass.: Warner Modular Publications, 1973).
Bender, L., *The Politics of Hostility* (Hato Rey, Puerto Rico: Interamerican University Press, 1975).
Benjamin, J. R., *The United States and Cuba: Hegemony and Dependent*

Development, 1880–1934 (Pittsburgh: University of Pittsburgh Press, 1977).
Bernardo, R. M., *The Theory of Moral Incentives in Cuba* (University, Ala.: University of Alabama Press, 1971).
Black, J. K., *et al.*, *Area Handbook for Cuba* (Washington, DC: US Government Printing Office, 1976).
Blackburn, R., 'Prologue to the Cuban Revolution', *New Left Review*, no. 21 (Oct 1963) 52–91.
Bonachea, R. E., and Valdés, N. P., Introduction to *Revolutionary Struggle: The Selected Works of Fidel Castro* (Cambridge, Mass.: MIT Press, 1972).
—— (eds), *Cuba in Revolution* (New York: Doubleday, 1972).
Boorstein, E., *The Economic Transformation of Cuba* (New York: Monthly Review Press, 1968).
Bowles, S., 'Cuban Education and Revolutionary Ideology', *Harvard Education Review*, XLII, no. 4 (Nov 1971) 473–501.
Casals, L., 'On Popular Power: The Organisation of the Cuban State during the Period of Transition', *Latin American Perspectives*, II, no. 4 (1975) 78–88.
Castro, F., *Fidel Castro Denounces Sectarianism* (La Habana: Ministry of Foreign Relations, 1962).
——, *Fidel Castro Speaks*, ed. Martin Kenner and James Petras (New York: Grove Press, 1969).
——, *Discursos*, 2 vols (La Habana: Instituto Cubano del Libro, 1976).
Constitution of the Organs of People's Power (New York: Center for Cuban Studies, 1976).
Constitution of the Republic of Cuba (New York: Center for Cuban Studies, 1976).
'Council of Ministers', in *Granma Weekly Review*, 12 Dec 1976, p. 5.
Cuba: The Educational Movement (Geneva: UNESCO, 1970).
Domínguez, J. I., *Cuba: Order and Revolution* (Cambridge, Mass.: Harvard University Press, 1978).
——, 'The Civic Soldier in Cuba', in Catherine Kelleher (ed.), *Politico-military Systems* (Beverley Hills: Sage, 1974).
——, 'Institutionalization and Civil–Military Relations', *Cuban Studies*, VI, no. 1 (Jan 1976) 39–66.
——, 'The Cuban Operation in Angola', *Cuban Studies*, VIII, no. 1 (Jan 1978) 10–21.
——, 'Cuban Foreign Policy', *Foreign Affairs*, LVII, no. 1 (1979).
Dumont, R., *Is Cuba Socialist?* (New York: Viking, 1974).
Estatutos del Partido Comunista de Cuba (La Habana: Departamento de Orientación Revolucionaria del Comité Central del PCC, 1976).
Fagen, R. R., 'Charismatic Authority and the Leadership of Fidel Castro', *Western Political Quarterly*, XVIII, no. 2 (June 1965) 275–84.
——, *The Transformation of Political Culture in Cuba* (Stanford, Calif.: Stanford University Press, 1969).
First Congress of the Communist Party of Cuba: Collection of Documents (Moscow: Progress Publishers, 1976).
Foner, P. S., *The Spanish–Cuban–American War and the Birth of American Imperialism* (New York: Monthly Review Press, 1972).
Gonzalez, E., *Cuba Under Castro: The Limits of Charisma* (Boston, Mass.: Houghton-Mifflin, 1974).

———, 'Complexities of Cuban Foreign Policy', *Problems of Communism*, XXVI (Nov–Dec 1977) 1–15.

———, 'The United States and Castro: Breaking the Deadlock', *Foreign Affairs*, L (July 1972) 722–37.

Guevara. E., *Venceremos: The Speeches and Writings of Che Guevara* (New York: Simon and Schuster, 1969).

Harnecker, M., *Cuba: Dictadura o Democracia?* (Mexico City: Siglo XXI, 1975). [French ed.: *Cuba: Dictature ou Démocratie?* (Paris: Maspero, 1976).]

Horowitz, I. L., (ed.), *Cuban Communism*, 3rd ed. (New Brunswick, N.J.: Transaction, 1978).

Huberman, Leo and Sweezy, Paul, *Cuba: Anatomy of a Revolution* (New York: Monthly Review Press, 1960).

———, *Socialism in Cuba* (New York: Monthly Review Press, 1969).

Jackson, D. B., *Castro, the Kremlin, and Communism in Latin America* (Baltimore: Johns Hopkins University Press, 1969).

Junta Central de Planificación, Dirección Central de Estadística, *Anuario Estadístico de Cuba* (La Habana, annual).

LeoGrande, W. M., 'Continuity and Change in the Cuban Political Elite', *Cuban Studies*, VIII, no. 2 (July 1978) 1–32.

———, *The Development of the Party System in Revolutionary Cuba*, Monograph no. 6 of the Northwestern Pennsylvania Institute for Latin American Studies (Erie, Penn., 1978).

———, 'The Politics of Revolutionary Development: Civil–Military Relations in Cuba', *Journal of Strategic Studies*, I (December 1978) 260–94.

———, 'Cuba's Socialist Democracy in Theory and Practice', forthcoming in *Studies in Comparative Communism*.

Lockwood, L., *Castro's Cuba, Cuba's Fidel* (New York: Macmillan, 1967).

Marguez, G. G., 'Cuba en Angola: Operación Carlota', *Proceso*, Jan 1977.

Matthews, H. L., *Fidel Castro* (New York: Simon and Schuster, 1969).

———, *Revolution in Cuba* (New York: Charles Scribner's Sons, 1975).

Mesa-Lego, Carmelo, *Cuba in the 1970's*, 2nd ed. (Albuquerque: University of New Mexico Press, 1978).

——— (ed.), *Revolutionary Change in Cuba* (Pittsburgh: University of Pittsburgh Press, 1971).

———, 'Ideological, Political, and Economic Factors in the Cuban Controversy on Material vs. Moral Incentives', *Journal of Inter-American Studies and World Affairs*, XIV, no. 1 (Feb 1972) 49–111.

O'Connor, J., *The Origins of Socialism in Cuba* (New York: Cornell University Press, 1970).

Olsen, V., 'Confluences in Social Change: Urban Women and Health Care', *Journal of Interamerican Studies*, XVII, no. 4 (Nov 1975) 398–408.

Paulston, R., *Cuban Rural Education* (Pittsburgh: Pittsburgh University Press, 1973).

Ritter, A. R. M., *The Economic Development of Revolutionary Cuba: Strategy and Performance* (New York: Praeger, 1974).

Roberts, C. P. (ed.), *Cuba, 1968: Supplement to the Statistical Abstract of Latin America* (Los Angeles: UCLA Latin American Center, 1970).

Roemer, M., 'Development of Medical Services under Social Security', *International Labor Review*, CVIII, no. 1 (July 1973) 1–24.

'La Selección del Trabajador Ejemplar', *Cuba Socialista*, no. 9 (May 1962) 129–32.

Silverman, B., *Man and Socialism in Cuba: The Great Debate* (New York: Atheneum, 1973).

Smith, R. F., *The United States and Cuba: Business and Diplomacy 1917–1960* (New York: Bookman Associates, 1960).

Sobre los Organos del Poder Popular (La Habana: Departamento de Orientación Revolucionara de Comité Central del PCC, 1976).

'Theses of the 13th Workers Congress of the CTC', *Granma Weekly Review*, 2 Sep 1973, pp. 7–12.

Thomas, H., *Cuba: The Pursuit of Freedom* (New York: Harper and Row, 1971).

Valdés, N. P., 'Health and Revolution in Cuba', *Science and Society*, XXXV, no. 3 (1971) 311–35.

Zeitlin, M., 'Castro and Cuba's Communists', *The Nation*, CXCV, no. 14 (3 Nov 1962) 284–9.

——, *Revolutionary Politics and the Cuban Working Class* (New York: Harper and Row, 1970).

10 Czechoslovak Socialist Republic

ALEX PRAVDA

Together with the German Democratic Republic, Czechoslovakia is the most industrially developed and Westernised of the countries under communist rule. Largely because of their strategically sensitive location, the Czech lands of Bohemia and Moravia have a long and crisis-ridden history. More than four centuries of independence came to an end with the defeat of the Czech nobility at the battle of the White Mountain in 1620. Thereafter the Czechs were absorbed into the Hapsburg Empire and became an important part of its successor, the Austro-Hungarian Empire. The collapse of Austria–Hungary in the wake of the First World War opened the way to the realisation of Czech nationalist aspirations for independence, which had steadily grown over the previous half century. The Paris Peace Conference created a new Czechoslovak state, incorporating the Czechs with the less numerous and economically and culturally less developed Slovaks, who had experienced a millennium of harsh Hungarian rule.[1]

The First Czechoslovak Republic was proclaimed on 28 October 1918 and lasted for twenty years before its large German minority (3 million of a total population of 14 million) made it easy prey to Hitler's expansionist policies. Consigned to the German sphere of influence by its Western allies at Munich in September 1938, Czechoslovakia was occupied and a German Protectorate of Bohemia and Moravia was established in March 1939. In Slovakia the presence of considerable anti-Czech nationalist sentiment facilitated the creation of a puppet fascist state under Monsignor Jozef Tiso.[2]

Minority problems notwithstanding, the First Republic was the most successful of the successor states. While the others degenerated into authoritarianism or dictatorship, Czechoslovakia managed to sustain relative prosperity and a Western style multi-party democracy. This

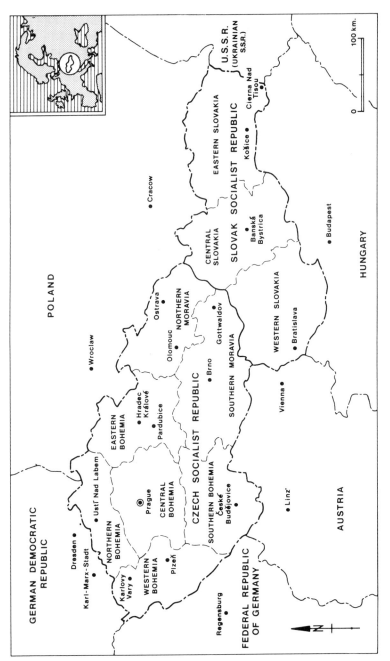

Czechhoslovakia: republican and provincial boundaries

achievement should be ascribed in large part to Czech democratic traditions and to the qualities of the Republic's leaders, above all to the first President (1919–35), T. G. Masaryk, whom Czechs still regard as the embodiment of humanitarianism and democracy. Even in 1968, after twenty years of Communist Party rule, Czechs considered the First Republic to be 'the most glorious period' in their history.[3]

THE CZECHOSLOVAK COMMUNIST PARTY AND ITS RISE TO POWER

A Czech social-democratic party was established in 1906 and became the strongest political party in the pre-1914 period, a prominence it maintained in the First Republic until 1925. The party was increasingly weakened by acute internal strife, which led to the formation of the Czechoslovak Communist Party (CCP) in 1921 by a group of left social democrats headed by Bohumir Šmeral. Initially the Party retained strong social-democratic traits, but by 1929 the Comintern had successfully engineered its Bolshevisation. At the Party's Fifth Congress, Šmeral was replaced as Secretary-general by Klement Gottwald, and the Party's mass membership was reduced to a Leninist hard core. Despite their open opposition to the First Republic, the communists were able to operate politically with little restriction and achieved considerable electoral success throughout the 1920s.[4] As German pressure mounted after 1935, so Moscow's line brought the communists closer to the Beneš government; except for the years of the Molotov–Ribbentrop pact (1939–41), Gottwald consistently supported the integrity of the Czechoslovak State. Such support was reinforced by Eduard Beneš's wartime agreement with the Soviet Union, and in 1945 the communists joined the National Front coalition government, which was headed by Beneš and included all but the most right-wing of the pre-war parties. As the most well organised party in the coalition, offering the most vigorous and acceptable programme of socialism plus democracy, the CCP attracted a good deal of popular support. In the 1946 elections, the last free and competitive elections to be held in Czechoslovakia, the Communist Party polled 38 per cent of the vote, double that of its nearest rival, Beneš's National Socialist Party.[5] Electoral success did not strengthen Gottwald's commitment to parliamentary democracy, and the Party concentrated on building up influence within key organisations. By 1947 the worsening international situation had helped to polarise forces within the National Front and hasten the demise of an independent Czechoslovak democratic road to socialism. Moscow vetoed the acceptance of aid under the Marshall Plan and encouraged Gottwald to adopt a more aggressive line. Conflict with the non-communist parties came to a head in February 1948 over communist infiltration of the security police. Faced with token opposition, the CCP organised a coup that had the trappings of a popular take-over.[6]

THE STALINIST PHASE, 1948–62

The February coup marked a break with democratic tradition and signalled the end of a 'Czechoslovak road to socialism'. The May 1948 constitution proclaimed the State to be a People's Democracy. Institutional continuity was maintained, but only in form, as all political and mass organisations were rapidly reduced to 'transmission belts' for the CCP. The economy underwent a process of Sovietisation. Nationalisation of industry, which had been embarked upon in 1945, was speedily completed, and a centralised planning system introduced, the first five-year plan running from 1949–1953. Rapid and forced collectivisation brought half of all agricultural land into collective ownership by 1956. Such radical political and economic restructuring was accompanied by a massive social upheaval: over 100,000 professionals and white-collar workers were downgraded to manual jobs and their positions were taken by members of the ascendant working class.[7] Between 1949 and 1955, over 136,000 communists and non-communists suffered arrest, imprisonment or internment in labour camps. At Stalin's prompting and under Soviet guidance, Gottwald embarked in 1950 upon a series of political trials involving some of the most prominent of his own colleagues. Perhaps precisely because of the domestic strength of the Czechoslovak Party, these trials were the most extensive in the Soviet bloc, culminating in 1952 in the execution of the former Secretary-general of the Party, Rudolf Slánský, and ten of his thirteen co-defendants, on charges of Titoist and Zionist treason and conspiracy.[8]

When Gottwald died, in 1953, he left his successors – Antonín Zapotocký as President and Antonín Novotný as First Secretary of the Party – the most Stalinised of the East European states. Czechoslovakia was hardly affected by the Soviet 'New Course', and even the Twentieth Congress of the CPSU (1956) caused only mild ferment among students and writers but brought no change in the Party's line. Novotný, who on

Zapotocký's death in 1957 added the presidency to his list of offices, was among the staunchest supporters of Soviet policy towards Poland and Hungary. In 1960 a new constitution declared in self-confident tones that Czechoslovakia had reached the stage of socialism, which placed it ahead of all its East European fellows along the road to communism.[9]

STALINISM UNDER STRAIN, 1962–8

From the Party's Twelfth Congress (December 1962) the seemingly stable system began to exhibit signs of strain. Under pressure from Khrushchev's renewed drive for de-Stalinisation, the political trials of the early 1950s were re-examined. Apart from the tensions that this created within the leadership, many of whose members were directly implicated, the rehabilitation and release of Slovak communists (including Gustáv Husák) imprisoned for 'bourgeois nationalism' fuelled Slovak resentment of Czech domination.[10] However, the main destabilising factor was the economy.

Poor industrial and agricultural performance led to the abandonment of the third Five year Plan in August 1962; in 1963 there was an actual decline in national income. The gravity of the situation forced a reluctant leadership to appoint a commission headed by a leading Party economist, Ota Šik, to find ways of solving these difficulties. Šik's scheme involved the replacement of the existing command economy with a synthesis of plan and market which would allow far greater enterprise autonomy and would make investment, wages and prices dependent in part on market forces. A watered-down version of Šik's reform proposals was approved by the Party leadership in September 1964 for phased introduction starting in 1965.[11] As the implementation of reform met with continual bureaucratic obstruction, so Šik and others came to realise that the economy could not be substantially refashioned without enabling changes in the political power structure, which in turn involved the removal of Novotný.

Two other developments helped to weaken Novotný's position and to increase the pressure for change: intellectual dissent and Slovak nationalism. In 1966–7 the general renascence of intellectual activity which had been developing since 1963 became explicitly political. At the Fourth Writers' Congress in June 1967, Ludvík Vaculík, Václav Havel, Antonín Liehm and others attacked all forms of censorship and accused the Party of stifling cultural freedom. Reprisals against the writers served to heighten tension between the regime and the intellectual community.[12]

The perennial problem of Slovak nationalism had a more direct political impact. By his tactless rejection of mounting demands for greater political and economic equality for Slovakia, Novotný earned the undying hostility of the powerful Slovak lobby within the Party. At Party Central Committee sessions in October and December 1967 and January 1968, the divisions, not only over Slovakia, but also over the 1950s trials and economic reforms, erupted into unprecedented conflict. At the December session Šik called for radical reforms within the Party and for Novotný's resignation from the first-secretaryship. Finding himself under attack in the Party Presidium and outnumbered in the Central Committee, early in January Novotný tendered his resignation as First Secretary. His successor, Alexander Dubček, the First Secretary of the Slovak Party, was not the most outstanding but was the most widely acceptable of the candidates put forward.[13]

REFORM AND INTERVENTION, 1968-9

The two months following the change-over at the top gave little indication of impending radical change. Only after the effective suspension of central censorship on 4 March did the public debate begin that was to become the most distinctive hallmark and achievement of the Prague Spring.[14] A rising chorus of criticism of the old regime and its leaders brought Novotný's resignation as President on 21 March; his successor, General Ludvik Svoboda, was the safe rather than the popular choice. At the first Central Committee meeting to be held under Dubček's leadership (28 March to 5 April) Novotný and his main supporters lost their Presidium seats; by the end of April reformers held most of the top positions. Oldřich Černík became Prime Minister, Josef Smrkovský Chairman of the National Assembly and František Kriegel Chairman of the National Front. On 10 April the Party published its Action Programme, which included proposals to democratise the Communist Party and its relations with government and mass organisations; its declared objective was to build 'a new profoundly democratic model of Czechoslovak socialism conforming to Czechoslovak conditions'.[15] However welcome, such general intentions, and many of the proposals put forward in the programme, sounded over-cautious to a public participating in an open debate which had already raised more radical demands, including the institutionalisation of political opposition. Similarly, the re-emergence of political pluralism overtook the often slow and measured changes in structure and personnel taking place within the National Assembly, the National Front, government bureaucracy, the trade unions and even the Party.[16]

Precisely at a time when Dubček and his colleagues found themselves under domestic pressure to radicalise the Party's reforms, they began to come under growing external pressure to move in the opposite direction. The first open warnings from Czechoslovakia's socialist allies came at a meeting of the Warsaw Pact in Dresden in March and they were repeated by Soviet leaders throughout May and June. Attempts by the Czechoslovak leaders to slow down the progress of democratisation evoked popular fears of regression which were expressed most forcefully in Vaculík's '2000 words' published on 27 June.[17] Signed by sixty leading intellectuals, this call for grass-roots resistance to any backsliding brought heavy censure from Czechoslovakia's allies. Warnings about the dangers of anti-socialist forces thriving in a climate of 'excessive freedom' culminated in the Warsaw letter of 15 July, which demanded that the Party reassert control over the media and over non-communist organisations. Similar demands were reiterated by Soviet leaders when they met the full Presidium of the Czechoslovak Party at Čierna nad Tisou between 29 July and 1 August. The Czechoslovak leaders agreed to clamp down on the press and on the more radical of the new organisations, including the revived Social Democratic Party. These pledges were reaffirmed two days later at Bratislava by an agreement signed with the Soviet Union, the GDR, Bulgaria, Poland and Hungary. It was generally assumed that the crisis was over.[18]

The invasion of Czechoslovakia by a quarter of a million Warsaw Pact troops (this soon increased to 600,000) on the night of 20 August therefore took all, including Dubček, by surprise. The intervention was probably timed to prevent the holding of the CCP's Fourteenth Congress, scheduled for early September, which would have approved new Party rules and would have launched a more thoroughgoing democratisation of the political system.[19]

Central to the reasons for using armed intervention at all was Soviet and East European alarm at the CCP's relaxation of control over the media and over political organisations. Failing to understand that the Czechs might be able to combine democracy with political stability more successfully than the Poles, let alone the Russians, Soviet leaders assumed that developments were leading to a loss of Party control and a general breakdown of order. But, even given a more optimistic analysis, the creation of democratic socialism under communist party auspices must have seemed a threat to the *status quo* in the GDR, Poland, Hungary and the Ukraine.

A collaborationist Czechoslovak Revolutionary Workers' and Peasants' Government, which was probably part of the original intervention scenario, failed to materialise and the Soviet leaders had to negotiate in Moscow (23–26 August) with leaders whom they had initially arrested. Under extreme pressure, the Czechoslovak side signed the Moscow Protocols, which provided for the temporary stationing of troops and specified the measures Moscow considered necessary to restore 'normality'.[20] 'Normalisation' proved extremely difficult in a situation in which nationalism now reinforced popular support for reform. In Slovakia the task was made easier by the Slovaks' preoccupation with federalisation, which came into effect on 1 January 1969, giving them republican status and parity with the Czechs. In the Czech lands, however, the press, trade unions and students led resistance to 'normalisation', climaxing in the demonstrations following Jan Palach's protest suicide in January 1969. In late March, ice-hockey victories over the USSR sparked anti-Soviet demonstrations which were taken by Moscow as final evidence of Dubček's inability to restore control. At the Central Committee plenum in April he was replaced as First Secretary by Gustáv Husák.[21]

'NORMALISATION', 1969–76

Husák embarked on a gradual but thorough reversal of what had happened from January 1968 to April 1969. Tight central control was reimposed over all aspects of public life; within a year all leading reformers had been replaced. In the course of 1970, all communists were screened and approximately half a million were deprived of their Party membership. The purge extended to all mass organisations; altogether 5 million (half the adult population) were put through the mill, and an estimated million were demoted or lost their jobs.[22]

With reformists extirpated at all levels, the Party leadership at the official Fourteenth Congress in May 1971 (as distinct from the Fourteenth Congress held clandestinely in Prague on 22 August 1968) found itself presiding over a cleansed but severely depleted stock of cultural, academic, political and managerial resources. Moreover, opposition to 'normalisation' persisted. In the build-up to the November 1971 elections, a group of dissenters calling themselves the Socialist Movement of Czechoslovak Citizens appealed to electors to register their dissent by not voting or by spoiling their ballot papers. This incident finally induced Husák, who had opposed the use of political trials, to give way to hard-liners such as Vasil Bilak, Alois Indra and Antonín Kapek. In July–August 1972 ten trials took place, involving forty-seven 'oppositionists' – second-rank figures from the Prague Spring as well as dissenters of more recent vintage – who received sentences ranging from nine months to six and a half years.[23] These reprisals brought a lull in resistance. Party membership was successfully built up and the majority of the population seemingly anaesthetised into materialistic introspection by stable prices and steadily rising wages. Addressing the Fifteenth Party Congress in April 1976, Husák, who in 1975 had also taken on the office of President from an ailing Svoboda, could afford to adopt a somewhat conciliatory line towards the reformists.[24]

DISSENT AND HUMAN RIGHTS, 1977–8

The relative calm and apparent resignation of the population was soon broken by a new kind of development. Since 1973 the focus of dissent had slowly shifted from political-reform based opposition to human-rights centred protests. In January and October 1974, in his only public utterances since 1969, Dubček condemned the regime for its violation of human rights; the following April, the writer Havel attacked the fear and corruption on which normalisation was founded.[25] The signing of the Final Act of the Helsinki Conference on Security and Co-operation in Europe and, more directly, the publication in late 1976 of two UN covenants which Czechoslovakia had recently ratified prompted 242 communists and non-communists to issue Charter 77. The Charter described itself as an 'informal association of people of various convictions and beliefs and professions united by their respect for civil and human rights'; they did not intend to become a political opposition but merely wanted to document breaches of human rights and to conduct 'a constructive dialogue' with the authorities. The Charter declaration detailed how fundamental rights such as freedom of work, speech and organisation and freedom from fear were violated by the Husák regime.[26]

Predictably, the authorities launched a media offensive and attempted to rouse mass condemnation of the Chartists. But most workers refused to condemn something they were not allowed to read, and, instead of extinguishing the movement, the regime's attack helped to swell the number of signatories, which stood at nearly 1000 in early 1978. The Chartists are a remarkably heterogenous group: while the majority are professionals or ex-professionals who have been demoted to manual work, many hundreds of engineers, technicians and workers have also been willing to risk arrest by signing the document. The movement also covers a broad spectrum of opinion, as is reflected in its spokesmen. Of the first team, one, Jiři Hájek, was a former reformist communist and Minister of Foreign Affairs under Dubček; one, Václav Havel, was a leading non-communist playwright; and one, Jan Patočka, was a non-communist philosopher. The spokesmen in 1978 were Jaroslav Săbata (a reformist communist), Ladislav Hejdánek (an evangelical Christian philosopher) and Marta Kubišová (a pop singer). Since September 1977 the various streams within Charter 77 have become more distinct.[27] The only important group who do not figure in the Charter are the Slovaks. The fact that there is only a handful of Slovaks among the signatories reflects the general absence of overt dissent in Slovakia. For, despite the administrative recentralisation that has taken place since 1971, the Slovaks have experienced rising economic prosperity, heightened political prestige and a less repressive normalisation policy than that applied in the Czech republic.[28]

Charter 77 has had considerable international impact. Its documentation of political persecution alerted world opinion to post-Helsinki conditions in Czechoslovakia and elicited support from the European communist parties. Declarations of solidarity have also come from dissidents in Hungary, the GDR and Romania, and there has been active collaboration with Polish human-rights groups.[29]

In Czechoslovakia, the Charter shattered the relative stability which Husák had carefully nurtured between 1972 and 1976. Press campaigns, police action and the resort to political trials in late 1977 have failed to halt the movement. While it would be an exaggeration to say that Charter 77 threatens the regime's power, it increases its already heavy dependence on Moscow and the 70,000 Soviet troops still in Czechoslovakia. Soviet leaders seem to be content to keep Husák in office, balanced by Bilak, Indra and other hard-liners, as long as he can maintain political stability. Yet, with economic growth declining and dissent very much alive, Moscow cannot be entirely happy that, even after a decade of 'normalisation', Czechoslovakia continues to show signs of its traditional abnormality.

THE CZECHOSLOVAK COMMUNIST PARTY

Organisation

The CCP is organised along orthodox democratic centralist lines. In 1968, thoroughgoing democratisation of the Party was planned and a draft of revised statutes was published in August, but these never came into effect. The statutes currently in force are basically those adopted under Novotný's leadership at the Twelfth Congress in 1962. The lowest rung in the Party's hierarchy consists of over 43,000 primary organisations (*základní organizace*), over three-quarters of which are located in factories and offices, the remainder being based in collective farms, villages and neighbourhoods. The primary organisations are directly subordinate to district (*okresní*) and city (*městské*) organs, which are responsible, in particular, for supervising recruitment and ideological work. They are in turn controlled by the regional (*krajské*) organs, which bear overall responsibility for economic and political developments in their area. Both district and regional committees have five secretaries and an apparatus consisting of ten departments, covering political organisation, ideology, industry, agriculture, public administration, economic and technical administration, information and the People's Militia. In the Czech republic this apparatus of professional Party workers is under the control of the Central Committee apparatus in Prague; in Slovakia it comes under the direction of the Slovak Party Central Committee in Bratislava. The Slovak Party constitutes a territorial organisation of the Czechoslovak Party; as in the USSR the Russian Federation has no separate party, so in Czechoslovakia there is no Czech Communist Party, although Party federalisation was contemplated between 1969 and 1971.[30]

The Czechoslovak Party Congress (*sjezd*), which is elected indirectly and meets every five years, formally possesses supreme power. It lays down policy in all fields and elects the Central Control and Auditing Commission (fifty-one members) and the Central Committee. The Slovak Party follows the same pattern, holding its congress shortly before the Czechoslovak one. According to the statutes, the Central Committee (in 1976 there were 121 full and fifty-two non-voting members) runs the Party between congresses. While the Committee's quarterly meetings of two to four days' duration have provided an important forum for discussion of Party policy (except during the leadership crisis of 1967–8), they have never decided such policy. As is the case elsewhere in Eastern Europe, the plenums of the Central

Committee invariably approve proposals put forward by the Committee's Presidium.[31] Formally elected by and accountable to the Central Committee, the Presidium, together with its Secretariat, takes all major decisions. In 1978 the Presidium consisted of eleven full and two non-voting candidate members; the Secretariat comprised the Secretary-general, eight secretaries and two members.[32] The real power-house of the Party is the Central Committee apparatus, whose departments cover the whole range of Party, government and mass organisation activities. As of 1969 there were fifteen departments: Political Organisation; Ideology; Education and Culture; Party Work in the Mass Media; Economics; Party Work in Industry, Transport and Communications; Agricultural Policy; State Agencies; Social Organisations; Defence and Security Policy; International Policy; Political–Professional Unit (information-processing section); Economic Management and Administration; Secretariat of the Secretary-general; and the Central Control and Auditing Commission. There was also a department which acted as the main staff of the quarter of a million strong People's Militia, a volunteer force composed of communists at factory level.[33]

Membership

The Czechoslovak Party has always been large by Soviet and East European standards, comprising between $8\frac{1}{2}$ and 22 per cent of the population since 1948 (see Table 10.1). The periodic and large-scale fluctuations in its membership have been a result of alternative recruitment and purge. Open recruitment in the years immediately following 1946, together with the absorption of the social democrats in June 1948, created a massive party of 2·5 million. This figure was rapidly reduced by membership purges – begun in 1946 and culminating in 1948–50 – which excluded approximately 700,000 from Party ranks. Almost equally far-reaching purges were undertaken in 1970, in order to cleanse the Party of all reformist elements. Official figures for the numbers involved range from a low of 326,817 (67,147 expelled and 259,670 struck off) to a high of 461,751 (70,964 expelled and 390,817 struck off).[34]

Composition

Only very limited data are available on the composition of the Party after 1966. Like their colleagues in other East European states,

TABLE 10.1 Membership (including candidate members) of the CCP (as of 1 January unless otherwise specified)

	Membership	% of population (rounded)
1945 (July)	475,304	
1946 (July)	1,214,234	
1947	1,043,593	
1948 (1 Oct)	2,674,838	22
1951 (Feb)	1,677,443	
1956	1,417,989	
1962	1,657,021	
1966	1,698,002	12
1968	1,690,977	
1971	1,217,245	8·5
1976	1,381,090	
1978	1,473,112	10

Sources: 1946–71: G. Wightman and A. H. Brown, 'Changes in the Levels of Membership and Social Composition of the Communist Party of Czechoslovakia 1945–73' *Soviet Studies*, XXVII (1975) 397–414. 1976: *Rudé právo*, 16 Apr 1976. 1978: *Rudé právo*, 17 Mar 1978.

Czechoslovak Party leaders have long been anxious to attract greater numbers of working-class and young members. The need to do this became particularly acute in the wake of the 1970 purge, when the contingent of workers in the Party fell to a quarter and the average age of communists rose to forty-nine. However, by 1976 recruitment drives had successfully cut the average age to forty-four and raised the proportion of workers to a third (see Table 10.2).[35]

GOVERNMENT

The Constitution

Czechoslovakia has had two constitutions since the CCP came to power. The 1948 Constitution (promulgated on 9 June 1948) declared the state to be a People's Democracy and its provisions corresponded to this transitional stage of development. The Constitution currently in force was adopted on 11 July 1960 proclaims the elimination of all exploitation and vests all power in working people, who have both the duty

TABLE 10.2   Social composition of the CCP (percentage of total membership as of 1 January)

	Workers	Co-operative farmers	State farm workers	Professional/ white-collar workers	Pensioners
1962	33·4	6·4	2·6	45·6	13
1966	30·2	5·4	2·7	44·5	17·3
1968	30·4	5·2			
1971	26·1				18·7 (former workers only)
1976	34·8				

Sources: 1962–71: Wightman and Brown, in *Soviet Studies*, XXVII, 410, 414–15. 1976: estimate in Kusín, *From Dubček to Charter 77* (1978) p. 187.

and the right to work in the interests of the community. By claiming in 1960 that the country had entered a new stage of 'the construction of an advanced socialist society', the Constitution set Czechoslovakia ahead of all its East European counterparts along the road to communism. On 27 October 1968 the Constitution was amended to take account of the establishment of a federated Czechoslovakia, comprising the Czech and the Slovak Socialist Republics, which came into existence on 1 January 1969.[36]

Representative State bodies

The highest organ of State power and the supreme legislative body is the bicameral Federal Assembly, comprising the House of the People and the House of Nations. The House of the People consists of 200 deputies (137 from the Czech Republic and sixty-three from the Slovak) each representing approximately 75,000 citizens; the House of Nations includes 150 deputies, seventy-five from each republic. The republics have their own assemblies: the Czech National Council numbers 200 members and the Slovak National Council 150. All the above bodies are directly elected for a five-year term, which coincides with quinquennia of economic plans and Party congresses.[37]

    Elections to all representative State bodies are direct, secret and based on universal adult suffrage (eighteen years and above). All candidates stand on the joint platform of the National Front, an association of political parties and mass organisations headed by the CCP. Although more than one candidate may be proposed for each single-member constituency, electors are almost never presented with a choice on polling day. What element of choice exists is supposedly available during the selection process which in practice is closely controlled by the CCP through the National Front. Elections are highly organised mass mobilisation and propaganda exercises; the extremely high turnouts and positive votes achieved (see Table 10.3) add popular legitimacy to the regime.

TABLE 10.3 Czechoslovak election results, 1948–76 (percentage of electorate)

	30 May 1948	28 Nov 1954	12 June 1960	14 June 1964
Turnout	100	99·18	99·68	99·42
National Front vote	89·4	97·99	99·86	99·94

	26–27 Nov 1971	22–23 Oct 1976
Turnout	99·45	99·7
National Front vote		
House of the People	99·81	99·7
House of Nations	99·77	99·7

Sources: Dokumentačni přehled ČTK, 22 Sep 1976, and Radio Hvezda, 24 Oct 1976, cited in *Radio Free Europe Situation Report* (Czechoslovakia), 27 Oct 1976, p. 3.

Meeting biannually for two to three days, the Federal Assembly invariably passes the legislative proposals put before it by Party and government, making little if any use of constitutional powers to scrutinise and control executive performance. The Assembly elects a Presidium of forty from amongst its members (twenty from each chamber) to perform assembly functions between sessions; it also elects the Czechoslovak President for a five-year term of office. The President, who is commander-in-chief of the armed forces and head of State, represents the country in all international dealings and appoints the Federal government.[39]

The Federal government comprises a Prime Minister, eight deputy prime ministers, and sixteen ministers. Seven of the ministries – Foreign Affairs, National Defence, Foreign Trade, Fuel and Power,

Investment and Technical Development, and Transport and Telecommunications – cover sectors that fall exclusively within Federal competence. The Czech and Slovak Republics each have their own government, consisting of a Prime Minister, three deputy prime ministers and fourteen ministers, eight of whom preside over sectors – Building, Construction and Technology, Internal Trade, Forestry and Water Conservation, Culture, Education, Health, and Justice – that fall exclusively within Republican competence. Other spheres of governmental activity – notably law and order and the economy – come under joint Federal–Republican jurisdiction, though Federal powers to overrule Republican legislation and the highly centralised nature of economic planning and control militate to the advantage of the Federal authorities.[40]

Local government

The national committees are described in the Constitution as the organs of State power at regional, district and municipal level. As such, these committees administer health, culture, education, transport, general services and housing in their area. They play an important part in the national economy – their budgets constitute a quarter of the national budget – and employ one in four of all State employees. Control and supervision of these local-government bodies is the responsibility of local deputies. Elected every five years, these deputies are also seen as the most direct link between government and the population at large. The public also take part in the work of the national committees, via volunteer-staffed commissions which are conceived as bodies furthering the development of socialist self-government.[41]

Party–State relations

The leading role of the CCP within the polity is enshrined in the Constitution, which describes the Party as 'the vanguard of the working class' and 'the guiding force in society and the State'. The Party rules make this more explicit by stating that the Party's Central Committee 'regulates and supervises' the activity of all Party, government and mass organisation bodies, 'ensuring that they carry out Party policy'. In 1968, attempts were made to loosen and democratise the Party's leading role and increase the autonomy of State, government and other non-Party bodies. Under 'normalisation', particular stress has therefore been placed on the growing importance of the Party's leading role in an advanced socialist society, and recent years have seen the revival of the neo-orthodox concept of all non-Party organisations as 'transmission belts' for CCP policy.[43]

In line with other communist states, Party control is exercised indirectly by means of an extensive network of Party apparatus departments shadowing State and government operations, as well as through groups of communists who hold office in non-Party bodies. The CCP's overall control of appointments ensures that many of its leading officials are highly placed in the State, government and mass organisations, as is evidenced by the interlocking of offices at the apex of these hierarchies (see Table 10.4).

Mass organisations

All public organisations, from political parties to sports associations, are grouped within the National Front, which is described by the Constitution as 'the political expression of the alliance of the working people of town and country, led by the Communist Party of Czechoslovakia'. Established in 1945 as a broad political coalition, the Front has since 1948 served the Party as an election platform and as an additional means of controlling the activity of all non-communist organisations. The National Front includes four non-communist political parties – the People's Party, the Czech Socialist Party, the Slovak Freedom Party and the Slovak Revival Party – which are allowed to eke out a nominal political existence and use their small number of allotted Assembly seats and occasional ministerial portfolios to further CCP policy.[43]

The Union of Youth was created in 1970 as successor to the Czechoslovak Youth Union, which effectively disintegrated during the Prague Spring. At its Second Congress, in October 1977, the Union had 1,361,000 members between the ages of fifteen and thirty, organised in 42,812 primary groups. Recruitment is highest among secondary-school and university students, for whom membership carries certain trade-union-like advantages, and lowest among young workers and farmers, who received no career benefits from joining. Like its Soviet and other East European counterparts, the Union is supposed to educate its members in the spirit of Marxism-Leninism, to combat all bourgeois influences and to serve as a recruitment channel for the Communist Party, under whose leadership it operates. The six to fifteen year olds are catered for by the Pioneers. By a programme of scout-like activities, laced with Marxist-Leninist indoctrination, the Pioneer organisation

TABLE 10.4 Multiple holding of positions in Party, State, government and mass organisations in Czechoslovakia, August 1978

Party Presidium (full members)	Party Secretariat	Slovak Party	State	Government	Mass organisations
Gustáv Husák	Secretary-General		President		Chairman, National Front
Vasil Bil'ak	Secretary				
Petr Colotka		Presidium member		Slovak Prime Minister and Deputy Federal Prime Minister	
Karel Hoffmann					Chairman, Central Trade Union Council
Václav Hůla				Deputy Federal Prime Minister and Chairman, Federal State Planning Commission	
Alois Indra			Chairman, Federal Assembly		
Antonín Kapek					
Josef Kempný	Secretary				Chairman, Czech National Front
Josef Korčák				Czech Prime Minister and Deputy Federal Prime Minister	
Jozef Lenárt		First Secretary			Chairman, Slovak National Front
Lubomir Štrougal				Federal Prime Minister	

Source: Compiled from 'East European Leadership List', *Radio Free Europe Research*, supplement, 3 Aug 18, 1978, pp. 6–9.

prepares the very young for entry into the Union of Youth. Based in schools, the Pioneers number approximately half of all children between six and fifteen and, despite problems of understaffing, appear to be more successful than their senior partner, which is dogged by apathy.[44]

The origins of trade unionism in the Czech lands can be traced to the late 1890s, which saw the foundation of social-democratic, National Socialist and Christian union organisations. The first communist unions, the Red unions, were established in 1928, and, shortly after the end of the Second World War, in 1946, the Party oversaw the creation of the united Revolutionary Trade Union Movement. In 1968–9 the unions underwent considerable democratisation – demands were made for free union organisation and for an independent interest-promotion role. Many union officials were replaced by men willing to press for improvements in living standards rather than only for higher labour productivity, and it took three years to 'normalise' the situation.[45]

The trade unions are by far the largest of the mass organisations, their membership of 6·6 million embracing 97·1 per cent of the work force. All members belong to one of eighteen industry-based unions which are organised at factory and national level. Individual unions are co-ordinated by trade-union councils at district, regional and national level and are subordinate to the Central Trade Union Council in Prague (in Slovakia they come directly under the Slovak Trade Union Council). These central councils are elected every five years by their respective congresses; as in the Party, executive bodies, notably the presidia of the central councils, exert a dominant influence over policy. According to the current highly orthodox statutes, the unions are 'a school of good management and socialism' whose primary function is to ensure the fulfilment and over-fulfilment of production targets. Although trade unions are also supposed to defend members' interests and rights, greater stress is placed on their duty to defend workers against 'bourgeois ideologies, revisionism, dogmatism and opportunism'. In all its work the trade-union movement is pledged to advance Party policy, which is described as the 'basis of its activity'.[46]

INTERNAL AFFAIRS

Education

When the communists came to power in 1948, they took over a well developed educational system, particularly in the Czech lands, where compulsory elementary education had been introduced in 1869. As in all communist states, education is seen as a vital instrument for the eradication of bourgeois values and the creation of a new socialist man; the Constitution stipulates that all schooling must be 'directed in the spirit of the scientific world-outlook of Marxism-Leninism'. Education is also used as a means of social transformation. In the 1950s and early

1960s, discrimination against children from bourgeois backgrounds and in favour of those from manual workers' families helped to increase the proportion of working-class students from a quarter to a third.[47] Such class discrimination was discontinued in 1968 only to be resumed in 1970–1; at the time of writing, social origin and political loyalty of a student's family can count for up to one-fifth of the credits necessary to gain a place in higher education. While this policy may have facilitated the entry of working-class children into universities – they constitute 60 per cent of students in higher education – the massive political purges of teaching staff have severely damaged the quality of education that they receive.[48]

Under the educational reforms currently being introduced, schooling is compulsory between the ages of six and sixteen. All children have to go through two four-year cycles of elementary school; the practically inclined continue their education for a further two years, either at apprentice training schools or at ones offering vocational sandwich courses. The more academically oriented attend 'gymnasiums' from fourteen to eighteen; at these they prepare for entry into what are mostly four-year courses at the country's five universities and thirty-one other institutes of higher education, which in 1976–7 comprised 106 faculties and were attended by 168,310 students.[49]

Religion

The origins of Christianity in the Czech lands go back to the missionaries Cyril and Methodius in the tenth century, and a strong dissenting tradition can be traced to the Hussite movement 400 years later. In the Czech lands, the Protestant churches, the Czechoslovak church and the evangelical Czech Brethren constitute 13 per cent of the population, while in Slovakia only 9 per cent profess the Protestant faith. Roman Catholics constitute by far the largest religious community in the country, embracing approximately 40 per cent of Czechs and 60 per cent of Slovaks.[50]

Religious believers enjoy considerable formal rights: freedom of conscience and worship is constitutionally guaranteed and children are allowed to receive religious instruction as long as this is carried out after school hours. None the less, the authorities frequently violate these provisions and severely restrict the churches' activities. Partly because of the revival in religious activity in 1968–9, the period since 1971 has seen a sustained campaign to combat church influence. 'Legal' religious education has come under growing pressure and the small number of students attending the country's seven seminaries has been reduced to 350. Relations between the regime and the Catholic Church have improved since an accord was signed with the Vatican in 1973, but nine of the fourteen Catholic seats remain vacant. Despite administrative pressures and long years of anti-religious propaganda, only one in five Czechs and Slovaks professes atheism, and, there is evidence to suggest that a growing number of young people see in religion one of the safest and most satisfying outlets for dissent.[51]

Economy

A sound industrial base, constructed under Austria–Hungary and developed between the wars, made Czechoslovakia the most prosperous of East European Communist states until the early 1960s, since when it has ranked second to the GDR. The command economy, which was built up rapidly after 1948, was disrupted by the partial implementation of Sik's decentralising and marketising reforms between 1966 and 1969. By 1970, however, central controls had been restored over all major aspects of economic activity.[52]

Economic performance has borne up surprisingly well through the upheavals of 'normalisation', which involved the replacement of 40 per cent of all managers. During the Sixth Five-year plan (1971–5) industrial production grew at an average of 6·7 per cent per annum, and income and consumption rose by a quarter, while prices remained stable. To deal with problems of over-investment, financial inputs have been reduced and overall growth targets have been cut in the current Seventh Five-year plan (1976–80); industrial production grew by approximately 5½ per cent per annum in 1976 and 1977. Since the mid 1970s the economy has become increasingly weighed down by poor labour productivity, rising price subsidies and a growing trade deficit.[53] Heavily dependent on fuel and raw material imports from the Soviet Union, Czechoslovakia has had to bear the brunt of rocketing prices (Soviet oil doubled in price between 1974 and 1976), while its traditional exports (machinery, tools and general engineering products) have found it increasingly difficult to keep pace with competitors.[54] While the present trade deficit with Comecon and Western countries is small by East European standards, it underlines the problems of inefficient and low-quality production that have prompted several Czech economists to call for rationalisation and reform. In January 1978 a scheme was launched, on an experimental basis, to increase the role of material incentives and economic levers at the expense of central direction based on quantitative criteria. If it proves successful, this reform will be introduced nationally in 1981.[55]

Rapid collectivisation of agriculture in the 1950s brought stagnation and declining production, which were only reversed in the aftermath of major agricultural reforms introduced in 1966. Between 1966 and 1970 agricultural production grew by 4·8 per cent per annum, and, though this slowed in the 1970s, 1977 brought a record harvest and the sector succeeds in providing approximately 85 per cent of domestic needs.[56] Because of its key importance and sensitivity to interference, agriculture has suffered less than industry from the vagaries of 'normalisation'. However, the 1970s have seen a renewed drive against the very small private sector as well as continued merging of farms. The collective farms, which cultivate nearly 65 per cent of the country's arable land, fell in number from 6327 in 1969 to 2736 in 1975; the number of State farms fell from 343 in 1969 to 250 in 1975.[57]

EXTERNAL AFFAIRS

As a small country located between the Soviet Union and Germany, Czechoslovakia's foreign policy has always been determined by considerations of survival. Fear of Germany made Beneš look first to the Western allies and, after Munich, to the USSR. After 1947, alliance with the Soviet Union rapidly became total subordination of Czechoslovak foreign policy to that of Moscow. The 1968 invasion brought the traditionally Russophile Czechs and Slovaks into line with their anti-Soviet East European neighbours.[58] A treaty legalising the 'temporary' stationing of 70,000 Soviet troops in Czechoslovakia was ratified in October 1968 and a new Soviet–Czechoslovak friendship and mutual-collaboration agreement was signed in May 1970. The regime's lack of popular legitimacy and Husák's total dependence on Moscow have made Czechoslovakia the most overtly loyal of Warsaw Pact states. Taking a neo-Moscow line on all major international issues, from the Middle East and Africa through to China, Czechoslovakia has also provided unflagging support for Soviet policy in Comecon and within the international communist movement. The Czechs and Slovaks have become the most ardent advocates of the Brezhnev doctrine of limited sovereignty for East European states.[59]

The invasion of 1968 was followed by a period of diplomatic isolation. By 1972–3, however, the efforts of men such as the Foreign Minister, Bohus Chňoupek, had succeeded in renewing international contacts.

Western leaders, notably Harold Wilson and Willy Brandt, visited Prague, and Czechoslovak leaders began to be more freely received in Western Europe. Important headway was made in relations with Austria, the Vatican and, above all, with the Federal Republic of Germany. Long and difficult negotiations with the FRG were successfully concluded in 1973, an agreement between the two countries was signed in December 1973, and it was ratified the following July. Soviet pressure played an important part in making the agreement possible, and it is characteristic of the situation that Husák's visit to Bonn in April 1976 came only weeks before Brezhnev's own trip to the FRG.[60]

BIOGRAPHIES

Gustáv Husák, Secretary-general of the CCP, President of Czechoslovakia and Chairman of the National Front, was born into a smallholder's family in what is now part of Bratislava in June 1913. He joined the Slovak Communist Party at the age of twenty and played a leading part in its wartime underground activity, which culminated in the Slovak Uprising of August 1944. A strong advocate of Slovak autonomy, Husák became Chairman of the main executive body, the Slovak Board of Commissioners, a post he held from 1946 to 1950. In 1951 he came under attack for 'bourgeois nationalism' and three years later was sentenced to life imprisonment on that charge. Released in 1960, he worked as a manual labourer until partial rehabilitation in December 1963 allowed him to take up a research post at the Slovak Academy of Sciences. In April 1968 he became a deputy prime minister in Černík's new government and subsequently (May) the chairman of the government commission on federalisation.[61] Elected First Secretary of the Slovak Party in August 1968, Husák took a pro-Dubček line in the period immediately following the invasion. Because of his proven ability to keep the Slovak Party under tight control and to maintain a flexible middle position in political terms, Husák was chosen by Moscow to replace Dubček as First Secretary of the CCP in April 1969. In 1971 he became Chairman of the National Front and in May 1975 took over the presidency from an ailing Ludvik Svoboda.[62] Throughout the years since 1969, Husák has tried to steer a moderate course on treatment of ex-reformers and has had to contend with pressure for more extreme measures from hard-liners such as Indra and Bi'lak. So far he has managed to be sufficiently flexible to retain Moscow's support.

Jozef Lenárt, First Secretary of the Slovak Communist Party, member of the Presidium of the CCP and Chairman of the Slovak National Front, was born in Liptovská Porubka in central Slovakia in April 1923. He joined the underground Slovak Communist Party in 1943. After working in the lower echelons of the Party apparatus, he became Deputy Minister of Light Industry in 1951. On completing three years at the Higher Party School in Moscow, he became leading secretary of the Bratislava regional committee in 1956 and two years later was promoted to a secretaryship in the Slovak Party Central Committee. In 1962 Lenárt became Chairman of the Slovak National Council and a member of the Presidium of the CCP, and in 1963 Novotný appointed him Prime Minister of Czecholovakia. Because of his support for Novotný during the leadership crisis, Lenárt was replaced as Prime Minister in April 1968, but was given a Central Committee secretaryship.[63] Reportedly involved in the attempts to establish a collaborationist government during the invasion, Lenárt became Central Committee Secretary for Ideological Affairs and in May 1969 moved over to the Economic Department, also heading the Central Committee's Economic Commission. In June 1970 he became a full member of the Presidium and First Secretary of the Slovak Party, adding the chairmanship of the Slovak National Front to his offices in May 1971.

Lubomír Štrougal, Member of the Presidium of the CCP and Federal Prime Minister, was born in southern Bohemia in October 1924 and studied law at Charles University. Having joined the CCP in 1945, he worked in its south Bohemian apparatus from 1949, becoming leading secretary in 1955 and a member of the Czechoslovak Central Committee in 1958. After two years as Central Committee secretary in charge of agriculture, Štrougal was appointed Minister of the Interior in 1961, an office he held for four years. Between 1965 and April 1968 he once again was Central Committee Secretary for Agriculture. Štrougal was one of the most influential conservatives in the Černík government, holding the offices of Deputy Prime Minister and Chairman of the Economic Council. In November 1968 he entered the Czechoslovak Party Presidium as head of the newly-created Party Bureau for the Czech lands. When it was decided not to federate the Party, Štrougal was moved to the post of Federal Prime Minister. In 1974–5 he deputised for an ill President Svoboda, a responsibility which confirmed his political proximity to the Husák-led group of moderates within the Presidium.[64]

BASIC FACTS ABOUT CZECHOSLOVAKIA

Official name: Czechoslovak Socialist Republic (Československá socialistická republika).
Area: 127,877 sq. km. (49,200 sq. miles). (Czech Socialist Republic: 78,863 sq. km.; Slovak Socialist Republic: 49,014 sq. km.).
Population (31 Dec 1976 est.): 14,973,792 (Czech SR 10,158,434; Slovak SR 4,815,358).
Population density: 117 sq. km.
Population distribution (1975 est.): 66 per cent urban, 34 per cent rural.
Membership of the CCP (Komunistická strana Československa) in 1978: 1,473,112.
Administrative division: Czech Socialist Republic – 8 regions, 76 districts; Slovak Socialist Republic – 4 regions, 38 districts.
Ethnic nationalities (31 Dec 1976 est.) percentage of population:

	Czechoslovak SR	Czech SR	Slovak SR
Czech	64·1	94·0	1·1
Slovak	30·2	3·8	85·8
Hungarian	4·0	0·2	11·9
German	0·5	0·7	0·1
Polish	0·5	0·7	0·0
Ukrainian	0·3	0·1	0·8
Russian	0·1	0·1	0·1
Others	0·3	0·4	0·2

Population of major towns (31 Dec 1976 est.): Praha (Prague, the capital), 1,175,522; Brno (South Moravia), 363,171; Bratislava (capital, Slovak SR), 350,025; Ostrava (North Moravia), 316,990; Košice (East Slovakia), 180,792; Plzeň (Pilsen, West Bohemia), 162,902; Olomouc (North Moravia), 97,504.
National income by sector (1976 est.): industry, 66·5 per cent; construction, 12·5 per cent; agriculture and forestry, 8·3 per cent; transport, 3·9 per cent; wholesale and retail trade, 8·6 per cent; others, 0·2 per cent. [Source: adapted from *Statistická ročenka ČSSR 1977* (Prague, 1977) p. 127.]
Main natural resources: coal, iron, graphite, copper, lead, silver and uranium.
Foreign trade (1977, in thousands of Czechoslovak crowns): exports, 58,246; imports, 63,213; total, 121,459. [Source: *Statistické přehledy*, no. 5 (May) 1978.]
Main trading partners (1976 share of trade): USSR (34·1 per cent), GDR (11·7 per cent), Poland (8·8 per cent), Hungary (5·6 per cent), FRG

286   Marxist Governments

(5·6 per cent). [Source: *Statistická ročenka ČSSR 1977*, p. 435.]
Distribution of foreign trade (percentages):

	1976		1977	
	Imports	Exports	Imports	Exports
Socialist countries	69·8	74·2	69·9	73·4
USSR	32·6	33·9	33·9	34·3
Non-socialist countries	30·2	25·8	30·1	26·6
Advanced	25·0	18·2	23·5	18·4
EEC	13·8	11·4	13·2	11·4
Developing	5·2	7·6	6·6	8·2

[Sources: 1976 calculated from *Statistická ročenka ČSSR 1977*, pp. 434–5; 1977 calculated from *Statistické přehledy*, no. 5, 1978.]

National income by sector (1976 est.): industry, 66·5 per cent; construction, 12·5 per cent; agriculture and forestry, 8·3 per cent; transport, 3·9 per cent; wholesale and retail trade, 8·6 per cent; others, 0·2 per cent. [Source: adapted from *Statistická ročenka ČSSR 1977* (Prague, 1977) p. 127.]

Main natural resources: coal, iron, graphite, copper, lead, silver and uranium.

Foreign trade (1977, in thousands of Czechoslovak crowns, Kčs) [US $1 = approx. 5.64 Kčs]: exports, 58,246; imports, 63,213; total, 121,459. [Source: *Statistické přehledy*, no. 5 (May) 1978.]

Main trading partners (1976 share of trade): USSR (34·1 per cent), GDR (11·7 per cent), Poland (8·8 per cent), Hungary (5·6 per cent), FRG (5·6 per cent). [Source: *Statistická ročenka ČSSR 1977*, p. 435.]
Distribution of foreign trade (percentages):

	1976		1977	
	Imports	Exports	Imports	Exports
Socialist countries	69·8	74·2	69·9	73·4
USSR	32·6	33·9	33·9	34·3
Non-socialist countries	30·2	25·8	30·1	26·6
Advanced	25·0	18·2	23·5	18·4
EEC	13·8	11·4	13·2	11·4
Developing	5·2	7·6	6·6	8·2

[Sources: 1976 calculated from *Statistická ročenka ČSSR 1977*, pp. 434–5; 1977 calculated from *Statistické přehledy*, no. 5, 1978.]

Rail network (1976): 13,186 km. [Source: *Statistická ročenka ČSSR 1977*, p. 409.]

Road network (1976): 73,677 km. [Source: ibid.]

Universities, with student numbers 1976–7: Charles University, Prague (Universita Karlova), 21,338; Comenius University, Bratislava (Universita Komenského), 15,572; Purkyně University, Brno

(Universita J. E. Purkyňe), 8098; Šafařík University, Košice (Universita P. J. Šafaříka), 6537; Palacky University, Olomouc (Universita Palackého), 5199. [Source: *Statistická ročenka ČSSR 1977*, pp. 554–5.]

Foreign relations (1976): diplomatic relations with 115 countries [source: *Rudé právo*, 31 Mar 1976]; member of the UN (since 1945), Comecon (since 1949) and the WTO (since 1955).

NOTES

1. See J. S. Kirschbaum (ed.), *Slovakia in the 19th and 20th Centuries* (Toronto: Toronto University Press, 1973); S. Harrison Thomson, *Czechoslovakia in European History* (Princeton, N.J.: Princeton University Press, 1943); R. W. Seton-Watson, *A History of the Czechs and Slovaks* (London: Hutchinson, 1943); and A. H. Hermann, *A History of the Czechs* (London: Allen Lane, 1975).
2. See V. S. Mamatey and R. Luža (eds), *A History of the Czechoslovak Republic 1918–1948* (Princeton, N.J.: Princeton University Press, 1973).
3. A. H. Brown and G. Wightman, 'Czechoslovakia: Revival and Retreat', in A. H. Brown and J. Gray (eds), *Political Culture and Political Change in Communist States* (London: Macmillan, 1977) pp. 164, 179. Beneš, who was President from 1935 to 1938, came far lower in popular estimate in 1968.
4. P. E. Zinner, *Communist Strategy and Tactics in Czechoslovakia 1918–1948* (London: Pall Mall, 1963) pp. 63–7; and H. G. Skilling, *Czechoslovakia's Interrupted Revolution* (Princeton, N.J.: Princeton University Press, 1976) p. 7.
5. The National Socialists polled 18·3 per cent of the vote; in Bohemia the communists polled 43·8 per cent, in Moravia 34·5 per cent and in Slovakia only 30·4 per cent. See Zinner, *Communist Strategy*, p. 258.
6. For analyses of 1947–8, see Zinner, *op. cit.* ch. 11; P. Tigrid, 'The Prague Coup of 1948: The Elegant Takeover', in T. E. Hammond (ed.), *The Anatomy of Communist Takeovers* (New Haven, Conn.: Yale University Press, 1975) pp. 399–432; and V. V. Kusín, 'Czechoslovakia', in M. McCauley (ed.), *Communist Power in Europe 1944–1949* (London: Macmillan, 1977) pp. 73–4.
7. See J. Krejčí, *Social Change and Stratification in Post-war Czechoslovakia* (London: Macmillan, 1972) pp. 44–6, 157–9.
8. See F. Fëjto, *A History of the People's Democracies* (London: Pall Mall, 1971) pp. 7–8; and J. Pelikán (ed.), *The Czechoslovak Political Trials* (London: Allen Lane, 1971).
9. Skilling, *Czechoslovakia's Interrupted Revolution*, pp. 29–38; G. Golan, *The Czechoslovak Reform Movement* (London: Cambridge University Press, 1971) chs 1–6.
10. Ibid., pp. 17–24.
11. R. Selucký, *Czechoslovakia: The Plan that Failed* (London: Nelson, 1970); and Golan, *The Czechoslovak Reform Movement*, chs 4–7.

12. Skilling, *Czechoslovakia's Interrupted Revolution*, pp. 62–72; D. Hamšík, *Writers against Rulers* (London: Nelson, 1971).
13. Skilling, *Czechoslovakia's Interrupted Revolution*, ch. 4; Golan, *The Czechoslovak Reform Movement*, ch. 19; and V. Mencl and F. Ouředník, 'What Happened in January', *Život strany*, nos 14–19, 1968, trans. in R. A. Remington (ed.), *Winter in Prague: Documents on Czechoslovak Communism in Crisis* (Cambridge, Mass.: MIT, 1969) pp. 18–39.
14. Skilling, *Czechoslovakia's Interrupted Revolution*, ch. 8.
15. For text of the Action Programme, see Remington, *Winter in Prague*, pp. 88–139.
16. See Skilling, *Czechoslovakia's Interrupted Revolution*, chs 10 and 18; and A. Pravda, *Reform and Change in the Czechoslovak Political System January–August 1968* (London and Beverley Hills: Sage, 1975).
17. For text see A. Oxley, A. Pravda and A. Ritchie (eds), *Czechoslovakia: The Party and the People* (London: Allen Lane, 1973) pp. 261–8.
18. See Skilling, *Czechoslovakia's Interrupted Revolution*, pp. 304–13 and ch. 20; and P. Tigrid, *Why Dubček Fell* (London: MacDonald, 1971) ch. 5.
19. For accounts of the invasion and Soviet motivation, see Skilling, *Czechoslovakia's Interrupted Revolution*, ch. 21; and R. Lowenthal, 'The Sparrow in the Cage', *Problems of Communism*, XVII, no. 6 (Nov–Dec 1968), 2–28.
20. Tigrid, *Why Dubček Fell*, pp. 210–14; and V. V. Kusin, *From Dubček to Charter 77: A Study of Normalisation in Czechoslovakia 1968–1978* (Edinburgh: Q. Press, 1978) pp. 17–28.
21. For popular response to the invasion, see R. Littell (ed.), *The Czech Black Book* (London: Pall Mall, 1969).
22. Z. Mlynář, *Listy* (Rome), no. 7, 1975; Kusin, *From Dubček to Charter 77*, pp. 69–78, 170–8.
23. Ibid., pp. 162–9.
24. Husák, *Rudé Právo*, 13 Apr 1976.
25. See J. F. Triska, 'Messages from Czechoslovakia', *Problems of Communism*, XXIV, no. 6 (Nov–Dec 1976) 26–42; for Havel's letter, see *Encounter*, Sep 1975.
26. For the text of Charter 77, see B. Szajkowski (ed.), *Documents in Communist Affairs – 1977* (Cardiff, 1978) pp. 270–4; V. Prečan (ed.), *Kniha Charty* (Munich: Index, 1977) pp. 90–5; and Kusin, *From Dubček to Charter 77*, pp. 304–23.
27. See J. Kavan, 'One Year of Charter 77', *Labour Focus on Eastern Europe*, I, no. 6 (Jan–Feb 1978) 1–3, and 'Debate within Charter 77', *Labour Focus on Eastern Europe*, II, no. 3 (July–Aug 1978) 9–18; and Kusin, *From Dubček to Charter 77*, pp. 324–5.
28. Ibid., pp. 119–24; and see R. W. Dean, 'Three Years of Czechoslovak Federation', *Radio Free Europe Background Report* (Czechoslovakia) 1 Mar 1972.
29. See *Labour Focus on Eastern Europe*, I, no. 6 (Jan–Feb 1978) 4–6, and II, no. 4 (Sep–Oct 1978) 7.
30. Kusin, *From Dubček to Charter 77*, pp. 119–20; for Party structure, see O. Ulč, *Politics in Czechoslovakia* (San Francisco: W. H. Freeman, 1974) p. 29, and G. Husák, *Rudé právo*, 13 Apr 1976.

31. According to a count of agenda items between 1969 and 1977, the most frequently discussed issues were personnel and Party membership policy and the economy. See Kusín, *From Dubček to Charter 77*, pp. 189–90.
32. The office of First Secretary was restyled Secretary-general in May 1971 at the Fourteenth Congress of the CCP.
33. See *Život strany*, no. 1, 1974 cited in *Radio Free Europe Situation Report* (Czechoslovakia), 22 Feb 1978; for departments, see *Život strany*, no. 12, 1969, cited in Ulč, *Politics in Czechoslovakia*, p. 78.
34. G. Wightman and A. H. Brown, 'Change in the Levels of Membership and Social Composition of the Communist Party of Czechoslovakia 1945–73', *Soviet Studies*, xxvii, no. 3 (July 1975) 400–3, 414; and V. Bil'ak, *Rudé právo*, 13 Sep 1975.
35. The 1976 figures are estimates by Kusín – *From Dubček to Charter 77*, pp. 187–8.
36. See the constitutional law of 27 Oct 1968 in *Sbírka zakonů Československé socialistické republiky*, no. 41, 1968. The constitutions of 1948 and 1960 are translated in J. F. Triska (ed.), *Constitutions of the Communist Party States* (Stanford, Calif.: Hoover Institution Press, 1968) pp. 396–429 and 430–52.
37. Articles 29–31 of the law of 27 Oct 1968 (see note 36).
38. See J. Chovanec, *Zastupitelská soustava Československé socialistické republiky* (Prague, 1974) pp. 102–10; for the 1971 elections, see F. Dinka and M. J. Skidmore, 'The Functions of Communist One-Party Elections: The Case of Czechoslovakia 1971', *Political Science Quarterly*, Sep 1973, 395–422.
39. Articles 56–8, 61–5 of the law of 27 Oct 1968 (see note 36).
40. See *Chekhoslovatskaya Sotsialisticheskaya Respublika* (Moscow: Nanka, 1975) pp. 98–100; and Kusín, *From Dubček to Charter 77*, pp. 120–1.
41. Ulč, *Politics in Czechoslovakia*, pp. 79–80; article 86 of the Constitution, in Triska, *Constitutions*, p. 447; and *Chekhoslovatskaya Sotsialisticheskaya Respublika*, p. 101.
42. See M. Šimek, *Život strany*, no. 11, 1977, pp. 50–2; and *XIII sjezd Komunistické strany Československa* (Prague: Svoboda, 1966) p. 432.
43. Ulč, *Politics in Czechoslovakia*, pp. 24–7; article 6 of the Constitution, in Triska, *Constitutions*, p. 432; *Lidová demokracie*, 10 June 1972; and *Svobodné slovo*, 14 Jan 1972.
44. Ulč, *Politics in Czechoslovakia*, pp. 114–18; and *Dokumentační přehled ČTK*, 31 Aug 1977, cited in *Radio Free Europe Situation Report* (Czechoslovakia), no. 35 (5 Oct) 1977, pp. 5–9.
45. See A. Rozehnal, *Odborové hnutí v Československé republice* (New York, 1953); and M. Lowit, *Le Syndicalisme de Type Soviétique* (Paris: Armand Colin, 1971) pp. 292–309.
46. See K. Hoffmann, *Odborář*, nos 12–13 (June) 1977, p. 3, and statutes, ibid., pp. 44–52.
47. M. Chalupec, *Nová mysl*, no. 12 (June) 1966, cited in Ulč, *Politics in Czechoslovakia*, p. 105.
48. *Vysoká škola*, 8 Feb 1973; *Rudé právo*, 23 Oct 1974; and Kusín, *From Dubček to Charter 77*, pp. 97–8.
49. *Statistická ročenka ČSSR 1977* (Prague: SNTL ALFA, 1977) p. 552. For the education reforms currently being introduced, see *Učitelské noviny*, 23–

30 Mar 1976, cited in *Radio Free Europe Situation Report* (Czechoslovakia), 3 Nov 1976.
50. These figures refer to 1966–8; see Krejčí, *Social Change*, pp. 34–5.
51. See Kusin, *From Dubček to Charter 77*, pp. 218–19; and Prečan, *Kniha Charty*, pp. 125–9.
52. See Golan, *The Czechoslovak Reform Movement*, pt IV.
53. *Rudé právo*, 13–14 Apr 1976; *Statistická ročenka ČSSR 1977*, pp. 144, 649; and *Rudé právo*, 27 Jan 1978.
54. V. Holesovsky, 'Czechoslovak Economy in the 1970s', in Joint Economic Committee, Congress of the US, *East European Economies; post-Helsinki* (Washington, DC: US Government Printing Office, 1977) pp. 707–9.
55. E. M. Snell, 'East European Economies between the Soviets and the Capitalists', in Joint Economic Committee, Congress of the US, *East European Economies; post-Helsinki* (Washington, DC: US Government Printing Office, 1977) p. 22; RFE Czechoslovak Situation Report, nos 7 and 14, 22 Feb and 25 Apr 1978.
56. A trade deficit of 1,225,000 crowns in 1971 grew into one of 4,967,000 crowns by 1977; see *Statistická ročenka ČSSR 1977*, p. 434, and *Statistické přehledy*, no. 5 (May) 1978.
57. *Statistická ročenka ČSSR 1970* (Prague: SNTL ALFA, 1970) pp. 323, 325; and *Statistická ročenka ČSSR 1976* (Prague, 1976) pp. 340, 342. State farms cultivate 20·5 per cent of arable land and just under 15 per cent is in private hands.
58. On foreign policy before and through 1968, see Skilling, *Czechoslovakia's Interrupted Revolution*, ch. 19.
59. See Kusin, *From Dubček to Charter 77*, pp. 261–4; and J. Mrazek, 'The International Legal Relations of the Socialist Countries', *Nová mysl*, no. 2, 1976, trans. in *Radio Free Europe Background Report* (Czechoslovakia), 15 Mar 1976.
60. *Rudé právo*, 14 Apr 1978; for discussion of relations with the West, see Kusin, *From Dubček to Charter 77*, pp. 258–71.
61. *Kdo je kdo v Československu* (Prague, 1969) vol. I, pp. 12, 292; and *Kto je kto na Slovensku* (Bratislava, 1969) p. 170.
62. *Rudé právo*, 28 May 1975.
63. *Kdo je kdo v Československu*, p. 130; *Kto je kto na Slovensku*, p. 261; and 'The Czechoslovak Party Leadership', *Radio Free Europe Background Report* (Czechoslovakia), 28 Aug 1972, pp. 67–71.
64. Ibid., pp. 78–81; and Kusin, *From Dubček to Charter 77*, p. 193.

BIBLIOGRAPHY

Historical to 1948

Hermann, A. H., *A History of the Czechs* (London: Allen Lane, 1975).
Kirschbaum, J. S. (ed.), *Slovakia in the 19th and 20th Centuries* (Toronto: Toronto University Press, 1973).
Korbel, J., *The Communist Subversion of Czechoslovakia 1918–48* (Princeton, N.J.: Princeton University Press, 1959).

Kusín, V. V., 'Czechoslovakia', in M. McCauley (ed.), *Communist Power in Europe 1944–9* (London: Macmillan, 1977).
Mamatey, V. S. and Luža, R. (eds), *A History of the Czechoslovak Republic 1918–1948* (Princeton, N.J.: Princeton University Press, 1973).
Olivova, V., *The Doomed Democracy: Czechoslovakia in a Disrupted Europe, 1914–38* (London, 1972).
Seton-Watson, R. W., *A History of the Czechs and Slovaks* (London: Hutchinson, 1943).
Thomson, S. Harrison, *Czechoslovakia in European History* (Princeton, N.J.: Princeton University Press, 1943).
Tigrid, P., 'The Prague Coup of 1948: The Elegant Takeover', in T. E. Hammond (ed.), *The Anatomy of Communist Takeovers* (New Haven, Conn.: Yale University Press, 1975).
Zeman, Z. A. B., *The Masaryks: The Making of Czechoslovakia* (London, 1976).
Zinner, P. E., *Communist Strategy and Tactics in Czechoslovakia 1918–48* (London: Macmillan, 1963).

1948–68

Elias, Z. and Netik, J., 'Czechoslovakia', in W. E. Griffith (ed.), *Communism in Europe*, vol. II (Cambridge, Mass., 1967).
Golan, G., *The Czechoslovak Reform Movement* (London: Cambridge University Press, 1971).
Hamšík, D., *Writers against Rulers* (London, 1971).
Kusín, V. V., *The Intellectual Origins of the Prague Spring* (London: Q. Press, 1971).
Lőbl, E., *Sentenced and Tried: The Stalinist Purges in Czechoslovakia* (London, 1969).
Pelikán, J. (ed.), *The Czechoslovak Political Trials 1950–54* (London: Allen Lane, 1971).
Taborsky, E., *Communism in Czechoslovakia 1948–1960* (Princeton, N.J.: Princeton University Press, 1960).

1968–9

Czerwinski, E. J. and Piekalkiewicz, J. A. (eds), *The Soviet Invasion of Czechoslovakia* (New York: Praeger, 1973).
Dean, R. W., *Nationalism and Political Change in Eastern Europe: The Slovak Question and the Czechoslovak Reform Movement* (Denver, 1973).
Golan, G., *Reform Rule in Czechoslovakia: The Dubček Era 1968–69* (London: Cambridge University Press, 1973).
Kusín, V. V., *Political Grouping in the Czechoslovak Reform Movement* (London: Q Press, 1972).
—— (ed.), *The Czechoslovak Reform Movement* (London: Q. Press, 1973).
Pravda, A., *Reform and Change in the Czechoslovak Political System January–August 1968* (London and Beverly Hills: Sage, 1975).
Skilling, H. G., *Czechoslovakia's Interrupted Revolution* (Princeton, N.J.: Princeton University Press, 1976).
Sviták, I., *The Czechoslovak Experiment 1968–69* (New York, 1971).

Tigrid, P., *Why Dubček Fell* (London: MacDonald, 1971).
Windsor, P. and Roberts, A., *Czechoslovakia 1968* (London, 1969).
Zeman, Z. A. B., *Prague Spring: A Report on Czechoslovakia 1968* (London, 1969).

Collections of documents relating to 1968–9

Ello, P., and Lunghi, H. (eds), *Dubček's Blueprint for Freedom* (New York: Acropolis, 1969).
Littell, R. (ed.), *The Czech Black Book* (London: Pall Mall, 1969).
Oxley, A., Pravda, A. and Ritchie, A. (eds), *Czechoslovakia: The Party and the People* (London: Allen Lane, 1973).
Pelikán, J. (ed.), *The Secret Vysočany Congress: Proceedings and Documents of the Extraordinary XIV Congress of the Communist Party of Czechoslovakia* (London: Allen Lane, 1971).
Piekalkiewicz, J., *Public Opinion Polling in Czechoslovakia, 1968–69* (New York: Praeger, 1972).
Remington, R. A. (ed.), *Winter in Prague, Documents on Czechoslovak Communism in Crisis* (Cambridge, Mass.: MIT, 1969).

Social and economic

Feiwel, G., *New Economic Patterns in Czechoslovakia* (New York: Praeger, 1968).
Krejčí, J., *Social Change and Stratification in Post-war Czechoslovakia* (London: Macmillan, 1972).
Machonín, P., *et al.*, *Ceskoslovenska spolecnost* (Bratislava: Epocha, 1969).
Selucký, R., *Czechoslovakia: The Plan that Failed* (London: Nelson, 1970).
Šik, O., *Plan and Market under Socialism* (White Plains, N.Y., 1967).
——, *The Bureaucratic Economy* (White Plains N.Y., 1972).

1969–78

Chovanec, J., *Zastupitelská soustava Československé republiky* (Prague, 1974).
Grospič, J. (ed.), *Ceskoslovenská federace. Zákony o federativním uspořadání* (Prague, 1972).
Kusín, V. V., *From Dubček to Charter 77: A Study of Normalisation in Czechoslovakia 1968–78* (Edinburgh, 1978).
Pelikán, J. (ed.), *Socialist Opposition in Eastern Europe: The Czechoslovak Example* (London: Allison & Busby, 1976).
Prečan, V. (ed.), *Kniha Charty* (Munich: 1977).
Szajkowski, B. (ed.), *Documents in Communist Affairs – 1977* (annual: 1977–9, Cardiff: Cardiff University Press; 1980– , London: Macmillan).
Ulč, O., *Politics in Czechoslovakia* (San Francisco: W. H. Freeman, 1974) – contains much material from the pre-1969 period.

11 Socialist Ethiopia

PETER SCHWAB

Ethiopia, a self-professed socialist state since 1974, is situated on the Horn of Africa with direct access to the Red Sea in the north-east part of the continent. Its strategic geographical importance, with the ensuing implications for shipment of oil from Persian Gulf states to the USA and Western Europe, has made it a focal point of super-power interest in Africa. Thus, both the United States and the Soviet Union have defined Ethiopia as geographically central to their own national interests.

Between 1953 and 1974 the United States had an overriding interest in Ethiopia. In return for help in maintaining Ethiopia's external security, it was permitted to establish a military base in Kagnew Station, near Asmara, from which it monitored communications in Eastern Europe, tracked satellites, and gained direct access to the Red Sea.[1] In 1960 the United States secretly 'affirmed the continuing interest of the US Government in the security of the Ethiopian Government and its opposition to any activity threatening the territorial integrity of Ethiopia'.[2] Between 1953 and 1970, half of all United States military aid to Africa was sent to Ethiopia, and the amount of military aid during this period totalled $305 million.[3]

In 1974, after the revolution, the Soviet Union became the chief ally of Ethiopia, establishing its position even more securely when it gave military support to Ethiopia in the latter's wars against Somalia in the Ogaden desert, and against Eritrean secessionists.[4] Upwards of $875 million in military aid has been sent by the Soviet Union to Ethiopia since 1977,[5] the year in which the American presence in the country all but disappeared.

Never colonised by Europe, Ethiopia has historically been politically and culturally dominated by the Amhara of Shoa province, who, together with Amhara from other provinces and the other powerful ethnic group, the Tigre, constitute about one-third of the population. Inhabiting the northern provinces, both groups are Ethiopian Orthodox

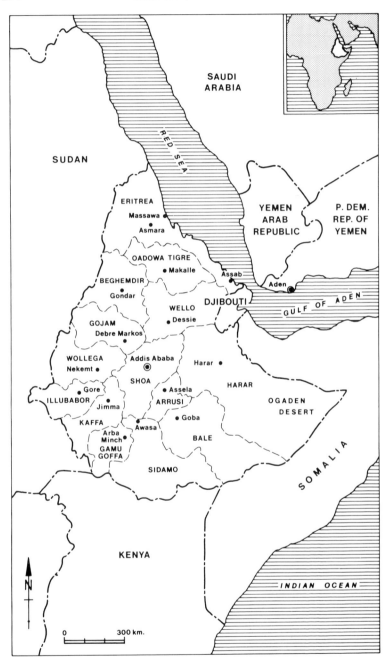

Ethiopia: provincial boundaries

Christians. The largest ethnic group are the Oromo, who constitute some 40 per cent of the population. They live in the south, and those that reside close to the Moslem population in the east have adopted Islam as their religion, while those living in the south-west have joined the Ethiopian Orthodox Church. The Somali, Moslems who predominate in the Ogaden in the south-east, were incorporated into the Empire in 1948, to the dismay of Somalia (which received its independence on 1 July 1960), which had historically considered the Ogaden culturally and politically part of its own territory. Eritrea, almost equally divided between Moslems and Christians, is a former Italian colony that was absorbed into Ethiopia in 1962. Because the only two outlets to the sea, Massawa and Assab, are in Eritrea, it is considered vital to Ethiopia's national interest. Since 1962 and 1970 respectively, the Eritrean Liberation Front (ELF) – a largely Moslem organisation – and the Eritrean People's Liberation Front (EPLF) – an organisation largely socialist – have been conducting a secessionist war in Eritrea.

Until 1974, when Ethiopia proclaimed itself a socialist state,[6] feudalism was the bedrock of the entire political and social system.[7] The landed class – made up of private landlords, a very small minority of the population – the Imperial Palace and the Ethiopian Orthodox Church owned some 80 per cent of all the arable land and imposed upon an oppressed class of tenant farmers and peasants a regime in which the latter held no legal, political, or economic rights. Under this feudal order, taxes were transferred illegally by landlords onto tenant farmers and evictions could and did occur without notice. More than 50 per cent of the produce was demanded as rent; a tithe was collected by landlords, despite its illegality; interest on loans supplied by landlords was frequently 100 per cent; and they demanded free services such as threshing and fence-building. The oppressed had little recourse to any higher authority, because governmental and legal structures were composed mainly of landlords. The landed elite was overwhelmingly Amhara.

1974–5: THE DEMISE OF FEUDALISM AND LIBERALISM

In the wake of civil disturbances reflecting overwhelming public concern over unemployment, increasing prices, soaring inflation, and a famine[8] which took the lives of some 200,000 people and was concealed by the Haile Selassie regime in order that Ethiopia should not lose international 'face', dissident military forces took over a number of cities

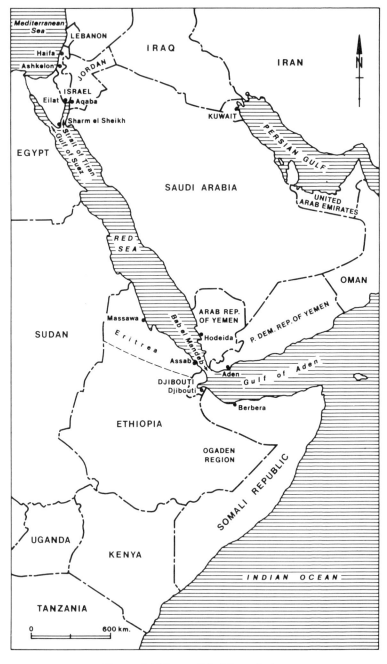

Horn of Africa: political boundaries

and towns in February 1974 and surrounded all public buildings in Addis Ababa. Calling for increases in military pay, land-reform programmes, and the dismissal of the Prime Minister and full cabinet, the junior officers who organised the revolt forced Emperor Haile Selassie to submit to their demands by early March. The newly appointed Prime Minister, Endalkachew Makonnen, a member of the Ethiopian aristocracy, appointed a new cabinet, promising to embark on a large-scale land-reform programme that would eliminate the worst elements of the feudal land system. Former Prime Minister Aklilu Habte Wold and many in his cabinet were placed under arrest on charges of corruption and self-enrichment at public expense. In April, civil authorities were again granted control by the military over Addis Ababa and Asmara. At the same time the military supported civilians in their successful attempts to obtain higher wages.

The more the demands of the military and civilians were met by the eighty-two year old Emperor, the more demands were generated. Shooting and violence began as upper-echelon officers who supported Haile Selassie tried in vain to put down the growing rebellion against his authority. In May the military insurgents made it clear that they remained unsatisfied with the slow pace of land reform. They demanded the further removal of leading political figures and as a result of their pressure the Emperor dismissed a host of officials, including the deputy military Chief of Staff, and a number of provincial governors.

Through the efforts of Foreign Minister Zewde Gebre-Selassie, a constitutional convention was called to formulate a constitution incorporating the demanded political reforms. The 120-man Dergue, the newly organised military co-ordinating committee formed to lead the opposition to the Emperor,[9] still felt that the emperor was dragging his feet and at the same time trying to organise opposition to the Dergue. The convention withered away into irrelevance and in July a large-scale round-up of government officials took place. Among those arrested by the Dergue were the President of the Imperial Crown Council, Ras (Prince) Asrate Kassa; Yilma Deressa, a former Minister of Finance, who had been a close ally of Haile Selassie and an advocate of land reform; Minasse Haile, former Minister of Foreign Affairs; the Minister of Defence, General Abiye Abebe; Iskander Desta, the Emperor's grandson; Endalkachew Makonnen; and the Keeper of the Royal Privy Purse, Abebe Retta. The Dergue forced the Emperor to appoint the liberal Michael Imru as Prime Minister, even though he was a member of the Amhara–Shoan aristocracy. By September 1974 some 150 Ethiopian leaders were imprisoned, among them all the Emperor's closest political allies, and many in his immediate family.

At this point decision-making within the Dergue was democratically organised. Committees within each military unit were composed of privates, non-commissioned officers and junior officers. Meetings were on a regular basis. Each of the forty units of the Army and police sent three members to the Dergue, which made decisions which accurately reflected the desires of the various military units.

The Dergue, in effective political control of Ethiopia, was faced with the issue of what to do about Haile Selassie, a man of international stature[10] despite his leading a government that brutalised its own peasant population under the aegis of feudalism. With their identity purposely kept publicly unknown, but supported almost totally by the rank and file of the military, the members of the Dergue argued fiercely among themselves. While the liberals in the Dergue supported a constitutional monarchy with political power in the hands of an elected parliament, the radical elements envisaged a complete restructure of the social and political system and demanded the removal of the Emperor. The radicals were successful in this respect and on 12 September 1974 Haile Selassie was deposed and arrested (he died on 27 August 1975 in mysterious circumstances).

The Dergue created a Provisional Military Administrative Committee (PMAC) to take over control of the government apparatus. Since the Dergue was based on the concept of democratic decision-making, it was necessary to create a separate entity to avoid power disputes among its members. The first two chairmen of the PMAC were purposely chosen from outside the Dergue. Lt Gen. Aman Michael Andom became its first Chairman. An Eritrean and reformist liberal, he believed that, in order to end the conflict in Eritrea, the Dergue should negotiate with the secessionists. Michael Imru, the deposed Prime Minister, became the Dergue's political adviser.

It is at this point that the counter-revolution began. It came from both the Left and the Right. Within the Left were those purists who felt that a Marxist state should not be controlled by a military committee but should be organised from the grass roots, with the military being merely the arm of the people. A number of student groups, intellectuals, and elements of the labour movement who had originally supported the Dergue now stood opposed to the government takeover. The Dergue moved quickly and arrested the three top officials of the Confederation of Ethiopian Labour Unions (CELU): Beyene Solomon, Gidey Gebre and Fisseha Tsion Tekier. Also arrested was Dr Eshetu Chole, a brilliant intellectual who was revered by students of the Left and by the leadership of the CELU.[11] Students who opposed the Dergue were arrested. The self-imposed secrecy of the membership of the Dergue prevented public discussion of the ideological backgrounds of its membership, but it is clear that extensive discussions took place within the Dergue over the future ideological framework through which it ought to operate. In late 1974 the liberals were still in control, and thus the Dergue continued to arrest the purist Marxists who on ideological and political grounds opposed the military's acquisition of power.

There was also counter-revolution from the Right. The Tigre Liberation Movement (TLM), led by the aristocrat Ras Mengasha Seyyoum, fought against the Dergue claiming that it was a terrorist elite clique. The Ethiopian Democratic Union (EDU), created by former Amhara aristocrats disenchanted with the Dergue's leftism, sought to restore the monarchical system but under a liberal parliamentary leadership. Individual acts of violent opposition from landlords and scions of the *ancien régime* also took place, on a non-organised basis. The Dergue moved quickly to eliminate this opposition, and, in order to set an example, on 24 November 1974 fifty-nine Ethiopian notables were executed, among them the two former prime ministers Endalkachew Makonnen and Aklilu Habte Wold, together with Ras Mesfin Seleshi and Rear Admiral Iskander Desta. Also executed was the Chairman of the PMAC, Aman Michael Andom. Marxists were gaining ascendancy in the Dergue and the liberal elements were being eliminated, branded as counter-revolutionaries. In December the Dergue declared Ethiopia a socialist state.[12]

On 4 March 1975 the Dergue proclaimed that 'all rural land shall be the collective property of the Ethiopian people'.[13] Many businesses and all banks and insurance companies were nationalised, as the Dergue and its governmental apparatus, the PMAC, were intent on securing a greater share of the national wealth for the traditionally neglected peasantry. In commenting on the land-reform programme, Ethiopian Foreign Minister Dr Feleke Gedle-Giorgis maintained that it was the 'main gain of the Revolution, together with the efforts which are being made to create a socialist [state] on Marxist-Leninist principles'.[14] Land reform was made the immediate economic–political goal and was the basis of the new economic programme. The announcement of the land distribution which would presently take place was met with great enthusiasm, particularly in the south, where land had always been seized by the northern Amhara nobility.

The land-reform programme was the major element of the Policy Guidelines on Ethiopian Socialism issued by the Dergue on 20

December 1974. According to the Guidelines, rural land was henceforth to be cultivated via collective farms, and farmers would be organised by the Government to ensure effective production rates. Socialism was the primary goal and would provide effective control over the financial institutions and the means of production. Reserved exclusively for State control were the following sectors: communications; leather and rubber manufacturing; electricity, gas, and water; basic industries; salt-mining; exploitation of precious metals; petroleum-refining. State-private participation would be permitted in tourism; manufacture of synthetic materials; large-scale construction; the paper and pulp industry; the processing of meats, fruits and vegetables; mining of chemical and fertiliser materials; and mining of ferrous and non-ferrous metals. Private enterprise would be allowed exclusive rights in food-processing, quarrying, grain-milling, wood-manufacturing, the weaving and knitting industry, cottage industry, small-scale construction, wholesale and retail trade, surface transportation other than rail, and entertainment services.

In effect Ethiopia was embarking on a new economic policy and massive land reform was to be its centrepiece. 'Ethiopia Tikdem' ('Ethiopia First') was defined by Policy Guidelines as 'Ethiopian socialism'. The 1975 land-reform programme was then, and is still, the main achievement of the Dergue. It met a long desired need in the peasant population and as such was warmly acclaimed. It also signified that the Dergue was moving away from the concerns of structure towards the process of meeting the economic needs of its population. The Policy Guidelines on Ethiopian Socialism and the land-reform proclamation were together a major indication that socialism in Ethiopia was to be based on the alteration of property rights moving from a private to a collective system useful for economic progress.

When the Dergue and PMAC took power in September 1974 a bitter ideological struggle ensued within the leadership of both groups. Although initially kept within the framework of discussion, it inexorably moved to the level of violence and bloodshed. Aman Michael Andom's execution was only the beginning, and within three years more than half the original 120 members of the Dergue were executed.[15] The violence became progressively more pronounced as Mengistu Haile Mariam, a Marxist, moved towards and eventually attained the primary position within the Dergue.

By early 1975 the liberals within the Dergue, who had advocated the imposition of a liberal democracy based on the Western model, had lost out to the self-professed Marxists. But the bloodshed continued as

Marxists violently disputed among themselves how best to attain a state based on the principles of Marx and Lenin. The transition to a Marxist state was extremely problematical, because of the desire to move quickly from feudalism to Marxism. The classical stages as formulated by Marx lent themselves less adequately to the Ethiopian situation than did the experience of the Russian revolution and the actions and political theory of Lenin.[16] In addition, the civil war in Eritrea and the imminent war between Ethiopia and Somalia over the Ogaden brought into the open the whole question of nationalities, national interest, and communist internationalism.[17] The inherent contradictions between nationalism and internationalism were fought over within the Dergue. In early 1975 the only thing clear was that Marxists had gained control of the Dergue, but everything else was still in a state of flux.

1975–6: ECONOMIC PROGRAMMES AND CONSOLIDATION

On 21 March 1975 the Ethiopian monarchy was abolished. Between September 1974 and March 1975 liberals and Marxists within the Dergue had been debating this issue within the context of the future ideology of Ethiopia.

The primary goal of the Dergue was to establish a people's government, 'to hand power over to the people',[18] and to that end it moved rapidly to enforce the Nationalisation of Rural Land Proclamation of 4 March 1975. The new law provided for the establishment of peasant associations throughout the country to organise collective farms, distribute land to former tenants and landless persons for personal cultivation, and to handle the economic and social problems inherent in this radical agrarian-reform programme. Each peasant family was granted the free use of a plot of land of less than ten hectares, and the State advocated the establishment of collectives to advance agricultural and economic production. The peasant associations served in a co-ordinating role, but they also served as a 'form of mass democratic organisation'.[19] According to Berhanu Bayih, a member of the Standing Committee of the PMAC, the peasant associations send local delegates to district and provincial levels to organise the implementation of land reform. 'They exercise the functions of local self-administration. They have their own executive bodies, judicial bodies, and security agencies. Self-defence detachments have been set up. . . . Their members have been given some military training and provided with weapons.'[20] Such training was considered necessary because of the opposition to the land-reform programme, particularly by landlords in the south, and farmers in the north who did not want their traditional land-tenure systems disrupted.

Although peasant associations are theoretically under the authority of the Ministry of Land Reform, in practice, as Berhanu Bayih implies, they acted independently of a national government body. In September 1977 the All-Ethiopian Peasant Association (AEPA) was founded to co-ordinate the activities of the many peasant associations, which together had organised over 7 million peasant farmers.

Landlords whose land was taken from them could appeal to a peasant association for compensation – in the form of the restoration of a portion of their former land – if they agreed to cultivate the land themselves. No financial compensation whatsoever was to be paid for appropriated rural land. To assist the implementation of the land-reform programme, colleges and secondary schools were shut and students were forced to go into the countryside to aid the peasant associations; this programme was commonly known as *zemecha* ('campaign') and was singularly unpopular among the students, whose commitment to the new regime was by no means certain. Many students tried to organise peasants against the Government and as a result many were arrested. The *zemecha* was not a notable success.[21]

Peasants in the south were elated with the new programme, but in the north, where much of the land was held under ancient communal land-tenure systems, many peasants, particularly in Gojam province, rebelled against the proclamation, which they viewed as a destruction of their traditional rights. (Land was held in common by descendants of the original person first granted usage rights and where title remained unfixed. Land, however, was individually farmed.) Even under the regime of Haile Selassie, Gojam had caused major problems to the government, when the latter attempted to impose land taxes upon the province. In the north also, the Afar, under the leadership of Sultan Ali Mirreh Hanafare, opposed the new programme. As nomads, they were unwilling to accept any fundamental alteration in the usage of their grazing lands. The Afar Liberation Front was secretly established in March and its well armed population battled with the military and peasant associations when attempts were made to nationalise the land. Individual landlords throughout Ethiopia, but particularly in the south, often refused to go along with the programme, and they were summarily executed. The EDU, from its main headquarters in London, also opposed the manner in which the agrarian land-reform was being carried out.

It is hardly surprising that most of the groups who fought violently against land reform were often precisely those elements who had benefited under Haile Selassie's regime. Overall, the land-reform programme was welcomed by the peasant population, although the enforcement of the policy was often carried out too rapidly. The establishment of the AEPA was an attempt by the Government to correct abuses of the system. But the problems inherent in the implementation of land reform could have been resolved much more easily had not the Dergue been beset by its adversaries of the Left and Right in Addis Ababa, and by opponents in Eritrea and the Ogaden. (On 29 October 1978 the National Revolution Development Campaign and Central Planning Supreme Council was established by the Dergue to organise more efficiently the broad masses of farmers.)

Because of growing opposition to its rule, the Dergue had to concentrate on strengthening its own power, and at the same time it was struggling with internal dissent over the degree of violence necessary to impose Marxism on Ethiopia. When the Dergue first took power, in 1974, decisions were as far as possible made on a democratic basis. But, as the Marxists gained power within the Dergue, those that were seen by Mengistu Haile Mariam, the Dergue Chairman, as opposing his brand of Marxism were labelled counter-revolutionaries. By 1975 democratic decision-making was being rapidly undermined as power moved to the hard core of Marxists within the Dergue. Mengistu, the real power behind the Dergue, firmly believed in imposing Marxism from above and using any amount of violence necessary for the successful achievement of a socialist state:

Our struggle is a calculated and scientific attempt to neutralise the power of the reactionary forces which are trying to destroy our revolution at its very birth. Those who have been dispossessed have reacted . . . and are being successfully fought by the broad masses. Counter-revolutionary elements . . . have been conducting a wide range of terror in all parts of the nation.

The revolution has an obligation to those who have been deprived and oppressed for centuries. Its goal is to build a socialist society in which justice, freedom, equality and the respect of human rights prevail.[22]

Mengistu, like Lenin, was willing to force the population to accept socialism, believed in a leadership cadre, and was absolutely unwilling to await the democratic revolution that would evolve from a protracted people's struggle. Mengistu thus moved to consolidate his power, and to eliminate his enemies within the Dergue and PMAC who were more 'purist' than he.

Mengistu Haile Mariam centralised his power on three fronts. He stepped up the elimination of those who opposed him, he created a political structure in the urban centres to administer to the needs of the urban population, and he laid down new guidelines for the revolutionary process.

Beginning in late 1975 and continuing through to September 1976, Mengistu moved against his opponents on the Left. Six Dergue leaders were either imprisoned or shot, and in July 1976 eighteen people were executed, including Major Sisay Habte, the Third Vice-chairman of the PMAC. Some 100 members of the Dergue and military officials who worked along with it in subordinate capacities were executed between July and September 1976.[23]

On 26 July 1975 Proclamation No. 47 was issued.[24] The proclamation nationalised urban land, and also allowed urban inhabitants to become members of a co-operative or urban dwellers' association, the 'kebelle'. Each urban area is divided into sections administered by a kebelle overseeing between 200 and 500 households.[25] In Addis Ababa 294 associations were established. Each kebelle has the power to make political and administrative decisions in its neighbourhood and to see to it that these decisions are carried out. It also has a judicial body composed of three members to enforce its regulations. According to article 30 of the Proclamation, 'no person who has exhausted his right of appeal at the kebelle judicial tribunals may lodge an appeal to the ordinary courts of law'. According to Norman J. Singer, 'the creation of the kebelle courts was presumably an attempt to introduce into the urban areas a set of courts that would be more responsive to the needs of the ordinary people'.[26] Disputes over housing allotments and urban land are the most typical of the cases heard. Individuals are appointed to a kebelle by the Dergue or elected by the community. The kebelles, in their power and structure, are similar to the *barios* in Angola.

Initially the kebelles functioned as a local political–judicial organisation. But in 1976 Mengistu Haile Mariam, in an attempt to secure his own power, called for the kebelles to go on the offensive and administer 'revolutionary justice' to counter-revolutionaries. Summary execution in the form of revolutionary justice clearly undermined the original purpose of the kebelles. 'It was no longer necessary to bring a dispute to the tribunal as long as there were other forces like the kebelle guards who were willing to administer justice summarily'.[27] As a result of

Mengistu's directive, many kebelles have far exceeded their authority, by abusing their power over those inhabitants under their control. The establishment of urban dwellers' associations was a valid political concept in that it drew the urban population directly into revolutionary activity of a judicial nature. But after 1976 the kebelles turned into instruments of violence, and as a result popular support was replaced by fear.

New guidelines for the ongoing revolution were publicly revealed on 21 April 1976. The Ethiopian National Democratic Revolution Programme (ENDRP)[28] was designed to consolidate the gains of the revolution. The programme set as its objectives the 'total eradication of feudalism, bureaucratic capitalism, and imperialism from Ethiopia . . . ; to build a new people's Ethiopia and lay a firm foundation for a transition to socialism'. It also maintained that the 'historical rights . . . of every nationality would be given equal respect'. A one-party revolutionary state based on socialism was the ultimate goal. A Political Bureau or Provisional Office for Mass Organisational Affairs (POMOA), under the leadership of Haile Fida, a French-educated Ethiopian Marxist, was created to advise the Dergue. According to Berhanu Bayih, the ENDRP is the basic Ethiopian document laying down guidelines for the revolutionary process:

> It establishes Ethiopia's entry upon the path of socialist orientation and sets as the goal of the national democratic stage the formation of a people's democratic republic led by the working-class party. When we call our country 'Socialist Ethiopia' we do not mean that we have already built up a socialist society. We are now at the stage of national democratic revolution. And we are aware that it will take much time before we can go over to socialist construction.[29]

Ethiopia has at present five Marxist-Leninist parties acceptable to the Dergue: the All-Ethiopian Socialist Movement, the Marxist-Leninist Revolutionary Organisation, the Revolutionary Seded, the Labour League, and the Revolutionary Struggle of the Oppressed Peoples of Ethiopia (see Figure 11.1). Although the goal of the Dergue is the creation of a one-party state, Berhanu Bayih maintains that it will not force a unity of the five parties 'from the top' but will encourage the parties to organise eventual unity by themselves, thus becoming the 'vanguard of the proletariat'.[30]

One must analyse the ENDRP in the light of established objectives rather than from the perspective of present day events. The programme

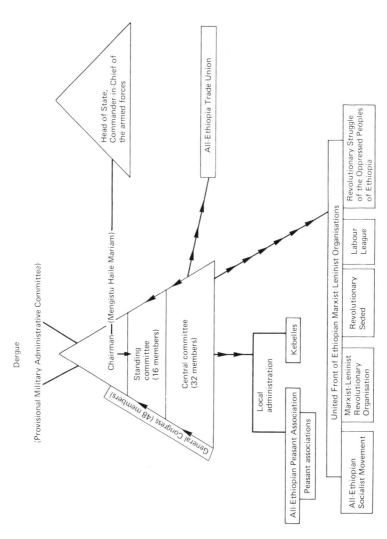

Dergue
(Provisional Military Administrative Committee)

Head of State,
Commander-in-Chief of
the armed forces

Chairman — (Mengistu Haile Mariam)

All-Ethiopia Trade Union

Standing
committee
(16 members)

Central committee
(32 members)

General Congress (48 members)

Local
administration

Kebelles

All-Ethiopian Peasant Association

Peasant associations

United Front of Ethiopian Marxist-Leninist Organisations

All-Ethiopian
Socialist Movement

Marxist-Leninist
Revolutionary
Organisation

Revolutionary
Seded

Labour
League

Revolutionary Struggle
of the Oppressed Peoples
of Ethiopia

FIGURE 11.1 Socialist Ethiopia: the political structure

is certainly the most formative exposition of the goals of socialist Ethiopia. It takes into consideration both structure and process and recognises the contradictions that must be dealt with. In admitting the existence of ethnic rebellions in eight of the fourteen provinces (Eritrea and Tigre went unmentioned) and maintaining that it would recognise the rights of nationalities, the Dergue attempted to deal with the problem of ethnic minorities. In September, Teferi Banti went even further and said that the Dergue would accept regional autonomy for Ethiopia's various nationalities.[31] Although the goal of socialism is the obliteration of national distinctions, the nationalities question in Ethiopia is so complex that recognition of its importance was taken into account. In essence the ENDRP clarified the revolutionary goals of Ethiopia, called for a party structure through which these goals could be attained, and considered the contradictions to the establishment of socialism in Ethiopia.

By the end of 1976, Mengistu Haile Mariam, Teferi Banti and Atnafu Abate were in firm control of the Dergue. They argued for a radical transformation of Ethiopia along the lines of the ENDRP. But ideological opponents continued to oppose the implementation of the programme. In addition, the civil war in Eritrea forced the government to keep 20,000 troops engaged in an attempt to maintain national unity (by 1976 the ELF and EPLF controlled about 95 per cent of the province and were clearly threatening to be fully successful in their secessionist drive).

1976–7: COUNTER-REVOLUTIONARIES AND THE MARXIST-LENINIST STATE

The power struggle within the Dergue reached its climax on 3 February 1977, when, at a meeting of the Dergue, seven of its leading members were killed by Mengistu Haile Mariam and his supporters. Among the dead were the PMAC Chairman, Teferi Banti, and Captains Alemayehu Haile and Mogus Wolde-Michael, all of whom in December 1976 had attempted to restrict the power of Mengistu and Atnafu Abate. Mengistu became Chairman of the PMAC, head of State, and Commander-in-Chief of the armed forces. Atnafu was put in charge of the people's militia, which in the rural areas was responsible for preserving order. Mengistu proceeded to centralise his authority by eliminating all his opponents within the Dergue and by combining the Dergue and the PMAC. Almost all power was in Mengistu's hands. But he and his Marxist cadre have been beset by a number of opponents.

The Ethiopian People's Revolutionary Party. Foremost among the opposition groups is the EPRP, which was organised in 1975 as a 'proletarian party' and is composed of urban intellectuals and college and secondary-school students. It maintains that a Marxist revolution cannot be directed through a military regime and argues that class contradictions can only be provoked through a period of multi-party democracy, during which time a people's revolution will take place.[32] It defines the Dergue's policy as 'adventurism' and claims to adhere to the theories of Mao Tse-tung, whose revolution was based on wide-ranging peasant participation.

Mengistu and his cadre refer to the EPRP as counter-revolutionary, maintaining that it is a 'white' group of Marxists, as distinct from the 'red' cadres of the Dergue, and claiming that it is an imperialist front.[33] To combat the execution squads of the EPRP, which killed scores of Dergue members and supporters, Mengistu created 'flame squads' to mete out their own form of immediate justice. From 1976 onwards the EPRP execution squads and the flame squads have fought on the streets of Addis Ababa, with scores of people on either side being murdered daily.

The EPRP is the most demonstrative opponent of the Dergue's form of Marxism and has been effective in killing members of the Dergue, although it has been ineffective in altering the direction of the socialist state. Its strength lies in Addis Ababa and in the townships of the south, where a large disaffected student body exists.

The Ethiopian Democratic Union. Although it disclaims any ideology,[34] with its membership made up largely of former aristocrats, the EDU group can be clearly defined as an organisation of the Right. It is based in London, but its fighters in Ethiopia are concentrated around Gondar and Dessie. It calls for democratically elected civilian rule. The Dergue has succeeded in wiping out many of the representatives of this group in Ethiopia, but, though generally ineffective, the EDU periodically engages in guerilla attacks.

The Tigre Popular Liberation Front. Distinct from the Tigre Liberation Movement, which is a rightist group, the Front is a Marxist organisation[35] fighting for the secession of Tigre from Ethiopia. The two Tigre liberation groups have prevented the Dergue from effectively controling Tigre.

The Confederation of Ethiopian Labour Unions. The Dergue has succeeded in arresting and executing most of the leadership of the CELU.[36] Although it publicly advocates a socialist platform, it claims that socialism must come about through 'volunteerism' of the people and that it must not be forced upon them. Despite its rhetoric, the CELU is a liberal group that had fairly close ties with the Haile Selassie regime, and its present call for class struggle and revolution of the masses seems very much out of character.[37] The philosophy it truly adheres to is difficult to ascertain. After 1977 it became relatively ineffective. On 8 January 1977 the regime set up the All-Ethiopia Trade Union to replace the CELU. Its first Chairman, Tewodros Bekele, was assassinated on 25 February 1977. The second Chairman was also murdered.

Students and intellectuals. Both groups claim that Ethiopia's present Marxist revolution is based on false consciousness, and that only full participation by the peasant masses can bring about scientific socialism. They have accordingly been harrassed by the Dergue. Thousands of students have been murdered or executed,[38] and intellectuals, who are greatly mistrusted by Mengistu, have been gaoled or executed. Even Haile Fida, who led the POMOA and was a leading member of the All-Ethiopian Socialist Movement, disappeared in 1977 and is said to have been executed.[39]

After the execution of Atnafu Abate in mid November 1977, Mengistu, in an attempt to consolidate his power further in the face of multiple opposition forces, altered the existing Dergue structure. The Dergue would continue to exist, but decisions would be made by a Standing Committee of sixteen members. A Central Committee of thirty-two representatives would make recommendations to the Standing Committee. The General Congress of the Dergue included all forty-eight members. Mengistu remained Chairman of the Dergue (now synonymous with the PMAC) and continued as head of State. Despite the structure of the Dergue, Mengistu eclipsed all its other members, made most of the decisions himself and 'assumed increasingly more of the trappings of power'.[40] No written constitution exists at present.

Right from its inception, the Ethiopian revolution had no coherent ideology. The old regime had disintegrated 'at the shouts of a few taxi drivers, workers and students'. Furthermore, in Ethiopia there was neither a classic Marxist-Leninist party nor a civil revolutionary movement. There was not even some kind of secret military group, like Nasser's Free Officers in Egypt. What was originally a spontaneous mass movement had been taken over by the armed forces and became an administered revolution. Mengistu emerged as its driving force and singularly important exponent.[41] What was in 1974 a democratically structured Dergue had in 1977 turned into rule by a single leader.

Even though Ethiopia is now referred to by its leadership as socialist, based on the principles of Marx and Lenin,[42] it would be accurate to suggest that the Ethiopian regime conforms more with Leninist-Stalinist principles than with those established by Marx. The rejection of the lengthy process of proletarian revolution, the use of an elitist cadre to establish communism from above through the use of force and, if necessary, violence, the attempt to jump from feudalism to communism without the intermediate stages claimed to be so necessary by Marx would appear to support this thesis.

Many writers have argued that Marxism was adopted by the military regime as a convenient political ploy. When this was challenged by the civilian opposition, and most militantly by a coalition of educated elite and organised labour, both proclaiming the Marxist creed and demanding a people's government, the soldiers' response was indiscriminate slaughter, which is still continuing in full force. This raises the problem of whether to accept the profession of socialist faith by one section of the elite, the military, and to reject the contention of the rest that the regime is simply a brutal dictatorship of arms which manipulates the symbols of an ideology that has great appeal for the masses.[43]

I would not agree with the civilian opposition. Though there is no question that there has been an abnormal utilisation of terror, and that Mengistu Haile Mariam has often killed opponents to achieve absolute power, it is also true that Ethiopia is only now emerging from an archaic feudal tradition. To move from this to communism requires a certain amount of upheaval, for, as Mao said, 'a revolution is not a dinner party'.[44] The replacement of feudal with communist structures necessitates a violation of the liberal orderly process. If a fundamental alteration of the socio-economic system is to come about and communism be created, then violence must occur. The programme of the EPRP would take generations, if not centuries, to mature and be fulfilled. Marxism can be more rapidly established in Ethiopia via the military and the policies advocated by Mengistu.

1977–9: WAR ON THE HORN OF AFRICA

In addition to being confronted with internal opposition, the Dergue had to face war on two fronts – the Ogaden[45] and Eritrea.[46]

In mid July 1977 the Western Somali Liberation Front (WSLF), with heavy military support from Somalia, stormed the Ogaden and captured 90 per cent of it. At this time Somalia, under socialist rule, was supported by the Soviet Union, and Ethiopia, which had broken with the United States, was helpless. The Soviet Union, however, feeling closer ideologically to Ethiopia and desiring an interest in Ethiopia and its Red Sea ports, agreed to supply Ethiopia with the military weaponry to defend itself. The USSR hoped to bridge the Somalia–Ethiopia dispute through common ideology, and at the same time it believed that it could maintain an interest in both countries. In November, however, Somalia expelled all Soviet advisers and closed the Soviet naval facilities in Berbera, overlooking the Gulf of Aden. As a result the Soviet Union tied itself more closely to Ethiopia. An extensive airlift of Soviet weapons – to the value, it is said, of $875 million – allowed Ethiopia, in March 1978, thoroughly to defeat and expel the Somalis. Cuba, which sent more than 16,000 military troops and advisers to Ethiopia to participate in the battle for the Ogaden, and the Soviet Union, which sent 1500 military advisers, secured a close relationship with Ethiopia by helping it in its hour of need. The GDR and the People's Democratic Republic of the Yemen also supported Ethiopia by sending military and technical advisers. By guerrilla warfare, however, the WSLF is still able to prevent Ethiopia from totally securing the area.

The ELF and EPLF, the two major secessionist groups in Eritrea, have fought Ethiopia since 1962 and 1970 respectively.[47] The Dergue has here continued the policy of Haile Selassie, which was to try to defeat the Eritrean secessionists by military means. In this instance the Dergue is caught in a major contradiction. As an advocate of socialism, recognition of national distinctions is contrary to its ideology, yet, as the ENDRP makes clear, differing nationalities are recognised. On 16 May 1976, one month after the ENDRP was made public, the Dergue unveiled its Nine-point Peace Plan for Eritrea. It called on progressive Eritrean forces to unite with Ethiopia in order to achieve the goals of the revolution. Point 2, however, affirmed 'the right of self-determination of nationalities through regional autonomy which takes due account of objective realities prevailing in Ethiopia'. The plan also called for full participation by Eritreans in the life of Ethiopia, urged negotiations with progressive Eritreans, and declared that it would aid the rehabilitation of Eritrea after the establishment of peace. Berhanu Bayhi, who was charged with the responsibility of pursuing an Eritrean settlement along the lines of the Peace Plan, claimed that autonomy was the only way of dealing with the nationalities issue. 'We believe that recognition of each nationality's right to self-determination and regional autonomy is the correct way to solve the nationalities question in line with socialist principles and Ethiopia's objective conditions'.[48]

Despite the rhetoric of the recognition of autonomy, the Dergue has consistently attempted to destroy the ELF and EPLF by military force. Though the Dergue has tried to soothe Eritrea by promising it some degree of autonomy, it is unwilling to give very much and is adamantly opposed to losing Eritrea and thus its Red Sea ports of Assab and Massawa – Ethiopia's only outlets to the sea. It has therefore struggled on against the ELF and EPLF, promising some autonomy but desiring full integration.

In fact the Dergue believes that the nationality issue in Eritrea can be solved by defeating the secessionists; but, because such a policy, publicly articulated, unifies the Eritreans even more, programmes such as the Peace Plan are revealed, in order to divide the Eritreans. By appealing to 'progressive' forces in Eritrea – namely, the EPLF – the Dergue hopes to weaken the entire movement. In April 1978 the ELF and EPLF agreed to consolidate their October 1977 political merger by uniting their combat units under joint military command.

Until July 1978, when Ethiopia recaptured a number of Eritrean towns, the ELF and EPLF together controlled 95 per cent of the province, with Asmara (the provincial capital), Assab, and Massawa remaining in Ethiopian hands. Between April and June, 3000 Cuban troops together with Soviet advisers were reported by the EPLF to have moved north to Eritrea from the Ogaden, in an attempt, in co-operation with Ethiopia, to destroy the secessionist movement. Ethiopia's national interest appears to come before its ideological link with the EPLF. It is very possible that the Cuban–Soviet–Ethiopian alliance will limit, perhaps even destroy, the effectiveness of the ELF and EPLF. Events through the summer of 1979 have shown this to be the case. Ethiopia would, however, still have to retain a large garrison in Eritrea for the forseeable future. Consequently it would remain a major force of opposition to the Dergue.

In increasing its military commitment in Eritrea, the Dergue has forced the ELF and the EPLF into an alliance that might not otherwise have been formed. As a result, the military situation confronting Ethiopia in Eritrea is, in the long run, as tentative as it was when Haile Selassie ruled the country. Only through Cuban and Soviet aid can the Dergue hope to vanquish the Eritrean secessionists. Although the Dergue would agree to limited autonomy, it is attempting to 'obliterate national distinctions' in Eritrea via militarism.

THE ECONOMY

Ethiopia's economy is basically agrarian, with little or no industry to speak of. Coffee is the primary export, with the richest farming areas found in Shoa province. The feudal land system prevented diversified agricultural development and left no room for industrialisation. As a result, Ethiopia has seen almost no industrial economic development.[49]

Since the revolution the Dergue has organised collective farms, and an adequate amount of food for self-sufficiency is grown. But the various internal and external wars prevent the Dergue from adequately coping with Ethiopia's economic stagnation.

Today the economy can only be described as post-feudal. Ethiopia is, and will be for some time, an agricultural nation and at some point its development will provide the basis for Ethiopia's industrial development. This will most probably occur when the political situation in Ethiopia becomes more settled.

BIOGRAPHY

Lt. Col. Mengistu Haile Mariam, Head of State, Chairman of the Dergue, Chairman of the PMAC and Commander-in-Chief of the armed forces, was born in 1941 in Addis Ababa. At seventeen he entered the Holeta military centre to train as a cadet, graduating in 1959 as a second lieutenant. He was then posted to the Third Army Division. He later travelled to the United States, where he studied industrial economics at the University of Maryland. His experience with racism in the US left him bitter, but his political insights deepened.[50] One military officer of the Haile Selassie regime maintained that Mengistu 'is deeply involved in political affairs and has evidenced hatred for the government. . . . He wouldn't shrink from taking part in a serious uprising when the situation is ripe.'[51] This comment was based on hindsight, as Mengistu had already participated in the abortive December 1960 coup led by the Imperial Guard.

A Shankella, Mengistu is said to despise the Amhara, who controlled Ethiopia for so many centuries. This feeling is partly owing to the fact that his mother worked as a servant to an aristocratic Amhara family and apparently was mistreated.

There is no person who is more of a true believer in the current revolution than Mengistu. After an attempt on his life he maintained that his enemies 'may succeed in assassinating me or other revolutionaries, but revolutionaries remain firm and ready to carry forward the banner of revolution. Regardless of who dies, our Revolution will continue. . . .'[52] A ruthless advocate of his Marxist political philosophy, he appears willing to eliminate any person or group who opposes his beliefs.

Mengistu is extremely well versed in the history of Ethiopia and is unusually articulate in relating the history of Ethiopia to present circumstances. There is no doubt that Mengistu has altered the history of Ethiopia. The revolution would most certainly have taken a different course without his presence. Haile Selassie's pardon of Mengistu's activities in 1960 allowed him to live to lead the revolution, much as Fulgencio Batista's decision not to execute Fidel Castro decided the future of Cuba. There is indeed historical linkage between Fidel and Mengistu.

Mengistu and his twenty-seven year old wife have three children.

BASIC FACTS ABOUT ETHIOPIA

Area: 1,221,900 sq. km (470,000 sq. miles).
Population (1978 est.): 29,400,000.
Population density: 24·1 per sq. km.
Population distribution (1978 est.): 10 per cent urban, 90 per cent rural.
Administrative division: 14 provinces.
Ethnic nationalities (1978 est.): Oromo (Galla), 40 per cent; Amhara, 19 per cent; Tigre, 16 per cent; Somali, 6 per cent; Sidamo, 6 per cent; Shankella, 4 per cent; Gurage, 2 per cent; Afar, 1 per cent; Saho, 0·5 per cent; Agau, 0·5 per cent; Falasha, 0·2 per cent; others, 4·8 per cent.
Population of major towns (1978 est.): Addis Ababa (the capital), 1,500,000; Asmara, 300,000; Diredawa, 100,000; Harar, 100,000.
National income by sector (1975 est.): agriculture and forestry 68 per cent; mining and manufacturing 3·2 per cent; construction 1·7 per cent; transportation and communication 4·2 per cent; retail and wholesale trade 7 per cent; small-scale industry and handicraft 3·9 per cent; others 12 per cent.
Main natural resources: small amounts of gold, manganese ore, quarry salt and platinum.
Main agricultural resource: coffee.
Foreign trade (1976): exports, $278 million; imports, $356 million; total, $634 million.
Main trading partners (percentage of trade): Japan (20 per cent); Italy

(18 per cent); USA (15 per cent – pre 1977); FRG (12 per cent); United Kingdom (9 per cent). (Since 1977 the USSR is a main trading partner, but its percentage of trade is unknown.)

Rail network: 1087 km.

Road network (1977 est.): 5880 km. all-weather roads.

Universities: 1, Addis Ababa University (formerly Haile Selassie I University), enrolls approximately 3000 students.

Foreign relations: close diplomatic and military ties with Cuba and the Soviet Union; member of the UN since its founding, in 1945 (before that, of the League of Nations); member of the OAU.

Sources: UN Industrial Development Organisation; UN *Yearbook of International Trade Statistics*; UN *Foreign Trade Statistics for Africa – Directions of Trade, 1975*; *Ethiopia Statistical Abstract*; *The World Almanac*; *Area Handbook for Ethiopia* (Washington, DC: US Government Printing Office, 1971). Figures on population, ethnic nationality and trade percentages are estimated from available sources and are not absolute. No census has ever been taken in Ethiopia and Ethiopian government figures are not always accurate.

NOTES

1. The Mutual Defence Agreement was signed on 22 May 1953. The United States was granted the right to build and maintain military bases in Ethiopia for ninety-nine years. It was permitted the use of Kagnew until 22 May 1978. The United States promised to defend Ethiopia from attack and to supply military advisers to help train the Ethiopian armed forces.
2. See *Hearings before the Subcommittee on United States Security Agreements and Commitments Abroad of the Senate Committee on Foreign Relations*, pt 8, Ethiopia, 1 June 1970, pp. 1903–4.
3. Note the testimony of David D. Newson, Assistant Secretary of State for African Affairs, ibid., p. 1888.
4. There is some debate as to how involved the Soviet Union is on the Eritrean front. It was extensively involved in aiding Ethiopia in the Ogaden war between July 1977 and March 1978.
5. *New York Times*, 10 Mar 1978.
6. Policy Guidelines on Ethiopian Socialism, a policy statement issued in Addis Ababa, 20 Dec 1974. The statement maintained that 'socialism means equality, the right to guide one's own destiny, the right to work and earn'.
7. For a thorough analysis of feudalism in Ethiopia, see Schwab, *Decision Making in Ethiopia* (1972).
8. Between 1973 and 1975, drought spread to famine beneath an official cover-up by the Haile Selassie regime. Some 200,000 people in eleven provinces were said to have died. According to the UN Food and Agriculture Organisation (1974) 2 million Ethiopians were made destitute by the famine.

Whole villages and districts were deserted, while life was shattered. The area most affected was Wello province. For a comprehensive account of the famine and its cover-up, see J. Shepherd, *The Politics of Starvation* (1975).

9. The full name of the Dergue, established on 28 June 1974, is the Co-ordinating Committee of the Armed Forces, Police and the Territorial Army.
10. For biographies of Haile Selassie, see Leonard Mosley, *Haile Selassie: The Conquering Lion* (Englewood Cliffs, N.J.: Prentice-Hall, 1965); Peter Schwab, *Haile Selassie: Ethiopia's Lion of Judah* (Chicago: Nelson-Hall, 1979).
11. Reports indicate that he was eventually executed.
12. See above, note 6.
13. Proclamation of the Nationalisation of Rural Land.
14. See 'An Interview with Ethiopia's Foreign Minister', *Horn of Africa*, I, no. 2 (Apr–June 1978) 3.
15. Colin Legum and Bill Lee maintain in *Conflict in the Horn of Africa* (1977) p. 18, that 'perhaps as few as 20' original members of the Dergue survive.
16. See Marx's analysis of the stages of feudalism and capitalism through which a state must pass in order to attain the communist ideal – K. Marx and F. Engels, *The Communist Manifesto* (1848). Lenin was unwilling to wait while Russia, just emerging from feudalism, passed through a period of bourgeois capitalism, and he justified a programme of bypassing this Marxist stage and seizing the opportunity to attain power. He emphasised the importance of the vanguard party and its leadership and was willing to force the masses to accept socialism. This policy was further developed by Stalin. See V. Lenin, *State and Revolution* (Moscow: Foreign Languages Publishing House, 1960).
17. The question of nationality in scientific socialism is best summarised by Lenin: 'The proletariat cannot support any consecration of nationalism; on the contrary, it supports everything that helps to obliterate national distinctions and remove national barriers; it supports everything that makes the ties between nationalities closer and closer or tends to merge nations. To act differently means siding with reactionary philistinism' – V. Lenin, *Questions of National Policy and Proletarian Internationalism* (Moscow: Progress Publishers, 1970) p. 28.
18. 'The Ethiopian Revolution: A Hard Period' (an interview with Berhanu Bayih of the PMAC), *World Marxist Review*, XXI, no. 4 (Apr 1978) 51.
19. Ibid., p. 51.
20. Ibid., pp. 51–2.
21. Brietzke, in 'Land Reform in Revolutionary Ethiopia', *Journal of Modern African Studies*, XIV, no. 4 (1976), discusses the *zemecha* failure in greater detail.
22. Interview with Mengistu Haile Mariam, conducted by Raph Uwechue, in *Africa*, LXXIX (Mar 1978) 16.
23. Legum and Lee, *Conflict*, p. 42.
24. The Government Ownership of Urban Lands and Extra Houses Proclamation.
25. J. M. Cohen and P. H. Koehn, 'Rural and Urban Land Reform in Ethiopia', *African Law Studies*, XIV, no. 1 (1977) 31.

26. J. O. Singer, 'Legal Development in Post-Revolutionary Ethiopia', *Horn of Africa*, I, no. 2 (Apr–June 1978) 23.
27. Ibid., p. 24.
28. See *The Ethiopian Revolution* (1978) for full text of the programme.
29. Interview with Berhanu Bayih (see note 18), p. 51.
30. Ibid., p. 54. In June 1977 the five groups merged into the United Front of Ethiopian Marxist-Leninist Organisations, but kept an independent status.
31. *New York Times*, 13 Sep 1976.
32. For a sustained analysis of the EPRP, see D. and M. Ottaway, *Ethiopia: Empire in Revolution* (1978).
33. Interview with Mengistu Haile Mariam (see note 22).
34. The EDU broadcasts regularly to northern Ethiopia over Radio Omdurman in the Sudan. See *EDU Advocate*, published in London.
35. See Legum and Lee, *Conflict*, for a comprehensive analysis of the Front.
36. For an overall view of its policies, see Statement of the CELU, issued in Addis Ababa, 5 June 1975.
37. For an extensive analysis of the contradictions within the CELU, see Marina Ottaway, 'Social Classes and Corporate Interests in the Ethiopian Revolution', *Journal of Modern African Studies*, XIV, no. 3 (1976) 481–5.
38. An excellent article discussing the mass killings of students is: An Observer, 'Revolution in Ethiopia', *Monthly Review*, XXIX (July–Aug 1977) 46–60.
39. Berhanu Bayih (see note 18) maintains (p. 54) that Haile Fida was a counter-revolutionary who claimed that 'the PMAC was doing nothing to save the country and the revolution'. His demise indicated the depth of the division within the revolutionary movement.
40. Legum and Lee, *Conflict*, p. 89.
41. To quote *Granma*, 22 Jan 1978, p. 8, 'It is evident today that although it is true that Marxism-Leninism in Ethiopia had not penetrated strongly enough to create a party or a movement, the universality of socialist ideas had indeed reached the middle officer class. One of them, the son of a slave, had known racial discrimination in the United States. . . . He had also known about the war in Vietnam, the Detroit fires started by the black masses, the student rebellion, the general unease that had led to the Watergate scandals, etc. Through his experience in the United States Mengistu began to see the world of today, with its uncontrollable increase of revolutions, rebellions and conflict. . . . The language in which the Communist Manifesto was written became the essence of truth to him. Without any hesitation he took sides with the exploited, the oppressed, the humiliated in Ethiopia. . . . What is more he decided to promote a movement for making demands within the armed forces. . . .'
42. See interview with Berhanu Bayih (see note 18).
43. See, for example, J. Markakis, *Class and Revolution in Ethiopia* (1978).
44. *Quotations from Chairman Mao Tse-tung* (Peking: Foreign Language Press, 1972) p. 11.
45. For background to the Ogaden dispute, see I. M. Lewis, *The Modern History of Somaliland* (London: Weidenfeld and Nicolson, 1965); and Mesfin Wolde Mariam, 'The Ethio-Somalia Boundary Dispute', *Journal of Modern African Studies*, II, no. 3 (1964).
46. Eritrea, which gives Ethiopia access to the Red Sea, has an area of 119,000

sq. km. and a population of 1,948,000, of whom some 56 per cent are
Moslem. Eritrea was captured by Italy in 1890 and became part of Italian
East Africa in 1936. It was occupied by British forces in the spring of 1941
and from then on was administered by the United Kingdom. On 2
December 1950 the General Assembly of the United Nations passed a
resolution by a vote of 46–10 recommending that Eritrea should 'constitute
an autonomous unit federated with Ethiopia under the sovereignty of the
Ethiopian crown'. The Federal government was to control 'defence, foreign
affairs, currency and finance, foreign and interstate commerce, and external
and interstate communications including ports'. The resolution envisaged
common citizenship and an Imperial Federal Council with Eritrean and
Ethiopian representation. The Eritrean government was to have 'legislative,
executive and judicial powers in the field of domestic affairs', and to be
responsible for 'all matters not vested in the Federal government, including
the power to maintain the internal police, to levy taxes, and to adopt its
budget'. On 16 September 1952 Britain formally handed over Eritrea to
Ethiopia. In May 1960 the central government at Addis Ababa announced
that the Eritrean government would henceforth be known as the Eritrean
Administration. On 14 November 1962 Eritrea was formally incorporated
into Ethiopia as one of its fourteen provinces. A noted work on the subject is
G. K. N. Trevaskis, *Eritrea, A Colony in Transition, 1941–1952* (London:
Oxford University Press, 1960).
47. The ELF, a largely Moslem organisation initially supported also by young
Christian intellectuals came into being in 1962. In 1970 it split into two
separate entities, the ELF–Revolutionary Council and the EPLF. The
ELF–Revolutionary Council desires self-determination for Eritrea, and
until 1977 demanded recognition as the sole representative of the Eritrean
people. See its appeal *Eritrea: A Victim of UN Decision and of Ethiopian
Aggression* (3 Dec 1971). The EPLF split off from the ELF because of
ideological and organisational differences. Its objectives include the establishment of a people's democracy with a planned national economy, the
nationalisation of all land and industry, the integration of the Eritrean
nationality, the support for all 'just and revolutionary' movements in Africa,
Asia, and Latin America. See its *National Democratic Programme* (31 Jan
1977). The EPLF is clearly the more precise in terms of its ideology, and it is
ideology rather than religious differences that set it apart from the ELF. The
EPLF is socialist, without religious orientation, while the ELF–
Revolutionary Council views itself as an organisation whose essential values
lie in Islam.
      In 1976 the EPLF itself split, when the Secretary-general, Osman Saleh
Sabbe, was thrown out by those elements of the EPLF who believed that he
had been sowing 'a reactionary line' by his 1975 attempt to establish unity
with the ELF. With the financial support of Saudi Arabia he established in
1976 the ELF–Popular Liberation Forces. Much smaller in terms of
adherents than either of the other two liberation movements, it is also far
more conservative, though it too demands secession from Ethiopia. For a
discussion of the split, see 'Eritrea in Struggle', *Newsletter of Eritreans for
Liberation in North America*, I, no. 8 (Mar 1977) 3. In late 1977 the EPLF
and the ELF–Revolutionary Council created a united front and in 1978

maintained that they would crush the ELF–Popular Liberation Forces unless it absorbed itself into the front. The merger came about because of the overwhelming force displayed by the Ethiopian–Soviet–Cuban alliance. The ELF–Popular Liberation Forces refused to join the united front.

48. Interview with Berhanu Bahih (see note 18), pp. 54–5.
49. The best work to date on the economy as it existed during the regime of Haile Selassie is Assefa Bequele and Eshetu Chole, *A Profile of the Ethiopian Economy* (Addis Ababa: Oxford University Press, 1969). The authors maintained at that time (p. 111) that 'the picture of the economic situation . . . is hardly flattering. . . . We are convinced that the road to development lies in a candid examination of the reality, however stark that reality may be, and in a conscious and determined effort to rectify the economic ills of the country. Admittedly there has been some development . . . yet . . . isolated advances represent the facade, not the substance of development'.
50. *Granma*, 22 Jan 1978.
51. As quoted in *Granma*, 7 May 1978.
52. Ibid.

BIBLIOGRAPHY

An extensive amount of literature on Ethiopia has been detailed in the Notes. The Bibliography lists books, articles and important government documents that relate to the Ethiopian revolution, but does not list the important news articles previously mentioned. Material helpful in understanding the process of government during the regime of Haile Selassie is also discussed in the Notes.

'An Interview with Ethiopia's Foreign Minister', *Horn of Africa*, I, no. 2 (Apr–June 1978) 3–6.
Brietzke, P., 'Land Reform in Revolutionary Ethiopia', *Journal of Modern African Studies*, XIV, no. 4 (1976) 637–60.
Cohen, J. M. and Koehn, P. H., 'Rural and Urban Land Reform in Ethiopia', *African Law Studies*, XIV, no. 1 (1977) 3–62.
ELF, *Eritrea: A Victim of UN Decision and of Ethiopian Aggression* (New York, 3 Dec 1971).
EPLF, *National Democratic Programme* (31 Jan 1977).
Ethiopian National Democratic Revolution Programme, issued in Addis Ababa, 21 Apr 1976.
The Ethiopian Revolution (New York: World View, 1978).
'The Ethiopian Revolution: A Hard Period', an interview with Berhanu Bayih, member of the Standing Committee of the PMAC, *World Marxist Review*, XXI, no. 4 (Apr 1978).
Farer, T. J., *War Clouds on the Horn of Africa* (New York: Carnegie Endowment for International Peace, 1976).
The Government Ownership of Urban Lands and Extra Houses Proclamation, in *Negarit Gazeta* (Addis Ababa), 26 July 1975.

Legum, C. *Ethiopia: The Fall of Haile Selassie's Empire* (New York: Africana, 1975).

Legum, C. and Lee, W., *Conflict in the Horn of Africa* (New York: Africana, 1977).

Markakis, J., *Class and Revolution in Ethiopia* (London: Spokesman Books, 1978).

Matatu, Godwin, 'Ethiopia's Finest Hour', *Africa*, LXXIX (Mar 1978) 17–26.

An Observer, 'Revolution in Ethiopia', *Monthly Review*, XXIX (July–Aug 1977) 46–60.

Ottaway, David and Mariana, *Ethiopia: Empire in Revolution* (New York: Africana, 1978).

Ottaway, Mariana, 'Social Classes and Corporate Interests in the Ethiopian Revolution', *Journal of Modern African Studies*, XIV, no. 3 (1976) 469–86.

Policy Guidelines on Ethiopian Socialism, Addis Ababa, 20 Dec 1974.

Proclamation of the Nationalisation of Rural Land, in *Negarit Gazeta* (Addis Ababa) 4 Mar 1975.

Schwab, Peter, *Decision Making in Ethiopia* (London: C. Hurst, 1972).

——, 'Human Rights in Ethiopia', *Journal of Modern African Studies*, XIV, no. 1 (1976) 155–60.

——, 'Cold War on the Horn of Africa', *African Affairs*, LXXVII, no. 306 (Jan 1978) 6–20.

Shepherd, Jack, *The Politics of Starvation* (New York: Carnegie Endowment for International Peace, 1975).

Singer, Norman J., 'Legal Development in Post-Revolutionary Ethiopia', *Horn of Africa*, I, no. 2 (Apr–June 1978) 21–7.

Statement of the CELU, issued in Addis Ababa, 5 June 1975.

Szajkowski, Bogdan (ed.), *Documents in Communist Affairs – 1977* (annual: 1977–9, Cardiff: University College Cardiff Press; 1980– , London: Macmillan).

Uwechue, Raph, interview with Mengistu Haile Mariam, in *Africa* LXXIX (Mar 1978) 12–16.

Valdes Vivo, Raul *Ethiopia's Revolution* (New York: International Publishers, 1978).

12 German Democratic Republic

HANS WASSMUND

PROBLEMS OF STUDYING THE GDR, AND THE STAGES OF ITS HISTORY

Given the radical ups and downs of German history in the twentieth century, the celebration of the thirtieth anniversary of the existence of the GDR is an achievement in itself. Although the 'first socialist state on German territory' has throughout its history been heavily dependent on the Soviet Union and has never reached any democratic legitimacy of its own in the Western sense, it has developed into an important element of stability and prosperity in the 'socialist camp'. Whereas the stages leading to the present state of affairs are seen by Marxist scholars as conforming to socialist logic, from the Western point of view various approaches to studying the regime can be discerned. During the 1950s the 'Soviet occupation zone' was analysed exclusively in terms of a rigid version of the concept of totalitarianism.[1] The goal of the scholars – most of them were refugees from East Germany – was to discredit the Ulbricht regime, isolate it internationally and picture it as something temporary that sooner or later would be integrated into the Federal Republic of Germany (FGR) and the Western power bloc.

After the building of the Berlin Wall in 1961, developments in the GDR were increasingly seen as leading to a status of relative self-reliance and the building of a separate statehood. The GDR was examined more and more in terms of what it was, and there was a striving for objectivity: social-science concepts were applied and efforts were made to collect as much empirical data as possible. Scholars and journalists slowly moved away from an aggressive tone and sometimes primitive anti-communism in their analysis and turned to spreading basic information on the politics, economics and society of the other

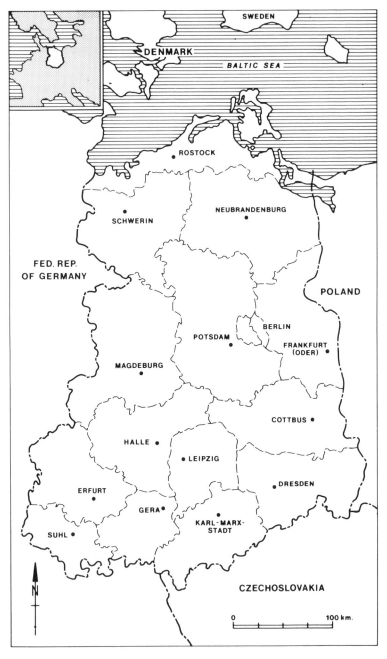

German Democratic Republic: provincial boundaries

German state. This sober delineation of the institutions, processes and structures of a state that was there to last was seen as essential in facilitating comparison of and competition between the two Germanies. Over the last decade the study of the GDR has increasingly become comparative: the forces at work in highly industrialised, complex, education- and achievement-oriented societies – be they called capitalist or socialist – came to the centre of attention. Research on the GDR became more and more interdisciplinary, the importance of methodology grew and the data base expanded. The results of these efforts were used on the one hand for arguments of the convergence of systems because of growing functional similarities of post-industrial societies, and on the other hand to demonstrate the superiority of the home system, with 'scientific' material in the intra-German confrontation and 'proof' of advantages in the worldwide rivalry between East and West. Thus, whereas various approaches to the study of the GDR are used side by side, at the same time the emphasis has switched from an analysis stressing system differences (in the 1950s) to one stressing the system itself (beginning in the 1960s). The favourite approach of recent years is one of system comparison.[2]

The approach used by Peter Christian Ludz, the leading West German expert on the GDR, seems to satisfy both of the basic prerequisites of serious scholarship dealing with communist regimes: it looks at the empirical material in the context of historical development and critically applies it to the further evolution of the system, and it tries to understand the regime in terms of its own standards, development, and vision of the future, always confronting them with the reality.[3]

Scholars from the GDR itself, on the other hand, have no difficulties whatsoever in analysing the history of their system and the present state of affairs. The evolution after 1945 is subdivided into very clear-cut stages, each with its own historical logic and socialist dynamic.

The period 1945–9, with its far-reaching restructuring of one part of German society, the radical elimination of all links with the past and the forceful establishment of Soviet-type socialism as the example to follow, is characterised as the *anti-fascist, democratic resurgence*. It ended on 7 October 1949 with the establishment of the GDR and the retreat of the Soviet Union from some of its responsibilities as an occupation force. The proclamation of the GDR was interpreted as an attempt to overcome the division of Germany which the Western powers had enforced on all Germans through the foundation of the Federal Republic. In addition, it was argued that the camp of socialism could be expanded, because the new quality of the State would allow for the transition from the democratic to the socialist stage of revolution in Germany.

The phase of development from 1950 to 1961 is called the period of *transition from capitalism to socialism*. During this period the final integration of the GDR into the Eastern bloc took place; various sectors of society were radically altered (witness the total collectivisation of agriculture, in 1960); and the 'protection of the State border' by the building of the Wall through Berlin in August 1961 brought consolidation.

The period after the Sixth Congress of the ruling Socialist Unity Party of Germany, the Sozialistische Einheitspartei Deutschlands (SED), in 1963 is characterised as *comprehensive construction of socialism*. In it a new economic policy, with special emphasis on flexibility and productivity, the broad use of advanced science and technology, and the increased self-confidence of the Ulbricht leadership, as expressed in claims of the model character of the GDR brand of socialism, were of special importance.

In the 1970s (particularly following the Eighth Congress of the SED in 1971) attention has been concentrated on the *formation of the developed socialist society*. Internationally new conditions came into existence, with the worldwide recognition of the GDR as a separate German state, the increased rivalry with West Germany and the necessity for a total sealing-off (*Abgrenzung*) in ideological matters, to prevent the population from being infected with Western ideas. Internally this period brought the transition from Ulbricht to Erich Honecker and his crew of pragmatists, a new realism in economic matters and an emphasis on ideological indoctrination, coupled with a total subordination to the Soviet Union in all matters.[4]

This clear-cut and all embracing interpretation of the history of the GDR is only one result of the monopoly of the SED leadership in all ideological and political matters. It has always claimed exclusive competence to proclaim the truth in all theoretical questions, to set undisputed guidelines for all spheres of life and to have its will executed without any restrictions.

BASIC PRINCIPLES AND THE ROLE OF THE SED

The dominating role of the Party is not only the result of long practice, but also has been fixed once and for all by the basic documents that underlay the GDR's political system. For example, the very first sentence of the Party Programme unanimously adopted at the SED's Ninth Congress, in May 1976, reads; 'The SED is the conscious and organised *avant-garde* of the working class and the labouring people of the socialist GDR.'[5] In the autumn of 1974, celebrating the twenty-fifth anniversary of the GDR, the 1968 constitution was readopted, but with a number of significant amendments. Its first sentence reads; 'The GDR is a socialist state of the workers and peasants. It is the political organisation of the labourers in town and countryside, under the guidance of the working class and its Marxist-Leninist party.'[6]

Whilst the overwhelmingly strong position of the Party in the society and relative to the State is rigidly fixed, the two governing principles of its inner life give at least the appearance of flexibility, decentralisation of power and democratic procedures. The fundamental organisational principle, *'democratic centralism'*, is defined in the Party statutes as follows:

1. All party organs from the bottom to the top are democratically elected.
2. All elected organs of the Party are obliged to give regular reports about their activities to the organisation that has elected them.
3. All resolutions passed in the higher Party organs are binding for all the subordinate ones, strict Party discipline is to be practised and the minority, or a single Party member, has to submit to the resolutions of the majority in a disciplined manner.[7]

For all directing and managing functions, the 'principle of collectivity' has to be applied: 'All leading cadres must consider and decide in the collective the problems confronting the Party, the measures to be taken and the planning of activities'.[8]

The way in which these principles are applied underlines the absolutely dominant role of the Party leadership, which controls and directs the entire economy and society of the GDR. The strictness and effectiveness of application of directives from a small, top Party clique may be explained historically and in terms of German political traditions. The Party leadership came to power by force and through the good offices of the Soviet occupation administration. The land was ruined by war, the territory was divided and large strata of society were opposed to the Soviet path of socialism, which was thought to be alien to Germany. The profound transformations that were to be brought about in all spheres of life in a short period made necessary the absolute concentration of power in a few hands. In addition, the Prussian tradition of strict obedience to all orders 'from above', pushed to extremes during twelve years of Nazi totalitarianism, certainly helped the communist leaders to establish their system of tight control.

The goals of the Party leadership have been translated into the socio-political realm in the traditional manner, as practised in the Soviet Union from the very beginning of its existence; Marxism-Leninism is said to be an infallible tool of social analysis and to provide a scientific instrument to shape the future. Besides this characterisation of the ideology as a form of science, its absolutely binding character and the obligation of all Party members always to act in line with the leadership's directives are of crucial importance. In addition, it is claimed that, in a permanent process of adaptation, the unity of theory and practice is guaranteed through the creativity of the Party. The principle of partiality finally asks for an unconditional siding with the interests of the working class and socialism and the condemnation of all forms of revisionism and dogmatism and non-activist attitudes.[9]

The total process by which the will of the Party leadership is transformed into the political actions of the State and government is complex. The Party stands above the State and all social organisations, and has the right and the duty to direct all its moves and activities. Its leading role has been compared with the functions of a conductor, whose directions have to be strictly followed by all members of the orchestra without his playing any single musical instrument.[10] One means by which the will of the Party is transformed into political activity is multiple office-holding in the highest reaches of the Party, the State and the mass organisations. To give just one example, of the thirty-nine members of the 1972 Council of Ministers, twenty-five were also members or candidate members of the Central Committee of the SED.[11] In short, those who take the decisions in the leading bodies of the Party also carry them through as the top functionaries of the principal governmental institutions.

Closely linked to this system of multiple office-holding is the unlimited right of the Party to determine with its cadre policy which posts, at all levels, are held by whom. The Party is free to hire and fire all functionaries and defines the way they fulfil their duties. Finally, there is a doubling of all the apparatus. The Party branch guides and controls the equivalent section of the State apparatus and governmental agencies in the economic, social and cultural fields. This creates a necessity for permanent consultation and exchange of information between Party and State. With it goes much red tape, doubling of work, friction and tension, but also the guarantee that absolutely nothing happens without the approval of the Party.[12]

For more than a year after the unconditional surrender of Nazi Germany in May 1945, a relatively independent road to a special German brand of socialism was followed. The founding declaration of the Communist Party of Germany (Kommunistische Partei Deutschlands – KPD) on 11 June 1945 took into account both the very strong traditions of social democracy, especially on the territory of the Soviet zone of occupation, and the feelings of the Western powers, into whose zones of occupation the Soviet Union still hoped to extend its influence. The German communists therefore stated:

> We are of the opinion that it would be wrong to force the Soviet system upon Germany, as that would not correspond to the present stage of development in Germany. Rather, we are of the opinion that the most important interests of the German nation in the present situation call for a different road, the road of establishing an antifascist, democratic regime, a parliamentary republic.[13]

This line was followed up in February 1946 by one of the Party's leading intellectuals, Anton Ackermann, who argued in the theoretical journal *Einheit:*

> The development towards socialism in Germany will doubtlessly carry a specific character. In other words, the strong particularities of the historical development of our people, the political and national individuality, the special traits of its economy and culture will find an unusually clear expression.[14]

Two developments in the international sphere brought hopes of an independent German road to socialism to an abrupt end: the disintegration of the wartime four-power alliance, leading to an open confrontation over Germany in 1947–8; and the outbreak of the ideological and power political conflict between the Soviet Union and Yugoslavia in 1948, added to a tightening of control from Moscow and to the Soviet Union's refusal to allow the states under its control to develop an independent line.

The SED, which came into existence through a merger in April 1946 of social-democratic forces (bringing into the union a clear majority of some 680,000 members) and just over 600,000 KPD members, in just two years totally changed its character. While the fusion of the two leftist workers' organisations had been brought about by a combination of measures from above (promises and compromises by and agreements between the leaders) and by demands from below (the wish of the masses to overcome the traditional rift in the German labour movement, and not to repeat the mistakes of the Weimar Republic, which had led to the common suffering of social democrats and communists in Hitler's concentration camps and the wish to tackle the tremendous task of overcoming fascism and building a democratic and socialist Germany), the drastic change in the Party in 1948 came about on orders from Moscow alone. The former mass party (with a peak membership of more than 2 million in 1948) gave way to an elitist cadre party 'of the new type'. Instead of there being an equal share of former members of the Social Democratic Party and the KPD in all important positions of State and society, the social democrats were now persecuted and chased out of office, and 'social democracy' was suddenly attacked as the principal ideological sin. Instead of the development of a 'German third road to socialism' (avoiding the faults of American capitalism and the Stalinist version of socialism), there was a total bolshevisation of the SED, with complete subordination to orders from Stalin.[15]

With the reorientation of the Party went a speeding up of the process of transforming the State, the economy and all structures of society to conform with the Soviet model. There was no longer any hesitation in introducing all the characteristics of the Soviet political system in Germany and in concentrating, for that purpose, total power in the hands of the Party bureaucrats. The federal structure of the GDR was abolished (and fifteen *Bezirke*, or districts, were introduced instead), resources mostly concentrated on the heavy-industry sector, 'suspicious elements' were 'purged', and a massive drive towards a total change of the structure of society was started. The Second Congress of the SED, in 1952, proclaimed that the 'construction of socialism' would take place over the next ten years.

Walter Ulbricht, who had been trained in Moscow and who was at the head of a small group of German communists who started the building of a 'new Germany' in May 1945,[16] almost fell from power when his superior Stalin died in March 1953. He faced an uprising affecting large sections of the population and, especially, three months later a revolt of workers. Since the new Soviet leadership thought it impossible to allow his overthrow, they sent in tanks, and the result was that the June 1953 events actually strengthened Ulbricht's position.[17]

As the self-proclaimed First Secretary of the SED Central Committee, he ruled the GDR with a combination of flexibility (a dedicated Stalinist surviving all the anti-Stalin moves after the Twentieth Congress of the CPSU) and harshness (brutally supressing all intellectual and political opposition). The relentless drive towards the destruction of all traditional forms of power and organisation and the constant pressing ahead to create a modern socialist industrial state strictly following the Soviet example laid the basis for a consolidation of the Party's power in the late 1950s and early 1960s.

The pressure on the GDR population to reach an accommodation with the regime and to conform to the will of the Party was enormously increased by the building of the Wall through Berlin in August 1961 and the sealing off all possibilities of flight to the West. Once the exodus of the best and the brightest (more than 200,000 leaving each year) had been halted, the SED could afford to take measures in order slowly to integrate more and more of the people into the social and political system. The SED created mechanisms of consultation and strove, by emphasising the importance of high standards of living, encouraging pride in the State's achievements and seeking to forge a new national self-consciousness, for an identity of the goals of the population with those of the Party.[18]

In the SED itself tensions and conflicts grew as the Party began to turn away from outwardly more totalitarian methods and attempted to find new ways of governing an increasingly complex industrial society. One reason for the growing difficulties of the Party rested in the fact that Walter Ulbricht concentrated an enormous amount of power in his own hands and, along with the 'old guard', showed signs of inflexibility and dogmatism. Ulbricht was known for his ability to manipulate different factions of the Party so as to confirm his own pre-eminence, but during the 1960s there emerged two major, fundamentally different groups labelled by Ludz the 'strategic clique' and the 'institutionalised counter-elite'.[19] In the former were the old, Moscow-trained, ideologically dogmatic leaders relying on force and their long experience as bureaucrats at the centre of power. In competition and partial conflict with this established elite of apparatchiks stood the younger Party functionaries, with university education in economics and sciences and with a pragmatic outlook laying emphasis on the need for efficiency and for rapid modernisation by means of science, improved communication and reformed methods. Previously the SED leadership, and not only the master tactician Walter Ulbricht, had been able to cope with the tensions and conflicts in the Party and prevent them from becoming dysfunctional for the overall system. They had succeeded in coordinating 'technical-functional and ideological-political authority'

(Ludz) and enlisting the co-operation of the 'dogmatists' and the 'pragmatists', despite the generation gap, differences of outlook and the 'organisational conflicts of interest among various bureaucracies of the party, the state and the economy'.[20]

One result of the need to balance the various interests of society and the tensions between groups is the increase in the membership of all the principal bodies of the political system of the GDR. After Erich Honecker succeeded Ulbricht, in May 1971, the Political Bureau, the very centre of power, was enlarged. At present it has nineteen full members and eight candidate members, who usually meet once a week. They determine basic policy directives relative to all aspects of political life.

In 1976, at the Ninth Congress of the SED (the Congress now meets every five years and is defined as 'the highest organ of the Party'), a Central Committee of 202 persons (including 145 full members) was elected. This usually meets every four months and can be regarded as a sort of Party parliament. It confirms the decisions of the Political Bureau, and the Central Committee Secretariat executes all the decisions of the Party, transforms the guidelines into concrete policies and keeps control over State, society and economy. The apparatus of the Central Committee consists of more than 2000 high-calibre experts. The various activities are run by some forty heads of subdivisions of the Secretariat, most of whom are at the same time members of top Party bodies.

At the Ninth Congress of the SED the Party had just over 2 million members (every sixth citizen over eighteen years), of which, according to official figures, 56 per cent were workers and 20 per cent members of the intelligentsia (in terms of the total population this represents a severe under-representation of the working class) (see Tables 12.1 and 12.2). Less than a third of the Party members are women; and to improve the age average a massive influx of young members has been arranged in recent years with 43 per cent of new members being under the age of forty. The educational standards of Party members have improved impressively: every fourth Party member holds a university or higher vocational schooling degree and almost 94 per cent of the leading cadres of the Party functionaries belong in this category.[21] Against this increasing professional and academic expertise of the Party, the leadership over the past couple of years has stressed its proletarian origins, sought to revitalise Marxism-Leninism, initiated campaigns for ideological indoctrination of the population, and very strictly defined the limits of ideas thought to be hostile to the GDR version of socialism.

TABLE 12.1 Membership of the SED

Year	Membership
1946	1,300,000*
1947	1,856,000
1950	1,750,000
1953	1,200,000
1954	1,400,000
1957	1,500,000*
1962	1,680,000*
1966	1,800,000*
1971	1,909,659
1976	2,043,697

* Very approximate figures.
Sources: P. C. Ludz, The Changing Party Elite in East Germany (Cambridge, Mass.: MIT Press, 1972) p. 197; D. Childs, East Germany (New York: Praeger, 1969) p. 27; H. Rausch and T. Stammen (eds), DDR – Das politische, wirtschaftliche und soziale System (Munich: Verlag C. H. Beck, 1974) p. 214; Protokoll der Verhandlungen des IX Parteitages der Sozialistischen Einheitspartei Deutschlands, vol I (Berlin: Dietz Verlag, 1976) p. 136; Aus dem Bericht des Politburos an die 5. Tagung des ZK der SED – Berichterstatter; Genosse Erich Honecker (Berlin: Dietz Verlag, 1977) p. 31. Table kindly supplied by Dr Leslie Holmes of the University of Kent at Canterbury.

TABLE 12.2 Social composition of the SED (percentages)

	Industrial workers	Peasants	White-collar workers	Others
1947	48·1	9·4	22·0	20·5
1957	33·8	5·0	42·3	18·9
1961	33·8	6·2	41·3	18·7
1966	45·6	6·4	28·4	19·6
1971	56·5	5·9	17·1[a]	20·5
1976	56·1	5·2	20·0[a]	18·7

[a] This figure includes members of the intelligentsia. The figures for 1971 and 1976 are the percentages of intelligentsia only, and it is not clear from the sources whether or not this includes 'employees' (Angestellte)
Sources: Rausch and Stammen, DDR, p. 219; Protokoll des IX Parteitages der SED, vol. I, p. 136; Kleines politisches Wörterbuch (Berlin: Dietz Verlag, 1973) p. 777. Table kindly supplied by Dr Leslie Holmes of the University of Kent at Canterbury.

The SED remains absolutely convinced of its leading role and its ever-increasing importance as a guiding force. In the Party Programme of May 1976 it defined the task of the Party as that of 'politically guiding the social development in the GDR on the basis of a scientifically founded strategy and tactic. As the tasks of guiding and planning all aspects and forms of the social process become more far-reaching and complicated, so the role of politically directing society through the Marxist-Leninist party is increased'.[22]

MASS ORGANISATIONS AND OTHER POLITICAL PARTIES

Despite the absolute centralisation of power at its top, the SED has always carefully tried to give the appearance of heading a pluralistic, democratic regime. This is evidenced by the existence and activities of a variety of political parties and mass organisations. The 'National Front' unites 'all forces of the people in common action for the construction of a socialist society'.[23] But the dominant role of the SED, its authority on all questions of importance and its right to fill positions with candidates of its own choice, has to be unconditionally recognised by all other forces of society. Independent moves or spontaneous initiatives, not to speak of real opposition, are not permitted and the multiplicity of parties and organisations is a mere formality. The non-SED parties and the mass organisations are represented on the ruling bodies and develop far-reaching activities in a number of fields, but they cannot and would never do anything that is against the directives and the will of the SED. The National Front has become an important link between State and society, bringing together the various strata of the population and furthering the feeling of togetherness by discussions about, and agitation and mobilisation for the solution of, political problems. Its theoretical basis is the supposed identity of interests and goals of all groups of society. In their role of conveying the will of the SED to all members of society, including those a communist party would otherwise not reach, neither the other parties nor the mass organisations forming a 'united bloc' with the SED should be underestimated. The Confederation of Free German Trade Unions (*Freier Deutscher Gewerkschaftsbund* – FDGB), for example, with over 8 million members, which includes 95 per cent of the total work force, has 1·7 million elected functionaries and fulfils important tasks in the social field. It has to be heard in most cases before any action can be taken with regard to work places and working conditions, and it is the country's largest travel agency and organiser of holidays. According to the Constitution, the FDGB has the right of 'comprehensive codetermination in State, economy and society' and the right to initiate legislation in the People's Chamber (Volkskammer).[24]

Through child and youth organisations, the GDR leadership reaches young people, directing them by a combination of political indoctrination and sports and hobby activities. The Free German Youth (Freie Deutsche Jugend – FDJ), with just over 2 million members, has influence over about 75 per cent of those aged between fourteen and twenty-five, and the pioneer organisation 'Ernst Thälmann' organises, with 1·9 million members, almost all the youngsters aged between six and fourteen. Making young people convinced socialists, preparing them for jobs, giving them a pre-military training and preaching to them intolerance towards class enemies and the imperialist camp are among the major functions of these organisations.[25] The 'unity of socialist patriotism and proletarian internationalism' is seen as the basis of the ideological education, and the role of the FDJ has been defined as one of 'active supporter and the fighting reserve of the party'.[26]

Second to FDGB in number of members is the 5-million-strong Association for German–Soviet Friendship, which expresses the extremely close ties in all fields between the two countries. The Association for Sport and Technology has about 16,000 basic units and sections, is subordinated to the Ministry for National Defence and gives a paramilitary training and basic scientific education, combined with sporting activities.[27]

There seem to exist three basic reasons why the SED allows a plurality of political parties. First, it gives the appearance of a truly democratic, multi-party regime. Secondly, the integration of bourgeois groups of society into the system is eased if they have organisations of their own. Thirdly, the ideological purity and social homogeneity of the cadre party of the working class, with its emphasis on discipline, can be sustained.

From the very beginning the political groupings have been united in an anti-fascist democratic bloc which can only make decisions unanimously. Representation on the different parliamentary bodies has been divided up among the various political parties, and the National Front only presents united lists of candidates (*Einheitsliste*) to the voters at elections. The leading role of the SED was originally based on patronage by the Soviet Military Administration. The other parties were later, after they had recognised the leading role of the SED in all matters, allowed to exist in a subordinate position. They have no independence and perform subsidiary functions of integrating and educating those that have difficulty in becoming direct and unconditional supporters of the communist regime. The Christian Democratic Union in the GDR has about 112,000 members, the Liberal Democratic Party of Germany 75,000. Those two parties help the traditional supporters of the principles of Christianity and liberalism to identify with the new system. The National Democratic Party (85,000 members) and the Democratic Farmers' Party (92,000) were only founded in 1948, on the initiative of the SED, which hoped that they would reach strata of society which it was unable itself to reach, enabling it to distribute responsibilities for the regime on many shoulders while still keeping tight control.[28] All the parties and mass organisations in the GDR have unconditionally recognised the absolute leadership of the SED and in their programmes and policies are loyal supporters of and strictly adhere to all actions and goals of the only political force that counts in the GDR.

THE STATE STRUCTURE: PEOPLE'S CHAMBER, STATE COUNCIL AND COUNCIL OF MINISTERS

In the GDR the State is seen as the main instrument in executing the will of the SED. Its job is to convert the political directives issued and basic principles espoused by the Party leadership into concrete political actions and to guide and plan the development of society on the lines scientifically elaborated by the Party.[29]

The various activities of the State column of the political system of the GDR are founded on two basic principles, of which the first is *socialist democracy* seen as a qualitatively new and historically the highest type of democracy. Unlike Western democracy this type opens the way to real participation by all people in the creation of a society corresponding to the wishes (presumed identical) of all groups and individuals. The second principle, in contrast to the liberal democratic principle of a separation of powers into an executive, legislature and judiciary, acting as mutual checks and balances, is the *concentration of power*. After the socialist revolution has overcome all the divisions and conflicts of society, this concentration, it is argued, expresses the superiority of the socialist form of government, as described by Marx after the Paris Commune of 1871.

According to the Constitution and ideologically, the People's Chamber (Volkskammer) is 'the highest power organ of the State (oberstes staatliches Machtorgan) deciding on the fundamental questions of State policy' (article 48).[30] It has 500 elected members, including the sixty-six members from Berlin who have a special status, and it appoints all the government organs of the GDR: the State Council (Staatsrat), the Council of Ministers (Ministerrat) and the National Defence Council (Nationaler Verteidigungsrat), an organ providing the leaders of the regime with unlimited powers in cases of emergency. In addition it appoints the judges of the Supreme Court and the Supreme Public Prosecutor. The members of the People's Chamber are elected every five years, on the basis of a single list of candidates presented to the voters by the National Front. All seats are allocated in advance to the different components of the Front (the SED 127, the other bloc parties' 52 each, the FDGB 68 and the Democratic Women's League of Germany (Demokratischer Frauenbund Deutschland) 35. Most of the representatives of the mass organisations are at the same time loyal members of the SED, so its majority is not in the slightest way endangered even in this politically unimportant body. In the elections of 17 October 1976 (see Table 12.3 for election results for 1946–76)

TABLE 12.3 GDR election results 1946–76[a]

	Entitled to vote	Votes cast	Votes for National Front candidates	Percentage[b]	Negative and invalid votes
1946	11,000,000[c]	9,780,652	4,658,483[d]	47·63	5,122,169
1949	13,533,071	12,887,234	7,943,949	61·64	4,943,285
1950	12,331,905	12,139,932	12,088,745	99·58	51,187
1954	12,085,380	11,892,849	11,828,877	99·46	63,972
1958	11,839,217	11,707,715			
1963	11,621,158	11,533,859			
1967	11,341,729	11,208,816	11,197,265	99·90	10,751
1971	11,401,090	11,227,535	11,207,388	99·82	20,147
1976	11,425,822	11,263,431	11,245,243	99·84	18,118

[a] These data exclude voting in East Berlin, since East Berlin deputies do not have full rights in the People's Chamber.
[b] This figure is the percentage of support amongst those voting; all percentage have been calculated by the compiler.
[c] Approximate.
[d] This figure refers to votes for the SED only – the unified National Front list was not at this time a part of East German electoral practice.

Sources: S. Dörnberg, *Kurze Geschichte der DDR* (Berlin: Dietz Verlag, 1965); *Keesing's Contemporary Archives*; R. F. Staar (ed.), *Yearbook on International Communist Affairs*. Table kindly supplied by Dr Leslie Holmes of the University of Kent at Canterbury.

11,263,431, or 98·58 per cent of the eligible 11,425,822 voters, took part, and the list prepared by the National Front received – as usual – the support of more than 99 per cent of all valid votes.[31] With a single exception (fourteen members of the Christian Democratic Union voting in 1972 against the abortion bill), the People's Chamber has from the very beginning voted unanimously on all issues. If the Parliament of the GDR were to have any real political power, it would have to meet much more often (at present it meets usually only five to seven times a year), and would have to do more legislative work (at present it passes about a dozen laws a year).[32] As it stands, it is no more than an organ of acclamation for decisions taken in the leading groups of the SED, and serves to give the governmental institutions the appearance of being elected by representatives of the highest democratic body: the people.

The People's Chamber elects the State Council (comprising twenty-four members and one secretary), which between the rare parliamentary sessions fulfils all the functions of the People's Chamber. After the death in 1960 of the first President of the GDR, Wilhelm Pieck, Walter Ulbricht transformed the State Council into a political body that fitted his taste for a concentration of decision-making power, and had unlimited oversight of all State matters. Instituted as an organ of the People's Chamber, it was in political reality far superior to it, setting its functions, determining its business and interpreting its pronouncements. The dominance of the SED was maintained in the State Council: Walter Ulbricht served as Chairman, and of its twenty-four members, fifteen were at the same time members of the SED Central Committee.

The political importance of the State Council was drastically downgraded after the death of Ulbricht in August 1973. Willi Stoph was moved from his influential position as Chairman of the Council of Ministers to that of head of the State Council. In October 1976, after further reshuffling of the top positions, Erich Honecker added the chairmanship of the State Council to his long list of important posts.[33]

The Council of Ministers was for the first twenty years of its existence a cabinet for economic matters only, but according to the present Constitution it is the government of the GDR: 'On behalf of the People's Chamber it directs the centralised realisation of State policy' (article 76). The political importance of the Council of Ministers has been increased at the cost of that of the State Council. Its forty-two members head the various ministries and other governmental institutions, such as the Planning Commission, the Council for Agriculture and the State Bank. To facilitate the decision-making process, a sort of 'inner cabinet' has been formed: The Presidium of the Council of Ministers is made up of the sixteen people who run the State. The Council has a large and highly specialised apparatus at its disposal. Its main task is to oversee and co-ordinate the manifold activities of all levels of the governmental administration, from the centre to the local echelons. The Council of Ministers consists of thirty-eight members of the SED and one member each from the other 'bloc parties'. The absolute predominance of the SED in the State is in addition guaranteed by the fact that 'the Chairman of the Council of Ministers, his two first deputies and the representatives of the National People's Army and State Security are full members of the SED Political Bureau, and two deputy chairmen are Political Bureau candidates'.[34] (See Table 12.4 for membership of the Political Bureau in 1978.)

TABLE 12.4 Posts held by members of the Political Bureau of the SED, 1978

Full members

Hermann Axen	(Secretary of the Central Committee)
Friedrich Ebert	Deputy Chairman, Council of State; Vice-president of the People's Chamber
Werner Felfe	(First Secretary, Halle District)
Gerhard Grüneberg	(Secretary of the Central Committee)
Kurt Hager	(Secretary of the Central Committee); member, Council of State
Jochim Herrmann	(Secretary of the Central Committee)
Heinz Hoffmann	Minister of National Defence
Erich Honecker	(General Secretary of the Central Committee); Chairman, Council of State; Chairman, National Defence Council
Werner Krolikowski	(Secretary of the Central Committee)
Erich Mielke	Minister for State Security
Günter Mittag	Deputy Chairman, Council of Ministers
Erich Mückenberger	(Chairman, Central Party Control Commission)
Konrad Naumann	(First Secretary, Berlin District)
Alfred Neumann	First Deputy Chairman, Council of Ministers
Albert Norden	(Secretary of the Central Committee); member, Council of State
Horst Sindermann	President of the People's Chamber; Deputy Chairman, Council of State

Table 12.4 (*cont.*)

Full members	
Willi Stoph	Chairman, Council of Ministers; Deputy Chairman, Council of State
Harry Tisch	Member, Council of State; Chairman, FDGB Executive
Paul Verner	(Secretary of the Central Committee); member, Council of State

Candidate members	
Horst Dohlus	(Secretary of the Central Committee)
Werner Jarowinsky	(Secretary of the Central Committee)
Günter Kleiber	Deputy Chairman, Council of Ministers; Minister for General Machinery, Agricultural Machinery and Vehicle Construction
Egon Krenz	First Secretary of the Central Committee of the FDJ
Ingeborg Lange	(Secretary of the Central Committee)
Margarete Müller	Member, Council of State
Gerhard Schürer	Deputy Chairman, Council of Ministers; Chairman, State Planning Commission
Werner Walde	(First Secretary, Cottbus District)

Note. In addition, all of the above are members of the People's Chamber and the National Front. Purely Party posts are given in parentheses. (Table kindly supplied by Dr Leslie Holmes of the University of Kent at Canterbury.)

From 1964 to 1973 Willi Stoph was Chairman of the Council of Ministers, a position he resumed in 1976, replacing Horst Sindermann who became President of the People's Chamber. The GDR does not emphasise these movements at the top of the administration; instead it stresses the large number of people participating in the process of government: the nearly 8000 regional and local representative bodies are made up of some 195,000 elected deputies, and almost half a million citizens are active in commissions, councils and other groups. This is seen as testifying to the superiority of the GDR governmental structure relative to its Western counterparts. The people have a real chance to 'participate in the decisions, their execution and the control of the results'[35] and act according to the well-publicised slogan 'Co-work, co-plan, co-rule'.

ASPECTS OF THE SOCIAL STRUCTURE, THE EDUCATIONAL SYSTEM AND GROUPINGS OF DISSENT

The principal goals of a communist regime are the total restructuring of the society under its control, the permanent mobilisation of its people through measures of education and indoctrination, and, finally, strict adherence to the guidelines set by the Party and suppression of even the slightest signs of dissent. In the GDR, the restructuring of society got under way just a few weeks after the German surrender in May 1945. The expropriation of all private owners of large industries (the official line – that active Nazis and Nazi-sympathisers were to be punished – was very broadly interpreted), the redistribution of all farm land over 100 hectares (mainly given to farm workers and refugees from East Prussia and Pomerania) and the radical purging from all State bureaucracies of those discredited during the Nazi period (this process was especially strict in education, justice and the police) took little more than a year and entailed a drastic disruption of the traditional structure of German society.[36] The new rulers were perfectly willing to accept economic losses, governmental mismanagement and a lowering of educational standards through expelling the people they distrusted before they were able to replace them with experts of their own choice. Even before a new communist elite had been reared (mainly through 'peasant and worker faculties', in which people with an appropriate social background obtained rapid and intensive training[37]), the next strata of the traditional society came under attack. In the early 1950s most of the middle-level commercial, trade and artisan groups were forced to come under public ownership. Many members of this sector of society fled to the West, as did thousands of those who could not bear the strong anti-religious pressure which the regime brought to bear on all members of Christian churches. A last wave of refugees escaped the forceful restructuring of GDR society when the collectivisation of the countryside was completed in 1960.

Seeing that all roads to the West were blocked after 1961, and considering the GDR's advanced social system (medical care, social security, pensions) and high standard of living (GNP per capita is higher than in Great Britain and there are extremely low, State-subsidised costs for all basic needs, such as housing, food, transportation and even holidays), it becomes understandable that over the years a certain loyalty to the State and a feeling of pride in the socialist system has developed. This, taken together with the age structure of the GDR population (in 1975 42·8 per cent were under thirty years of age, and almost 50 per cent less than thirty-five) and the attempts of the leadership to improve services and bonuses, explains the steps towards relaxation of the constant pressure on the people and the degree to which the regime has been stabilised and consolidated.

In official statements, factors such as the high degree of security (of jobs; in case of illness; and in old age), the strongly marked sense of solidarity (in the house and job collectives, helping fellow pupils, and so on), and equality of opportunity (upward mobility through education and performance; standard levels of income; lack of extensive private property) are praised as important achievements of the GDR form of socialism, and many GDR citizens would agree. Also noteworthy is the emancipated status of women, who in the GDR represent 49·6 per cent of the work force and over 70 per cent of teachers. Women are entitled to twenty-six weeks' leave on full pay in the case of childbirth, and more than 30 per cent of SED members are women. But there is of course another side to this picture: the triple burden of working, being a mother (despite the system of kindergartens) and being a housewife is very often too great. Divorce and abortion rates are extremely high and the need (as is often the case) to work in order to balance the family budget produces stresses that lead to absenteeism and low working morale. Furthermore, the top positions in all fields are still reserved for men.[38]

The GDR's educational system, however, has been widely admired and praised, though its critics emphasise its inflexibility, its lack of variety, the stress of ideological indoctrination and the frequent practice of promoting according to social origin and socialist consciousness rather than knowledge and intelligence. Yet, if one takes as a starting point that any system of education has to fulfil the basic functions of transmitting norms and values, preparing young people for economic and political duties and to stand up for their country, the results in the GDR are rather impressive.

The basic principles on which the whole educational system rests are those of uniformity and centralisation; a close relationship between theory and practice; and emphasis on learning for life, with close links between the various educational institutions. The basic form of poly-technical school education is thus one that includes one day in a production plant each week, a basic training in working skills and an introduction to crucial problems of industry and agriculture. The polytechnical secondary school with a ten-year course of study stands at the centre of the GDR educational system. Even if the ideal of an 'evenly and harmoniously developed socialist personality' cannot be attained, the system is highly successful on the practical level of close co-operation between schools and firms and sound preparation for jobs; 99 per cent of those graduating are immediately integrated into production. Relatively few go on directly, after a tough selection procedure, to university level. However, three years of professional training coupled with part-time schooling are equivalent to two years at 'extended high school' (*erweiterte Oberschule*). Performance, socio-political activity and family background are crucial for advancement and (usually in that order) become more important the higher one goes. Admission to university-level institutions is strictly limited, and more emphasis is placed on raising the educational level – especially in the technical, mathematical and economic fields – through a well-structured system of adult education, including evening schools and correspondence courses.[39] To acquire additional qualifications, take refresher courses and step up the ladder of social prestige by obtaining a diploma is common enough under the GDR educational system. These efforts have had direct effects on production and efficiency, as is seen by the fact that 'The percentage of unskilled and semi-skilled workers in the total population decreased from 43·7 per cent in 1970 to 32·9 per cent in 1975, while that of skilled workers increased from 44·9 per cent to 53 per cent during the same period.'[40] In other words, the permanent shortage of workers is at least partially balanced by working hard to increase the qualifications of those who are already at work and to give a sound training to those entering the economic process.

That the educational system in the GDR is used by the State and the SED to encourage political orthodoxy, support for national goals and pride in the country's achievements is quite normal. Despite all this, however, there have always existed groups in GDR society that have remained outside the mainstream of official thinking and have not accepted what the tightly controlled process of political socialisation is supposed to imprint on them.

In the history of the GDR there seem to be four basic reasons for the development of groups of dissent and opposition and for the support they have received from sections of the population. The first is the rapidity and harshness with which 'socialism' was forced on the area of the Soviet zone. The second is the Stalinist version of socialism, with its fixation on a supreme leader or a small power clique and its lack of democracy, popular participation and political freedom. The third is the discrepancies between the socialism in theory and the reality of a bureaucratic, centralised, power- and stability-oriented State and its narrow-minded functionaries; and the fourth is the will to overcome the deformations of this sort of socialism, or at least to lessen the effects of the national division of Germany and to acquire greater freedom of thought and action, bound to legal rights.

Those taking the initiative in voicing opposition and dissent have very often been members of the intelligentsia: scientists, philosophers, writers, artists. A second group has been made up of young people – both convinced socialists searching for a 'third way' between East and West, and faithful Christians trying to combine the ideas of Christianity with those of socialism. A third group are politically conscious workers who have attacked the regime from a basis of social-democratic traditions. Finally, mention must be made of decision-makers from inside the party and State apparatus who, because they suffer from the wide gap between socialist theory and the daily reality, strive for an alternative.[41]

From the very beginning of the regime, groups of very different orientations have been discernible even inside the leftist parties. In the early days, the actual form socialism should have in Germany, the question of coalition and the tempo and exact nature of the restructuring of society were, along with other problems, heavily disputed. The point of view taken in these controversies greatly depended on, for example where one had survived the Nazi rule and the war: in exile in Moscow, underground or in concentration camps in Germany, or in Western countries with liberal democratic traditions.[42] The disputes were brutally ended in 1948 when the SED was transformed into a 'party of the new type' and purged of all 'adherents of social democratism', 'supporters of the capitalist road' and 'traitors to the cause of German national unity' – as those who were not willing strictly to follow the directives from Moscow and their forceful execution by the group around Walter Ulbricht were called. All leaders of non-communist parties and groups were manoeuvred into a position of powerlessness, and those segments of society who opposed their being dispossessed and discriminated against were forced out of the country.

All elements of opposition and dissent erupted from below the surface during the events of June 1953. They found expression in the demands immediately to retract the raising of the working norms, to relax the course of the economy, to slow down the rapidity of the transformation of society, to get rid of Ulbricht and to have free elections throughout Germany, as a first step towards national reunification.[43] Soviet tanks had to be called in to silence the uproar of thousands of demonstrators. The usual arguments against the rebels and their demands were uttered once the regime felt safe again: it was all the work of class enemies, of international imperialism and foreign secret services increasing their subversive activities, and of Western mass media providing a ready platform for anti-socialist hate campaigns.

In addition to the extent of the opposition and the degree of mass participation in the anti-regime demonstrations, what was new in the June 1953 revolt was the fact that high-ranking Party members and bureaucrats also insisted on a different political course. In their demands for a new leadership, a stronger consumer orientation of the economy and flexibility in the negotiations with the West to reach an agreement on the German problem, men such as W. Zaisser (a member of the Political Bureau and Minister for State Security) and R. Herrnstadt (editor of the SED daily paper *Neues Deutschland* and a Political Bureau member) were backed by high-ranking members of the Soviet leadership such as Beria and Malenkov.[44] Even so, the Soviet Union, afraid of the effects on its still unsettled East European empire, felt unable to make any concessions. The result of the eruption of opposition was thus, paradoxically, a stabilisation of the Ulbricht leadership in the GDR.

The leadership, however, had been warned once and for all, and it watched the mood of the people with extreme care. By a combination of harshness and flexibility it survived the repercussions of the anti-Stalin campaign begun at the Twentieth Congress of the CPSU. Important figures in the realm of politics (K. Schirdewan, F. Ölssner, W. Wollweber), in the field of economics (F. Behrens, A. Benary) and among the intellectuals (W. Harich, E. Bloch, R. Havemann) took up Khruschev's criticism of Stalinism and applied it to the special circumstances in the GDR. This critical analysis led to demands for a return to the humanistic and utopian foundations of socialism, for condemnation of Stalinist practices in all spheres of life, and for freedom of discussion and expression. The insistence on a special German way to socialism re-emerged, and the idea of a coalition with West Germany's Social Democrats, in order to re-establish the unity of the nation, was put forward. A turning away from dogmatism and rigidity and towards experimentation, democratisation, decentralisation, and consultation of the interests of individuals was sought.[45] Those opposing the policy of Ulbricht were a large and diversified group with strong support in the general population. But, with the lessons of the 1953 uprising in mind, things never reached the point where they would go completely or almost out of hand, as in Hungary or in Poland in 1956.

Up to the building of the Berlin Wall, opposition to the official policy line was mainly expressed by passive resistance or, in most instances, by a massive 'voting with the feet' i.e. fleeing to the West. Almost all of those to whom opposition to a socialist regime was a matter of principle had left the GDR by 1961. After the exits had been blocked, the efforts of the leadership to win the population over to its goals were at least partially successful. However, those who now attacked the regime were particularly dangerous, because they argued from exactly the same Marxist basis as the leadership and had in addition all the credentials of convinced communists.

Robert Havemann, a leading scientist, and SED member for decades and anti-fascist fighter who survived internment in a concentration camp, was and is one of them. During the winter term 1963–4 he delivered a lecture at the Humboldt University in Berlin, entitled 'Scientific aspects of philosophical problems'.[46] In this lecture he critically examined the relationship between science and dialectical materialism and reached with his new interpretation positions considered 'revisionist' by the Party. Awareness of the explosive character of his philosophical argument earned him a large audience of more than a thousand students. The professor lost his job, he was systematically isolated and many of his books and articles could only be published in the West. After his support for other intellectuals a dozen years later, he was confined to his house and is day and night carefully watched by police and militia.

Wolf Biermann, a singer of critical songs and a poet, was excluded from the stage for a decade and could not publish a word in the socialist country to which he had moved from the West. After a concert in the FRG late in 1976, he was not allowed to return and the GDR authorities stripped him of his citizenship and accused him of anti-socialist slander. His treatment by the leadership brought about spontaneous reactions from artists, intellectuals and writers. For many of those protesting, life in the GDR was made so unbearable that more than a dozen of the more prominent saw no alternative but to leave for the West.[47]

Rudolf Bahro, in his book *Die Alternative*,[48] which had to be published in the FRG, sums up his experiences as a manager in the economic-technical field in the GDR. This he characterises as working in a totally inefficient way, on a frustrating system of 'organised irresponsibility'. He very lucidly and stringently pinpoints the discrepancies between, on the one hand, the politico-economic arguments of Marx and Engels and the political ideas of Lenin before the October revolution and, on the other, 'socialism as it really exists' anywhere. The leadership did not attempt to argue with him or take his well based analysis as a theoretical challenge, but condemned him to eight years' imprisonment for being a Western spy.[49]

In addition to these well known names, there are hundreds who work against the various forms of repression and discrimination (priests and church groups, for instance), failure to fulfil the letter of the law and international agreements (those applying for emigration or the re-unification of families on the basis of the Helsinki accords, for example), the absence of socialism worthy of the name (for instance, those who wrote the 'Manifesto' of January 1978[50] seeking an end to the Soviet system in the GDR by replacing it by a combination of socialism, democracy and freedom, collaboration with the Eurocommunists and the re-establishment of German unity). All in all, the history of opposition and dissent in the GDR dates back as far as the regime itself, and criticism of the sort of socialism established in the GDR is bound to continue in the years to come.

THE ECONOMY

The economy of the GDR rests on the principles of socialisation of all means of production and centralised planning by the State. During the first years of the GDR's existence, its economy suffered from a large number of serious deficiencies and shortcomings: the extremely high level of reparation exacted, over a long period by the Soviet Union, the Russians' dismantling of crucial industrial plants and the escape of altogether more than 3 million, mostly young and well qualified, people to the West burdened the East German economy with a total loss of some 100,000 million marks.[51]

In addition, the lack of raw materials (except for brown coal), along with war damage (almost 45 per cent of the industrial sector was destroyed) and the imbalance between, on the one hand, food pro-duction and light industry, which were strong, and, on the other hand, a small iron and steel industry, amounting to just 7·3 per cent of the iron and steel industry of Germany as a whole, created serious difficulties. Finally, the economy suffered from the total interruption of its traditional trade routes, the end of industrial co-operation with the rest of Germany, and a lack of infrastructure – for instance, traffic routes from north to south, as against the traditional east-west links.

In addition to these factors directly resulting from the Second World War and the division of Germany, the political leadership introduced a number of measures which at least in the beginning seriously aggravated the situation: hasty expropriation of all large industries, in 1964; drastic redistribution of the ownership of agricultural land; forcible changes in trade and commerce; and the introduction of a gigantic Soviet-type bureaucracy at the top of a highly centralised and rigid planning system. After a two-year plan (1949–50), the State Planning Commission, founded in 1950, produced two five-year plans (1951–5 and 1956–60, the latter in fact ending in 1959), one seven-year plan (1959–65) and three more five-plans (up to 1980). Some weaknesses in the first half of the period were the one-sided efforts to increase the output of heavy industry only and the imbalances in economic development – as, for example, the dangerous neglect of consumer goods. The other deficiencies of the economic system stemmed from the fixing of all production goals and prices by the central apparatus, and – up to 1963 – a system of planning under which quantity and extensive economic growth were the only things that counted. This lead to a number of 'soft plans' which could easily be overfulfilled, with high bonuses being earned, and to the permanent under-utilisation of production factors and low working morale, because of 'deficits of raw materials, poor equipment procurement, lack of spare parts etc.' – all disruptive factors beyond the reach and control of the workers.[52]

After the building of the Berlin Wall, which stabilised the GDR economy and forced the people to reach accommodation with the State, a comprehensive economic reform was introduced in 1963 under the name 'New Economic System of Planning and Managing the Economy'. Drastic changes had become necessary, because the GDR economy was by far the most developed and differentiated of all the socialist economies, with the consequence that the Soviet example and the planning system of the Stalin era were inadequate and even dysfunctional to further progress. The main characteristics of the reform were greater flexibility in planning and management, improvement of the financial instruments for guiding and controlling ('economic levers'), the massive use of material incentives and of categories such as rentability and profit, greater worker participation and greater responsibilities for individual enterprises and their managers.

It seems, though, that with this overall modernisation of the economy too much has been attempted too fast. With the 'Economic System of Socialism' introduced in 1967 and practised during the last years of the Ulbricht's leadership,

economic planning was to be supplemented by, and even embedded in, social planning based on independent prognoses of societal development. Responsibility for economic decision making was in part removed once again from the lower management level. . . . Investment and research would henceforth be concentrated on 'those branches of the national economy which are structurally determinant' that is, on selected large projects.[53]

It soon became evident, though, that even the reduced goals – expressed in the principal slogan of competition with the West, as 'Catch up without overtaking' – could not be realised. The one-sided concentration on those sectors of the economy by which the 'scientific-technological revolution' could be rapidly advanced led to dangerous disproportions and discrepancies in overall economic development. In 1969 a slackening in even those branches that had been given special attention became visible. The Fourteenth Session of the Central Committee, meeting in December 1970, decided on a number of fundamental corrections in the economic course. The dangers of disregarding the need for balanced development of the economy and ignoring the people's demands for a steady supply of consumer goods were very drastically demonstrated to the SED leadership by the strikes breaking out in neighbouring Poland at that time and the toppling of Gomulka from power. The new directives from the GDR economy therefore aimed at – among other goals – increasing the supply of consumer goods and a step-by-step stabilisation of the energy sector.[54] In other words, an era of economic consolidation was to be initiated, the high expectations raised by the various reforms had to be lowered, and economic stability was to be attained by structurally balanced growth. In the five-year plan 1971–5 important steps were taken to overcome the disproportions in the economic structure and to tackle two major obstacles to successful economic development: first, serious energy problems and scarcity of raw materials, and, secondly, the low levels of efficiency and productivity in most spheres of the economy.

These efforts, though, were very seriously hampered by the drastic worldwide rise in raw-material prices – especially for crude oil – and the increase in the GDR's foreign trade with the Western industrial countries, its net debt to which by the middle of 1976 stood at an estimated $3500 million.[55] The close links in all fields with the other socialist states and especially the GDR's membership since 1950 of Comecon have meant that two-thirds of the GDR economy is bound up with these partners. Half of the GDR's total trade with the socialist camp and a third of its total foreign trade (which in 1975 amounted to 26,500 valuta marks or $5000 million) are with by far its most important economic partner, the Soviet Union. While imports from the super-power are mainly raw materials, such as oil, gas, coal and cotton, or semi-manufactured products, exports from the GDR are predominantly of products of the highly developed optical, electronic, chemical and precision-tool industries, plus other machinery and technical equipment.[56]

Looking at the foreign-trade situation of the GDR in greater detail reveals a trend dangerous to its economic stability:

> The relative importance of the socialist countries as trading partners declined, while that of the Western industrial countries increased. . . . Imports from the Western industrial countries grew much faster than exports to them, and the imbalance intensified the GDR's shortage of hard currency. Although the share of all the socialist countries in GDR imports averaged 76 per cent in 1961–5, it dropped to 72·2 per cent in 1966–70, and to only 65 per cent in 1971–5. Imports from the Western industrial countries for these periods averaged, respectively, 20·1 per cent, 23·9 per cent and 30·9 per cent of total GDR imports. On the export side, the GDR sent to all the socialist countries 76·9 per cent, 74·6 per cent, and 72·7 per cent of its total exports in the three periods, and it sent the Western industrial countries 19 per cent, 20·8 per cent and 23·2 per cent, respectively![57]

The effects these developments have on the GDR economy can be studied by looking at the trade relations between the two German states. The FRG has insisted of its EEC partners that they allow a special form of intra-German trade. Since by this arrangement the GDR is practically a hidden member of the EEC, these special German relations have always been particularly advantageous to the GDR. After the Soviet Union, the FRG is the largest economic partner of the GDR, and the increase in intra-German trade has been steady, reaching, for example, 12 per cent more in 1976 than in 1975. One result for the GDR has been, though, that in order to compete on the world market it has to import high-grade machinery and extremely costly technological know-how from the West. Despite improvements in its ability to pay for these essential imports, mainly with consumer-good products, the situation remains extremely precarious for the GDR, whose total debt to the FRG alone has reached DM 2600 million in 1975.

The continual worsening of its foreign-trade situation has led the GDR to take a number of drastic internal measures. There have been constant drives to reduce imports and to economise on the consumption of raw materials. In addition, there is massive emphasis on the need to increase the value and quality of production, and one campaign follows another to stimulate competition and to create moral and material incentives for higher productivity and better utilisation of machinery. The recentralisation of management and planning after the abandonment of economic reforms has brought no satisfactory solution to the task of running an industrially highly developed and modern economy with a large, centrally guided bureaucracy. Despite the persistent difficulties of obtaining information, co-ordination, accounting and keeping a viable balance between the various parts of the national economy, the plans for the future of the GDR are extremely ambitious: for the period 1976–80 an overall GNP growth rate of 30 per cent, a 30 per cent increase in labour productivity and a 35 per cent increase in industrial production are envisaged.[58] More than 240,000 million marks are provided for investments. Much of this is used to further scientific and technological progress, which is seen as essential to achieving the goals. 8000 million marks are to be spent on the other major area which the GDR sees as essential to its economic future: the strengthening of economic links with the Soviet Union and the socialist community as a whole. For the longer-term prospects, though, one can agree with Rüdiger Thomas, who sees further economic achievement as dependent on the extension to all parts of the national economy of a concern for profits and rentability; continued reform of the price system; the improved information flow; the creation of mechanisms of competition and improvement of material incentives; improved flexibility of the economic apparatus; and a viable balance between the interests of the individual production units and those of the economy as a whole.[59]

FOREIGN POLICY PROBLEMS AND CONCLUSION

All foreign policy activities of the GDR rest on certain basic assumptions and guiding principles. For example, throughout its history the GDR has shown unquestioned submission to the Soviet policy line in all matters; indeed, over the years this subjection has even grown, finding its expression in all the basic documents of Party, State and the mass organisations.[60]

In addition, according to the arguments of Marxist-Leninist ideology, the fact that exploitation, profit interests and antagonistic contradictions between the classes are eliminated under socialism makes socialist foreign policy 'by its very nature' peaceful, constructive and in accordance with the interests of all people and nations. The principal goals of foreign policy are the maintenance and furthering of the most favourable external conditions for the internal construction of socialism, the creation of world peace, the strengthening of the socialist camp and the weakening of imperialism.[61]

Put in a less abstract way, over the last three decades the GDR has striven for close relations with the Soviet Union, for acceptance as a respected and reliable member of the socialist bloc, for Western recognition of existence as an independent state, and for the extension of its influence in selected countries and regions of the Third World.

The principles governing the GDR's foreign policy dealings can be seen to differ according to the context.

1. In the community of socialist states the principles of *socialist internationalism* are applied. Since all the countries belonging to the socialist camp share the same political, economic, military and ideological traits and work for the common goal of establishing socialism worldwide, they were also able to develop interrelations of a 'new type'. This includes what is called a 'new dialectic of nationalism and internationalism' – the right to interfere in internal affairs to prevent clear and present danger from a socialist member state, and the highest possible degree of integration and co-operation, because of common socialist aims.

In political reality, of course, the Soviet Union is the absolutely predominant power, giving all the commands, determining the road to follow, fixing prices and enforcing its will – if necessary with tanks. The GDR, because of its internal instability, its dependence on military protection, its open borders and its permanent competition with the FRG, never even tried to increase its independence or to follow its own national line. On the contrary, the leadership, aware of the suspicions that the other members of the socialist camp would entertain of a German state, sought, acceptance by the strictest loyalty to the Soviet Union and by a special eagerness to please its partners: the recognition, less than a year after the GDR's foundation, of the Oder-Neisse line as Poland's western border, and the GDR's enthusiastic participation in the 1968 intervention in Czechoslovakia are only two examples.

Once a member of the supreme bodies of the Warsaw Pact (1956) and of Comecon (1950), the GDR worked hard towards further integration, to increase co-operation and to improve co-ordination. For its full participation as an equal member it was perfectly willing to accept certain checks, such as the complete control that the Supreme

Command of the Warsaw Pact has over all GDR military forces, or the right of the Soviet commanders of the 400,000 foreign soldiers permanently stationed in the GDR to declare a state of martial law or conduct military manoeuvres without previous consent of the GDR authorities.[62] Over the years, not only has the GDR reached a status of equality with other members of the socialist camp, but, in addition, because of its strict adherence to the Soviet line, its strong military, economic and technological potential and its continual working for further intergration and an even closer net work of bilateral contracts with the other socialist countries, it has become a sort of a junior partner of the Soviet Union.

2. Closely linked to the principles of socialist internationalism are those of *proletarian internationalism* and *anti-imperialist unity*. Whereas the former are applied in the scialist camp in the narrow sense, the latter are applied to foreign revolutionary movements, national liberation forces and newly established 'progressive' nation states. These diverse forces are regarded as natural allies of world socialism and can expect solidarity and help from the GDR.[63]

In relation to its own potential, and in view of its propaganda, the actual help that the GDR offers to countries of the Third World is very small indeed. In addition, aid to underdeveloped countries is given bilaterally only, and the handful of recipients are selected not for their need or political leanings (and sometimes even against the interests of the local communists), but for their strategic importance, their wealth in raw materials or – at least in the past – their willingness to break off ties with the FRG and turn to the other Germany.

With this concentration of the GDR policy on a few selected countries in the Third World (such as India, Brazil, Egypt and Congo) goes a specialisation in two sectors in particular: the educational and the military field.[64] Factors that have certainly helped the GDR in the eyes of many industrially less developed countries are its 'sympathetic size' (as compared with the size of the Soviet Union or China); its starting more or less from scratch after the war; the proof of the effectiveness of a planned economy, which brought about a second German 'economic miracle', and the appearance of a plurality of political forces ('bourgeois' parties, for example).

In the United Nations the GDR always votes with the Soviet Union and most of the Third World countries, condemning colonialism, racism and imperialism; in the North–South negotiations of the past few years it has firmly sided with the industrially underdeveloped countries, seeing

capitalist exploitation alone as responsible for the misery of the poor
Southern countries.[65]

Despite all its efforts to establish itself by words and deeds as the
good, progressive and forward-looking Germany and to discredit the
FRG as 'rotten', 'imperialistic' and 'militaristic', the GDR has not been
particularly successful in its continual striving for international recognition: in 1969–70 the GDR was recognised by a very few African
and Asian countries (such as Algeria, Somalia and Cambodia), which,
with the GDR's socialist brother countries, brought the number of
states recognising it, after twenty-three years of its existence, to a total of
thirty-two. However, in the year November 1972 to November 1973,
when the Basic Treaty on intra-German relations was concluded and the
FRG renounced its opposition to international recognition of the GDR,
sixty-eight states declared their willingness to establish official ties with
the GDR.[66]

3.   On the plane of foreign policy activities, the GDR applied the
principles of *peaceful coexistence*, with 'regulation of interstate relations
of socialist and capitalist states on the basis of equality of rights, the
mutual respect of sovereignty and territorial integrity, and non-
interference in internal affairs'.[67] To this co-operative formula is usually
added a willingness to develop international economic ties working to
the advantage of both sides and to seek the solution of all controversial
problems by peaceful means. However, these principles are also seen, in
the context of the continuing fight between socialism and capitalism, as a
more sophisticated way to fight the class enemy and do not assume a
perpetual truce on ideological matters.[68]

Despite its strong emphasis on the co-operative elements of these
ambivalent principles, the GDR was for some twenty years unable to
break out of its international isolation and to achieve official recognition
by Western powers. Except where it maintained full diplomatic
relations, its international ties amounted to little more than a few trade
offices (for instance, in Paris and London), some links between villages
(especially with some in France with communist mayors) and contacts in
sports and cultural affairs (with Scandinavian countries). Up to 1972
even its participation in United Nations sub-organisations such as those
concerned with environmental and medical questions was systematically prevented.[69] Only after the GDR, in response to massive pressure
from the Soviet Union, which was unwilling to see its new policy of
détente with the West endangered, had consented to the Four Power
Agreement on Berlin (1972) and the Basic Treaty on the regulation of

the special relations between the two German states (1973), did it break out of its isolation.

The achievement of full international recognition, with the GDR entering the United Nations in 1973 and signing the Helsinki accords two years later, did, however, demonstrate the ambivalence of the GDR's dealings with the West. On the one hand, it had at last become recognised as a separate and independent German state, its borders internationally guaranteed. This new international status had very positive effects on the internal stability and the legitimacy of the regime. On the other hand, though, the leadership had to cope with a massive influx of Western ideas, the development of new economic commitments, and the legal obligations stemming from treaties and agreements.[70] In addition, the GDR lost its special status, becoming thenceforth one socialist state among others, without finding any way of strengthening its position in its worldwide competition with the FRG, and became increasingly forced to tighten up its policy of demarcation (*Abgrenzungspolitik*) relative to the West.

4. Although the GDR strictly denies it today, most of its foreign policy dealings have been determined also by a fourth principle: *the creation of a united German socialist nation*. To overcome the international isolation in which it found itself during the 1950s and 1960s, to counter the denial of its own legitimacy and to veil its weakness relative to Western demands for free elections throughout Germany as a basis for national reunification, the GDR has always claimed to represent the real interests of all Germans, to hold the only key to a progressive and peaceful future for Germany as a whole, and by its own existence to be setting an example for a reunited state which the FRG will sooner or later have to join.

Since the end of its international isolation and its official recognition by the FRG as a separate state, the GDR has however, strictly denied that the intra-German relations have any sort of a special character. Whereas the FRG insists on the singularity of its relations with the GDR, because of common traditions, family ties and the continued strong feelings of togetherness of the Germans in East and West, the GDR insists that its relations with Bonn are no different in kind from these with all other capitals of capitalist countries.

The drastic changes in the GDR's attitude towards the German nation may be seen by comparing the 1968 Constitution with the amendments made to it a few years later. In a number of passages the GDR had been given responsibility 'to point to the whole German nation the way into a future of peace and of socialism', but in October 1974 all references to the continued existence of a single German nation were eliminated and the structural differences as well as the total separation of the two Germanies were emphasised. The achievements of the GDR have, it is now argued, produced a new socialist nation with an identity all of its own.[71] Instead of calling itself a 'socialist state of the German nation' that would take all steps possible to reach rapprochement with the FRG, with an eye to eventual unification on the basis of democracy and socialism, the GDR after 1974 missed no opportunity to repeat its vow 'forever and irrevocably to be allied with the USSR' and to stress that 'relations of eternal and inviolable friendship and fraternal mutual assistance in all fields' exist between the two countries.[72]

In the thirty years of its history the GDR has developed from a shattered and incapacitated section of the Third Reich to a model of stability and efficiency that is admired not only by its communist partners. Economically, technologically and militarily it has reached a leading position in the socialist camp and easily rates among the first dozen states in the world. As far as political respectability, legitimacy of the regime and popular support are concerned, the leadership is constantly prey to strong feelings of insecurity, fear and mistrust. The pragmatic, efficiency-oriented outlook of a dynamic, differentiated industrial society has not brought about any form of political liberalism, relaxation of the strains on society or unmixed feelings of comfort and satisfaction. The mere existence of the FRG was taken as a challenge which made necessary the total restructuring of all spheres of life.

The betrayal of socialist ideals, the vast discrepancies between the pretensions of socialism for the masses and the actual practices of a clique at the top of the Party are excused – if they are ever recognised at all – by reference to the sinister activities of enemies of the people, the continued existence of imperialism and the dangers stemming from world capitalism.

The two German states have come a long way since the defeat and division of their predecessor, 'the Reich'. They are the principal cause and major outcome of the Cold War. Both have reached, in unbelievably short periods of time, strong positions of power and prestige in their respective bloc systems. Their attempts in recent years to co-operate, to solve urgent problems of mutual interest by processes of give and take, possibly even to learn from each other (with regard to equality in the GDR, to freedom and liberty in the FRG, for example) and to regard the other side as a positive challenge could turn out to be steps in the right direction, helping to push the negative effects of the national division of Germany into the background and contributing to overcome East–West confrontation, so that efforts may be joined in tackling the dangers for mankind in our time and in the future.

BIOGRAPHIES*

Erich Honecker, Secretary-general of the SED and Chairman of the Council of State, was born in Neunkirchen (Saar) on 25 August 1912, the son of a miner. His father was an active functionary of the KPD and of the miners' union.

After attending elementary school, Honecker learned the trade of a roofer. He joined the Young Communist League of Germany (*Kommunistischer Jungendverein Deutschlands* – KJVD) and the trade union at the age of fourteen, and in 1929 he became a member of the KPD. The Central Committee of the KJVD delegated him to the school of the Communist Youth International in Moscow. Together with other young communists, Honecker was a member of the international work brigades which at that time helped to build the Magnitogorsk steel mill in the southern Urals.

After the establishment of the fascist dictatorship, Erich Honecker directed anti-fascist work among the youth in the Ruhr region, south-west Germany and in Berlin. In December 1934 he was elected to the Central Committee of the KJVD. Because of his anti-fascist activity he was sentenced to ten years' imprisonment in 1937.

He became a member of the KPD Central Committee in April 1946. The congress of unification of the KPD and the Social Democratic Party held in April 1946 elected him to the National Executive of the SED, the new party resulting from the merger. Since then Honecker has been a member of the Party's collective leadership.

Honecker was one of the co-founders of the FDJ and the Chairman of its Central Committee between 1946 and 1955. From 1949 to 1955 he was a member of the Executive Committee of the World Federation of Democratic Youth.

In 1950 he became a candidate member of the SED's Political Bureau. In the same year he became member of the National Council of the National Front and of its Presidium, and since 1949 he has also been a deputy in the People's Chamber of the GDR.

*Compiled by Bogdan Szajkowski.

After studying in the Soviet Union from 1955 to 1956, Honecker continued his work in the SED leadership in the fields of national security, sport, youth and female affairs. He was elected a member of the Political Bureau and Secretary of the SED Central Committee in 1958. In May 1971 he was elected First Secretary of the Central Committee of the SED. In the same year he became a member of the Council of State and Chairman of the National Defence Council of the GDR. In 1976 the Ninth Congress of the SED elected Honecker Secretary-general of the Party. Also in 1976 he was elected Chairman of the Council of State of the GDR.

Willi Stoph, Chairman of the Council of Ministers, was born into a workers' family in Berlin on 9 July 1914. He attended elementary school, became a stonemason and later foreman, and after a course of extramural studies a building technician.

In 1928 Stoph joined the KJVD, and thereafter he held various responsible posts in the youth movement. He joined his trade union that same year and the KPD in 1931. During the twelve-year period of Hitler's dictatorship he joined the illegal resistance struggle and continued in this during his military service.

Since 1945 Willi Stoph has held responsible posts relating to the economy and to establishing and strengthening the armed forces, and he has been prominent in the leadership of the State. Until 1947 he headed the Department of Building Materials Industries and the Construction Industry and till 1948 was head of the Central Department of Basic Materials Industries in the Central German Administration of Industry. He headed the Department of Economic Policy of the SED National Executive. He has been a member of the Central Committee since 1950 and was a Central Committee Secretary until 1953, when he was elected a member of the Political Bureau of the Central Committee. As a member of the People's Chamber (since 1950) he headed the Economic Committee. In 1952 he was appointed Minister of the Interior. He was Minister of National Defence from 1956, when the National People's Army was founded, until 1960, when he held the rank of General of the Army.

In 1954 he was appointed Deputy Chairman and in 1962 First Deputy Chairman of the Council of Ministers, and between 1964 and 1973 he was Chairman of this body. In 1973 he was elected Chairman of the Council of State of the GDR, and he continued in this post until 1976, when he was again elected Chairman of the Council of Ministers.

BASIC FACTS ABOUT THE GDR

Official name: German Democratic Republic (Deutsche Demo-
kratische Republik).

Area: 108,178 sq. km. (41,768 sq. miles).

Population (1971): 17,040,926.

Population density: 157·5 per sq. km.

Population distribution: 73·7 per cent urban, 26·3 per cent rural.

Ethnic composition: Germans 99·1 per cent.

Religious affiliation: Protestants 80 per cent, Roman Catholics 11 per
cent.

Population of major towns (1971): Berlin (East) (the capital), 1,088,827;
Leipzig 575,913; Dresden, 505,408; Karl-Marx-Stadt (Chemnitz),
301,820; Halle 248,561.

Gross national product (1970): $42,970 million ($2,490 per capita).

Net domestic product by sector (1970) [US $1 = approx. 2
marks]: agriculture – value 13,140 million marks (percentage of total
value 11·7), labour force 1,023,000 (percentage of labour force 12·4);
manufacturing – value 68,580 million marks (percentage of total
value 60·9), labour force 3,460,400 (percentage of labour force 42·1);
construction – value 9,247 million marks (percentage of total value
8·2), labour force 655,800 (percentage of labour force 8·0).

Main natural resources: lignite (250 million tons; world's largest
producer), potash, rock salt.

Foreign trade (1970): 20,357·2 million marks (mineral products 31·8 per
cent, metal products 36 per cent); exports, 19,240·2 million marks
(metal products 56·2 per cent, foods and light-industry products 21·3
per cent).

Main trading partners (1970): import sources – USSR 40 per cent,
FRG 9·4 per cent, UK 1·8 per cent; export destinations – USSR 38 per
cent, FRG 11·8 per cent, Netherlands 1·7 per cent.

Rail network (1970): 29,250 km.

Roads network (1970): 45,729 km.

Passenger cars (1970): 1,159,800.

Press, broadcasting, telecommunications (1970): 41 daily newspapers
(total circulation 7,608,000); 18 broadcasting stations, 2,100,000
telephones.

Education (1970): primary (ages 6–16) – 6000 schools, 13,000 teachers,
2·5 million students; secondary (ages 17–18) – 306 schools, 54,700
students; vocational, teacher-training – 1100 schools, 14,800 teach-

ers, 43,000 students; higher – 54 institutions of higher education, 13,800 students.

Health (1970): 27,255 doctors (1 per 626 persons); 190,025 hospital beds.

Foreign relations: diplomatic relations with over 112 countries; 60 diplomatic missions established in Berlin; member of Comecon and the WTO, and, since 1972, of the UN.

NOTES

1. L. B. Schapiro, *Totalitarianism* (London: Pall Mall, 1972).
2. W. Maibaum, 'Konzeptionen und Schwierigkeiten der DDR-Forschung', *Politische Bildung*, v (Apr 1972) 3–12.
3. P. C. Ludz, *Die DDR zwischen Ost Und West* (Munich: C. H. Beck, 1977) pp. 26–37.
4. R. Thomas, 'Materialien zu einer Ideologiegeschichte der DDR' in P. C. Ludz (ed.), *Wissenschaft und Gesellschaft in der DDR* (Munich: Hanser, 1971) pp. 25–77.
5. Quoted in R. Thomas, *Modell DDR – Die kalkulierte Emanzipation*, 6th ed. (Munich: Hanser, 1977) p. 165.
6. Ibid., p. 185.
7. Ibid., p. 29.
8. Ibid.
9. G. Brunner, *Politische Soziologie der UdSSR*, vol. II (Wiesbaden: Akademische Verlagsgesellschaft, 1977) pp. 108–18.
10. Ibid., p. 101.
11. H. Horn, 'Das Regierungssystem der DDR', in H. H. Hartwich (ed.), *Politik im 20. Jahrhundert*, 4th ed. (Brunswick: Westermann, 1974) p. 297.
12. 'Staatsapparat', in Bundesministerium für innerdeutsche Beziehunge *DDR-Handbuch* (Cologne: Verlag Wissenschaft und Politik, 1975) pp. 822ff.
13. Quoted from Carola Stern, 'History and Politics of the SED 1945–1965', in W. E. Griffith (ed.), *Communism in Europe*, vol. II (Cambridge, Mass., and London: MIT Press, 1966) p. 64.
14. Part of the essay 'Is There a Special German Road to Socialism?' is reprinted in E. Deuerlein (ed.), *DDR – Geschichte und Bestandsaufnahme 1945–1970*, 5th ed. (Munich: DTV, 1975) 59.
15. D. Staritz, *Sozialismus in einem halben Land* (Berlin: Wagenbach, 1976) Chapters 4 and 8.
16. For an account of the beginnings of the 'Ulbricht group', see W. Leonhard, *Child of the Revolution* (Chicago: Regnery, 1958).
17. A. Baring, *Uprising in East Germany* (Ithaca, N.Y., and London: Cornell University Press, 1972).
18. H. Weber, *DDR – Grundriss der Geschichte 1945–1976* (Hanover: Fackelträger, 1977) pp. 77ff.

19. The argument has been developed in detail in his pioneering study *The Changing Party Elite in East Germany* (Cambridge, Mass.: MIT Press, 1972). The gist can be found in his *The GDR from the Sixties to the Seventies – A Socio-political Analysis*, Occasional Papers in International Affairs of Harvard University, no. 26 (Cambridge, Mass.: Harvard University Press, 1970) pp. 45–51.
20. Ibid., p. 37.
21. Thomas, *Modell*, pp. 30–3.
22. Ibid., p. 175.
23. K. Sontheimer and W. Bleek, *Die DDR – Politik, Gesellschaft, Wirtschaft* (Hamburg: Hoffmann and Campe, 1972) p. 75.
24. Thomas, *Modell*, p. 41.
25. H. Rausch and T. Stammen (eds), *DDR – Das politische, wirtschaftliche und soziale System* (Munich: C. H. Beck, 1974) pp. 74–8.
26. E. Honecker in *Neues Deutschland*, 19 May 1977.
27. Thomas, *Modell*, p. 44.
28. Ibid., pp. 40ff.
29. Ibid., p. 34.
30. Ibid., p. 35.
31. E. Waldman, 'Germany: GDR', in R. F. Staar (ed.) *Yearbook on International Communist Affairs 1977* (Stanford, Calif.: Stanford University Press, 1977) p. 26.
32. Sontheimer and Bleek, *DDR*, p. 107.
33. Waldman, in Staar, *Yearbook – 1977*.
34. Ibid., quoting from Bundesministerium für innerdeutsche Beziehungen, *Informationen*, no. 11 (Bonn, 1976).
35. Thomas, *Modell*, p. 39.
36. Staritz, *Sozialismus*, ch. 5.
37. For a literary treatment of this time, see H. Kant's novel *Die Aula* (Frankfurt a. M.: Fischer, 1968). Kant today is head of the GDR's writers' union (Schriftstellerverband).
38. I. Hanke, 'Die Sozialstruktur – Die Stellung der Frau', in Rausch and Stammen, *DDR*, pp. 67–74.
39. 'Einheitliches sozialistisches Bildungssystem', in *DDR – Handbuch*, pp. 224–45.
40. H. Zimmermann, 'The GDR in the 1970's', *Problems of Communism*, XXVII (Mar–Apr 1978) 29.
41. H. Weber, 'Der dritte Weg – Bahro in der Tradition der antistalinistischen Opposition', *Deutschland Archiv*, vol. XI (Sep 1978) pp. 921–7.
42. Staritz, *Sozialismus*, ch. 2.
43. Baring, *Uprising*.
44. H. Wassmund, *Kontinuität im Wandel* (Cologne and Vienna: Böhlau, 1974) p. 37.
45. H. Grebing, 'Die intellektuelle Opposition in der DDR seit 1956', *Aus Politik und Zeitgeschichte*, B 45 (12 Nov 1977) 3–19.
46. R. Havemann, *Dialektik ohne Dogma? Naturwissenschaft und Weltanschauung* (Reinbek: Rowohlt, 1964).
47. H. Kleinschmid, 'Das nützliche Korrektiv – Die geistige Auseinander-

setzung in der DDR findet im Westen statt', *Deutschland Archiv*, X (Oct 1977) 1011–17.

48. R. Bahro, *Die Alternative – Zur Kritik des real existierenden Sozialismus* (Cologne and Frankfurt a. M.: EVA, 1977).
49. I. Spittmann, 'Der Fall Bahro', *Deutschland Archiv*, X (Oct 1977) 1009–11.
50. 'Das "Spiegel-Manifest" und die Reaktion der DDR', *Deutschland Archiv*, XI (Feb 1978) pp. 199–219. An English version of the manifesto is to be found in B. Szajkowski (ed.), *Documents in Communist Affairs – 1977* (annual: 1977–9 Cardiff: University College Cardiff Press; 1980– , London: Macmillan) pp. 303–16.
51. Staritz, *Sozialismus*, pp. 14–21, and Thomas, *Modell*, p. 73.
52. Zimmermann, in *Problems of Communism*, XXVII, 5.
53. Ibid., p. 7.
54. Thomas, *Modell*, p. 83.
55. For both the raw-material prices and the debts, compare the figures in Zimmermann, in *Problems of Communism*, XXVII, 23.
56. Thomas, *Modell*, p. 92.
57. Zimmermann, in *Problems of Communism*, XXVII, 23.
58. Figures in Thomas, *Modell*, p. 85.
59. Ibid., p. 88.
60. P. J. Winters, 'Die Aussenpolitik der DDR', in H.-P. Schwarz (ed.), *Handbuch der deutschen Aussenpolitik* (Munich: Piper, 1975) p. 770.
61. W. Bruns, 'Sozialistische Aussenpolitik oder Aussenpolitik der DDR?', *Aus Politik und Zeitgeschichte*, B 19 (14 May 1977) 11.
62. Ludz, *The GDR from the Sixties to the Seventies*, p. 66.
63. Bruns, *Politik*, p. 7.
64. Cf. for details H. S. Lamm and S. Kupper, *DDR und Dritte Welt* (Munich and Vienna: Oldenbourg, 1976).
65. Bruns, *Politik*, pp. 19–24.
66. Ibid., p. 3.
67. Ibid., p. 12, quoting from an official GDR source.
68. B. von Rosenbladt, 'Aussenpolitik und internationale Beziehungen', in Rausch and Stammen, *DDR*, p. 272.
69. Thomas, *Modell*, p. 126.
70. To take just one example, the number of West German visitors in the GDR after years during which the GDR's population had been almost totally sealed off from direct contacts with 'Westerners' created tremendous problems for the GDR leadership. In 1977 almost 3 million West Germans and almost 3·5 million West Berliners were visitors to East Berlin and the GDR. 1·5 million one-day visits have to be added to this number, not to speak of the increase in telephone calls from West to East (half a million in 1969, 10 million in 1975). See for the figures the publications of the Federal Ministry for Intra-German Relations (Bundesministerium für innerdeutsche Beziehungen) quoted in Zimmermann, in *Problems of Communism*, XXVII, 36.
71. The problems related to the 'German nation' are dealt with in a wider historical context in P. H. Merkl, *German Foreign Policies, East and West* (Santa Barbara, Calif., and Oxford: Clio Press, 1974) ch. 2. For the most recent discussion, see Ludz, *DDR zwischen Ost und West*, ch. Sections II and III.

72. Quotations from the GDR Constitution and the Treaty of Friendship, Co-operation and Mutual Assistance with the Soviet Union of 7 Oct 1975, in Zimmermann, in *Problems of Communism*, XXVII, 34.

BIBLIOGRAPHY

1. German language publications

Of those publications cited in the Notes, the most important general surveys of different aspects of the GDR are repeated here in alphabetical order of authors or editors. They all include extensive bibliographies.

Bundesministerium für innerdeutsche Beziehunge *DDR-Handbuch* (Cologne: Verlag Wissenschaft und Politik, 1975).

Deuerlein, E. (ed.), *DDR – Geschichte und Bestandsaufaufnahme 1945–1970* (Munich: DTV, 1975).

Ludz, P. C., *Die DDR zwischen Ost und West* (Munich: C. H. Beck, 1977).

Rausch, H. and Stammen, T. (eds), *DDR – Das politische, wirtschaftliche und soziale System* (Munich: C. H. Beck, 1974).

Sontheimer, K. and Bleek, W. *DDR – Politik, Gesellschaft, Wirtschaft*, 4th ed. (Hamburg: Hoffmann and Campe, 1976).

Thomas, R., *Modell DDR – Die kalkulierte Emanzipation*, 6th ed. (Munich: Hanser, 1977).

To these have to be added studies concentrating on particular problems:

Bundesministerium für innerdeutsche Beziehunge, *Bericht der Bundesregierung und Materialien zur Lage der Nation*, 3 vols (Bonn, 1971, 1972 and 1974) (detailed comparisons between the GDR and the FRG).

End, H., *Zweimal deutsche Aussenpolitik* (Cologne: Verlag Wissenschaft und Politik, 1973).

Gasteyger, C., *Die beiden deutschen Staaten in der Weltpolitik* (Munich: Piper, 1976).

Hamel, H. (ed.), *BRD–DDR: Die Wirtschaftssysteme* (Munich: C. H. Beck, 1977).

Lapp, P. J., *Die Volkskammer der DDR* (Opladen: Westdeutscher, 1975).

Mampel, S., *Die sozialistische Verfassung der DDR* (Frankfurt a. M.: Metzler, 1972).

Pfeiler, W., *DDR-Lehrbuch* (Bonn: NVG, 1974).

Wettig, G., *Die Sowjetunion, die DDR und die Deutschland Frage*, 2nd ed. (Bonn: Bonn Actuell, 1977).

2. English language publications

General studies of the GDR include:

Childs, D., *East Germany* (New York: Praeger, 1969).

Dornberg, J., *The Other Germany* (Garden City, N.Y.: Doubleday, 1968).

Hanhardt, A. M., *The GDR* (Baltimore: Johns Hopkins Press, 1968).

Ludz, P. C., *The GDR from the Sixties to the Seventies* (Cambridge, Mass.: Harvard University Press, 1970).

Smith, J. E., *Germany beyond the Wall* (Boston, Mass.: Little, Brown, 1969).

Starrels, J. M. and Mallinckrodt, A. M., *Politics in the GDR* (New York: Praeger, 1975).

Steele, J., *Socialism with a German Face* (London: Cape, 1978).

Particular aspects of the GDR are dealt with in:

Baylis, T. A., *The Technical Intelligentia and the East German Elite* (Berkeley, Calif.: California University Press, 1974).

Birnbaum, K. E., *East and West Germany: A Modus Vivendi* (Farnborough, Hants.: Saxon Press, 1975).

Hearnden, A., *Education in the two Germanies* (Boulder, Colorado: Westview, 1976).

Herspring, D. H., *East German Civil–Military Relations* (New York: Praeger 1973).

Lippmann, H., *Honecker and the New Politics of Europe* (New York: Macmillan, 1972).

Ludz, P. C., *The Changing Party Elite in East Germany* (Cambridge, Mass.: MIT Press; Paris: Atlantic House, 1972).

——, *Two Germanies in One World*, Atlantic Papers, no. 3 (Paris: Atlantic Institute, 1973).

Schnitzer, M., *East and West Germany – A Comparative Economic Analysis* (New York: Praeger, 1972).

Schweigler, G., *National Consciousness in a Divided Germany* (Beverley Hills: Sage, 1975).

Sowden, J. K., *The German Question 1945–1973* (Bradford, Yorks: Bradford University Press, 1975).

3. Western Journals

Those regularly dealing with the GDR system include *Aus Politik und Zeitgeschichte, DDR-Report, Deutschland Archiv, Problems of Communism, Survey* and *Studies in Comparative Communism*.

13 Republics of Guinea-Bissau and Cape Verde

BASIL DAVIDSON

The republics of Guinea-Bissau and Cape Verde belong, politically, to the revolutionary trend that has been sweeping Africa in recent times. They were formed and are governed by the same integrated party or liberation movement, the Partido Africano de Independência de Guiné e Cabo Verde (PAIGC), whose leaders, while rejecting all doctrinal labels, whether Marxist or otherwise, have generally adhered to the principles of a Marxist analysis of history and society. If they may be said, notably in the thought and practice of their most outstanding leader, Amílcar Cabral, to have 'naturalised' this analysis to their own specific conditions and problems, they have also carried its approach and conclusions into original policies of form and content. Their claim is to have sought and found the social and cultural basis of reality, of local and indigenous reality, for programmes of unity and development capable of representing the collective interests of their populations. These are predominantly rural, although in thinking of the Cape Verdians one needs to bear in mind that the number of long-term Cape Verdian emigrants in urban situations abroad is not much smaller than the total population of the islands, and that links between emigrants and indigenes often remain close and even continuous.[1]

Long linked by historical and cultural ties, as well as by a common history within the Portuguese Empire, the two republics are pledged by the PAIGC to an eventual union on what will probably be a federal basis.[2]

In ecology Guinea-Bissau possesses strong contrasts. Its southern regions prolong the rain forest of the West African belt, the littoral consisting of sea creeks and semi-islands where tidal data are of daily

363

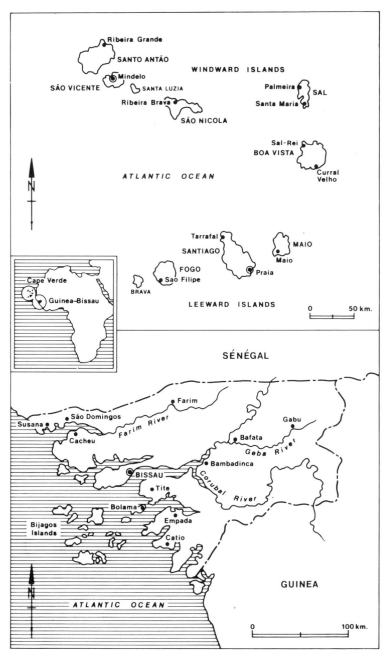

Republics of Guinea-Bissau and Cape Verde

concern. But the northerly regions, thin woodland dwindling into scrub and open savannah, are ecologically close to conditions in the *sahel*.[3] As in Cape Verde, there are no railways, but primitive road communications in the savannah areas were improved for military purposes by the Portuguese colonial power during the war of 1963–74. Road communications in the south remain poor or non-existent, while an effective network of communications by sea had still to be established in 1978, none having existed before save for the purposes of colonial administration and the movement of troops.

Guinea-Bissau's population is composed of four or five principal ethnic groups and more smaller ones. Portuguese is little spoken or understood, except in the capital and only considerable town, Bissau, but a specific creole, based chiefly on a Pepel-Mandjak syntax with a large intake of Portuguese words, is widely used and forms the basis for a national language.[4]

The Cape Verde republic consists of an archipelago of ten volcanic islands and five islets, divided traditionally into those to the windward (*barlavento*) and those to the leeward (*sotovento*), the largest population being on São Tiago, where also lies the capital, Praia. Originally of mixed origin and chiefly from the mainland of what the Portuguese used to call *los rios de Cabo Verde* (Guinea-Bissau and adjacent regions), the population has become specific and indigenous over the centuries, and is wrongly referred to as *mestiço* or mulatto. Though its principal ties have remained with Guinea-Bissau, the people of Cape Verde have long developed an indigenous culture and view of the world, being profoundly influenced by the ocean in which they live and by their copious emigration. Portuguese is widely understood, but the language of the country is an indigenous creole which is somewhat closer to Portuguese than is that of Guinea-Bissau.[5]

RECENT HISTORY

The origins of modern nationalism in these countries, as a reaction both against Portuguese nationalism and against colonial rule, have derived from longstanding grievances, a variety of forms of cultural protest and association, and a political trend influenced by corresponding movements in neighbouring colonies. All these took shape in elementary forms of political organisation during the 1950s, necessarily clandestine in the rigid circumstances of Portuguese intransigence and Salazarist chauvinism, and led by small groups of literate persons in the principal towns: persons who belonged, in so far as class definition is possible, to a colonial petty bourgeoisie. A decisive advance in political organisation, though still potential in any of its effects, was made in September 1956, when Amílcar Cabral and five others formed the clandestine PAIGC in Bissau; and from this time onwards, for reasons both geographical and otherwise, the mainland 'twin' became the chief centre and scene of action. This continued to be the case until 1974–5, when the Portuguese were finally obliged to withdraw from both countries and conceded their independence: to Guinea-Bissau on 10 September 1975, and to Cape Verde on 5 July 1975.[6]

Yet the culturally organic connection with Cape Verde remained vividly alive through these years of campaigning for independence. Two of the initial founders of the PAIGC had the same Cape Verdian father (although each had mainland mothers), while a third, afterwards President of the Cape Verde Republic, had come to Bissau when young from the island of Boa Vista. With the movement towards insurrectionary warfare in 1960 many young Cape Verdians, both men and women, rallied to the PAIGC and fought on the mainland in the years that followed. Thus, the present Foreign Minister of Cape Verde, Abilio Duarte, was a leading member of the mainland organisation; the Prime Minister, Pedro Pires, was a leading military commander; the Minister of Economic Planning, Osvaldo Lopes da Silva, was an artillery commander; and the same affiliation is true of many others. The same equally applies to Cape Verdian women who played leading roles on the mainland during the liberation war, including Carlina Pereira, Dulce Duarte and Maria das Dores.

Founded and led by the foresight and organising genius of Cabral, the PAIGC developed initially along the familiar lines of pressure for reform. Though severely hampered by the persecutions of the Salazarist system, this small organisation evolved a clandestine network of recruitment, and promoted urban strikes and demonstrations. These were seen both as a means of political education for protesters who were not yet nationalists, and as an instrument of peaceful pressure on the Portuguese. But it rapidly became clear to this leadership that peaceful pressure would bring nothing but renewed oppression, as indeed proved the case, and that more would be required. The turning point away from reformist concepts came in August 1959, when a strike of Bissau dockers, inspired by the PAIGC, was shot back to work with heavy losses. A month after this massacre, the leaders of the PAIGC declared for action against the colonial power 'by all possible means, including war'. From then onwards the PAIGC developed a revolutionary programme and practice.

Cabral thereupon established principles of thought and action which were to remain effective, with a gradually improving efficacy, until independence was secured fifteen years later. Their aims were to 'mobilise and organise the peasant masses who, as experience has shown, represent the main force in our struggle for liberation'; 'strengthen our organisation in the towns but keep it clandestine, avoiding all [further] demonstrations'; 'develop and reinforce units around our party of the Africans, of all ethnic groups, origins, and social strata'; 'prepare as many cadres [trained activists] as possible, either inside the country or abroad'; and take other and corresponding measures. A little later, early in 1960, Cabral transferred his head-quarters to neighbouring Conakry, capital of a now independent (ex-French) Guinea, and set about preparing to launch a war of liberation.[7]

Nothing like this could be attempted in the distant Cape Verde islands; and there, too, the situation was a somewhat different one. On the mainland, more than 99 per cent of all ethnic groups, save the Portuguese (the latter numbering around 3000), were subject to the rules of the *indigenato*, under which all civic rights were denied to those not considered to be 'civilised', while only the smallest handful, perhaps 0·3 per cent of Africans, were subject to the rules of 'assimilation', by which certain civic rights were granted.[8] It was therefore possible on the mainland to win ground among the vast bulk of the population on the basis of their grievances against the *indigenato*, providing as this did for forced labour and the forced cultivation of export crops as well as an all-pervasive system of colonial taxation. The Cape Verdians, by contrast, were in theory all exempt from the *indigenato*: in principle, at least, they were all Portuguese citizens. Yet the difference in practice was often very small,[9] a point which explains why the PAIGC rapidly became popular on the islands, even if it could survive as an organisation only in a tenuous clandestinity.

In Conakry Cabral continued to develop his plans. There he set up a school for militants, whom little by little he sent into Guinea-Bissau over the forest frontier with Guinea, after giving them a political and cultural education in what they should do there. He saw from the first that peasant support, leading to peasant participation, could derive only from linking local grievances to the wider aims of liberation. The core of his teaching at this stage and later was that no worthwhile progress could be made merely by achieving the outward trappings of inde-pendence, but that the peasant masses would measure their participa'tion only by the real and material advances they could make under PAIGC leadership. The early activists were told to learn local languages, get as close to the peasants as they could, and patiently explain the links between local grievances and united action to remove them. Several dozen young men and women followed these directives through 1960 to 1962, and were able, as was proved in the event, to win a substantial success. This lay at the foundation of the greater successes that were to follow.

In January 1963, having long measured their chances and refused a variety of pressures to 'begin' earlier, Cabral and his companions launched open warfare. Within months they had cleared the Portuguese from a number of forest regions and set up a series of guerrilla camps, under as many local guerrilla leaders. These initial gains then ran into difficulty, partly from Portuguese counter-offensives, and partly from guerrilla inexperience and indiscipline. Reverting to their precolonial heritage of culture and behaviour, a number of peasant commanders interpreted the war in ethnic or 'tribal' terms, fell back on the advice of diviners and oracles, and produced a situation of incipient chaos and division. All this came to a head late in 1963. Two events early in 1964 saved the PAIGC.

The first and crucial event consisted in the calling of a congress of all military and political leaders, totalling some 200, who met in the southern forest between 13 and 17 February 1964. At this first congress the leadership of Cabral and those most close to him was able to act, and as it proved decisively, against the fission of their movement into 'tribal' fragments; against destructive practices deriving from local religious belief; and against organisational confusion. A new political structure was agreed, the beginnings of a regular army were launched, tribunals were established to deal with indiscipline or crime; and, no less important for the outcome, plans were put into effect whereby the peasants in liberated areas were to elect a network of representative committees which, gradually, would acquire the attributes of local government within a modernising structure. These measures combined to put the movement on a sound basis, and meanwhile a second event confirmed the prospects of military success. A Portuguese attempt to recapture the liberated half-island of Como, off the ocean creek of Catio, was defeated after many weeks of fighting, and this place, together with its adjacent mainland areas, now became a central zone for the development of the PAIGC's political programme.[10]

MILITARY RECORD[11]

PAIGC success continued to grow until 1968, by which time the insurrectionary army and its supporting peasant militias had won and proved they could retain a more or less firm control of about half the rural areas, though not yet of any town or large settlement. Its regular army had grown from the initial 900 of 1964 to several thousand picked volunteers, was better trained and armed, and had commanders who were both skilled and highly disciplined. Most of its training was now conducted inside the country, but a trickle of militants continued to be sent abroad for training (initially to Algeria in 1963, a handful to China in 1964, and many more, afterwards, to the USSR and other countries in the Soviet bloc and to Cuba). After 1964 Cabral was able to win a little unofficial support in the West, a growing aid in non-military materials from Sweden (through its parastatal International Development Authority), and eventually a hearing at the UN and in the US Congress, as well as from a number of governments in East or West.

By late 1968 it was clear that the PAIGC was not going to be defeated, although the Lisbon dictatorship had concentrated an army of some 30,000 men in Guinea-Bissau as well as a small but still invulnerable air force. This meant that the war was now potentially won on the mainland; and, sure of this, Cabral and his companions set about improving their 'emergent state' in liberated areas while pushing further in the military field. In this last respect they pursued a consistent policy, defined by Cabral as follows:

> In order to dominate a given zone, the enemy is obliged to disperse his forces. In dispersing his forces, he weakens himself and we can defeat him. Then in order to defend himself against us, he has to concentrate his forces. When he does that, we can occupy the zones that he leaves free and work in them politically so as to hinder his return there.[12]

By 1969 the Portuguese army, though some seven times superior in numbers of fighting men, was thus distributed in more than a hundred fixed garrisons throughout the country, and most of these were besieged or sorely harassed by surrounding PAIGC units. The only superiority remaining to the Portuguese commander, General António de Spínola, was the air weapon; but this could not be decisive. Much napalm and fragmentation bombing was used by Spínola, but with little result.

There set in a certain 'balance' in the military field, with the

Portuguese unable to recover the large areas they had lost or prevent these areas from becoming larger still, but with the PAIGC unable to take any towns, much less Bissau itself. Concluding that he could never win by military means, Spínola now turned to political warfare and announced that he would promote a programme for a *Guiné melhor* (a 'better Guinea'), hoping by this means to outbid the PAIGC at its own game. To that end he made many promises, urged the formation of elementary schools, and even formed a 'nationalist movement' of his own, finding for it a figurehead in the person of a former PAIGC leader, Rafael Barbosa, whom the colonial police had arrested in 1962 and since kept under severe conditions.

No doubt unavoidably, these measures lacked the personnel, mental freedom and ideological initiative to ensure success. By this time, moreover, the liberated areas of the PAIGC were organised for self-rule through representative committees, were endowed with an elementary-school system already serving some 14,000 children, and possessed an elementary system of public health consisting of bush clinics staffed by local nurses trained in Europe as well as by a handful of local and Cuban doctors. The realities of an independent state were emerging from 'the grass roots', while the bulk of youthful men and women were volunteers in the military, social, or political organisations of the PAIGC. Already on foot were the embryos of youth, women's, and trade-union organisations which would take effective shape after 1974. Compared with all this, the promises of Spínola's 'better Guinea', accompanied as they were by continuous bombing and ground raids on the liberated areas, could seem no more than demagogy. They were, in any case, not believed.[13]

Another turning point came in 1973. In January Cabral was murdered in the neighbouring capital of Conakry by conspirators led by African agents of the Portuguese authorities in Bissau. But this murder, far from overwhelming the movement that Cabral had founded and led, was answered by anger and renewed effort. Major offensives were launched by the PAIGC in February. In March the PAIGC began to use SAM-7 ground-to-air missiles, Soviet supplied, with devastating effect on Spínola's air force. More fighting followed, and in July PAIGC artillery levelled the fortified strongpoint of Guileje, previously thought impregnable. By September, having carried through a general election by secret ballot and manhood suffrage in the liberated areas during 1972, the PAIGC called a second congress and declared the independence of their country, this declaration being quickly followed by wide recognition throughout the world. Full independence came a year later, following the Lisbon coup against the dictatorship, and all Portuguese forces were peacefully withdrawn by October 1974.

By local agreement with the Portuguese governor, the PAIGC established representatives in Bissau during July 1974, and began sending open emissaries to the Cape Verde islands in August. These at once set about the enlargement of a now effectively legal PAIGC in the islands. On 30 June 1975 a general election in the archipelago, held under Portuguese supervision, brought 85 per cent of the voters to the polls; of these, just over 92 per cent voted for the candidates of the PAIGC during an election in which no other parties took the field. Independence followed at once. As on the mainland, the colonial state had been destroyed. It now remained to build independent states.

POLITICAL IDEAS AND ORGANISATION

The working ideas of the PAIGC, evinced in a considerable body of theoretical and programmatic writings as well as in their practice, were and have remained the product of an anti-colonial nationalism reshaped and deepened by a Marxist analysis of local realities. They have therefore had to achieve originality, since no such analysis was to hand, save as a merely dogmatic and therefore unrealistic application of the 'classics'. Cabral's own approach may be seen, summarily, in two of his lectures, one in Milan in 1964 and the other in Havana in 1966, and was severely from the angle of African history.[14] He argued that the further unfolding of local history, after the long colonial interruption and reversal, must turn crucially upon raising the level of productive forces, and that this necessarily implied a system of production – more broadly, a whole culture – that could not be capitalist. The alternative could not properly be labelled socialist, since the cultural, productive and technological conditions for socialism must long remain absent in this extremely deprived country (with about 99 per cent of illiteracy even in the last years of the colonial period); but it would have to move in the direction of an eventual socialism. Meanwhile it could be described as a system designed to end all capitalist and customary forms of exploitation.

No just appreciation of the range and subtlety of Cabral's thought is possible here; and it is still early in the day to measure its historical importance. But attention should be drawn to some of Cabral's conclusions, applied as these were to the liberated zones during the war and since then to the whole country. He held that power must be returned to the masses from whom the colonial system had taken it. But these masses must at the same time be led out of the small enclosures of traditional thought and culture. A genuine liberation must therefore mean a revolution, but a dual one: against the culture and structures of the colonial system or of any prolongation of that system in a 'neo-colonial' form, but also, and equally, against all those aspects of traditional culture and structure – of pre-colonial culture and struc-ture – which could no longer serve an overall collective development within the modern world. To that end, as we have seen, the PAIGC used its liberated zones during the war to establish the groundwork of demo-cratic structures, modernising structures, within which the rural masses could mobilise themselves, increasingly, for social and cultural change.[15]

Taking over at the end of 1974, the PAIGC proceeded to apply the same approach to the whole country. Inheriting a wrecked economy, it was obliged to spend 1975 and most of 1976 in gaining a full insight into the country's situation and in beginning to bring purposive effort out of it. By the end of 1976 it was possible to hold a general election throughout the country, again, as in 1972 in the liberated areas, to regional councils, which in turn elected a People's National Assembly.[16] At the same time, the youth, women's and trade-union organisations, each seen as a mode of political and social mobilisation, were enlarged and reorganised, and a consistent effort began to be made in transform-ing the PAIGC itself into a more structured party with a registered membership and elective organs of its own.

These emergent structures were then discussed at length at a Third Congress of the PAIGC, held in Bissau during November 1977 in the presence of 305 militants from all levels and regions, and were redefined in a long analysis by the Secretary-general of the PAIGC, Aristides Pereira (also President of the Cape Verde Republic, his deputy as Secretary-general being Luiz Cabral, also President of the Guinea-Bissau Republic). Continuing to reject easy labels, Pereira defined the new regime in either country as being one of 'a liberation movement in power', and its ideological content as being 'the ending of the exploitation of man by man'.[17]

Its structures were a combination of two modes of organisation. The State itself was seen as consisting of an executive administration controlled by, but not identical with, the PAIGC, and powered, democratically, by a tiered network of representative committees and executives from the village base to the People's National Assembly. On the other hand, given that the State was 'born as the instrument of the PAIGC for the realisation of its programme', and that 'this could not have been otherwise', it remained the instrument of the PAIGC in the long transition to an advanced society. At the same time, the PAIGC itself possessed the structures of a party elected from the base, even if these structures had still to be perfected. A quadrennial congress elects a Supreme Council (Comité Supérior da Luta) of eighty-five persons, meeting once a year. This in turn elects an Executive Committee (Comité Executivo da Luta) of twenty-six persons, meeting every three months. Meanwhile the day-to-day conduct of affairs is entrusted to a Permanent Commission (Commissào Permanente) of eight persons (five from the mainland, three from the islands; see Table 13.1). A fourth congress will meet in 1981 and review these structures, as well as other essential problems (see Figures 13.1 and 13.2.)

There could be no confusion or identification between State and Party, Pereira affirmed, and there should be none:

> The subordination of State to Party, as provided in the basic texts of our two republics, can in no way mean the fusion of the two entities or the substitution of the first by the second. Each carries out functions

TABLE 13.1 Permanent Commission of Guinea-Bissau and Cape Verde, elected at the Third Congress of the PAIGC, Bissau, end 1977

Member	*Origin*	*Function*
Aristides Pereira	Cape Verde	President of the Cape Verde Republic; Secretary-general of the PAIGC
Luiz Cabral	Guinea-Bissau	President of the Republic of Guinea-Bissau; Deputy Secretary-general of the PAIGC
Francisco Mendes[a]	Guinea-Bissau	Prime-Minister (First Commissioner) of Guinea-Bissau
João Bernardo Vieira[b]	Guinea-Bissau	Minister of National Defence of Guinea-Bissau; Chairman of People's National Assembly
Pedro Pires	Cape Verde	Prime Minister of Cape Verde
Umarú Djaló	Guinea-Bissau	Chief of Staff of Armed Forces of Guinea-Bissau
Constantino Teixeira	Guinea-Bissau	Commissioner for Security of Guinea-Bissau
Abilio Duarte	Cape Verde	Foreign Minister of Cape Verde; Chairman of People's National Assembly

[a] Deceased, July 1978.
[b] Appointed Prime Minister of Guinea-Bissau in place of Francisco Mendes.

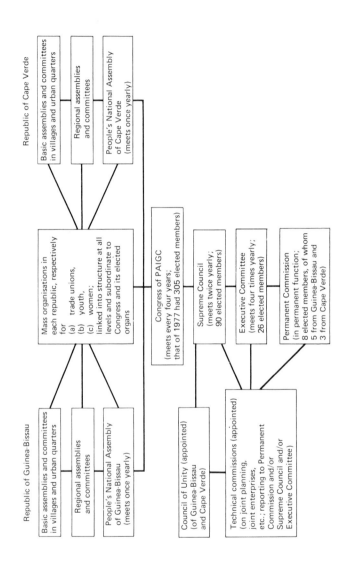

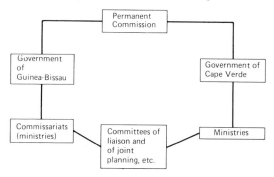

FIGURE 13.2 Essential administrative structure of Guinea-Bissau and
Cape Verde

which, although complementary, are different and use distinctive
ways and means. Their fusion or identification is as prejudicial to the
Party as to the State: for it would lead to inefficiency in their work; it
would create or increase bureaucratism [*o burocratismo*]; and it would
hamper Party activities in their duties. . . .[18]

Those who wish to make doctrinal comparisons may see this programmatic and practical organisation, as regards the nature of the State
and its relationship to its controlling party, as both a development from
the Leninist concept of 1917 (in *State and Revolution*, for example) and a
variant designed to ensure that the result should not lead to a
'monolithic party' identical with the State. The driving edge of the whole
programme, as revealed in Pereira's long analysis (itself in line with
Cabral's thought), was to develop and promote the political consciousness and self-development of the rural masses, whether through their
elective committees (their 'soviets', one might almost call them) or
through their participation in the PAIGC.

The same congress reaffirmed the aim of an eventual union between
the two republics, stressing that this must be the fruit of a gradual
process of complementary development and cultural convergence. All
relations between the two republics are meanwhile subject to the
Permanent Commission of the PAIGC (with, as noted, five members
from Guinea-Bissau and three from Cape Verde), supplemented by a
Council of Unity, which, in turn, has the duty of supervising the work of
a number of technical commissions. The latter were already at work in
1977 on measures to form a joint airline and shipping line, to ease and
remove tariff barriers, to compose the foundations of a common legal
system, and to forward a programme of cultural convergence.

INTERNAL AFFAIRS

Primitive public services on the islands, and practically non-existent ones on the mainland (outside the areas liberated during the war), defined the immediate tasks of 1975. One small secondary school existed in Guinea-Bissau, and there were two in Cape Verde. There was no system of higher education, either academic or vocational. In public health, independence found Guinea-Bissau with only three doctors, and the position was little better on the islands.

While makeshift methods were inevitable for the time being, planning of national educational and health services began in 1975. All private enterprise in these fields was abolished, though more as an earnest of what was intended for the future than because any such enterprise actually existed. Compulsory schooling for all would have to await the training of teachers and the building of classrooms; meanwhile the principles of such a system were debated and defined. Here again the first principle was to reject colonial models in favour of a modernising curriculum and structure suited to local realities.[19] In 1976 a beginning was made with mass literacy campaigning on the methods devised by the Brazilian educator Paolo Freire. In public health, some relief from the dearth of personnel was obtained from doctors sent from Portugal by an aid agreement, and these were later supplemented by medical personnel from Cuba. The corresponding situation on the Cape Verde islands was a little better so far as the principal urban centres were concerned; but outside these, as on the mainland, there were effectively no health services of any kind. Again as on the mainland, decentralisation was seen as the necessary key, together with an emphasis on preventive rather than curative medicine.

Law and order posed no special problem. Apart from a very local coup attempt in Bissau during 1975, immediately suppressed, no opposition appeared upon the scene, and each republic could reduce its security and defence services to a minimum; to this the only important exception lay in the need for additional fishery protection in the republics' territorial waters.

THE ECONOMY

Independence found each country in acute backwardness as regards all forms of modern industry and commercial enterprise. Only one modern manufacturing plant existed on the mainland, a brewery, and on the islands there was none of any economic weight. Meanwhile, hope of a rapid improvement from the disastrously low levels of rural production and external trade registered in 1974, whether in one country or the other, were greatly set back by the continuation of a nine-year drought on the islands and the onset of a severe drought in Guinea-Bissau during 1977.[20] The response in the islands was to combine an appeal for emergency aid, which was generously answered by a number of countries, notably the United States, with a long-term programme of water research and conservation, together with a long-term programme of afforestation. The same policy was applied on the mainland, and again with a substantial success, after the failure of the 1977 rice crop.

National planning was meanwhile put in hand, though much hampered by a lack of statistics and of statisticians.[21] Measures were taken to channel relatively high levels of foreign aid into appropriate forms of infrastructural investment. Whether in one country or the other, declared Pereira's programmatic analysis of November 1977, 'we must make very sure that we do not fall victims to a vicious circle such as would induce production for the external market at a rate faster than the expansion of our internal market'. More exports were essential, and would call for more investment, 'but the movement of our economy must, above all, be activated by an internal dynamism', arising from the activisation of internal resources, and not relying on an expansion won merely by the spending of foreign aid. 'Foreign aid must remain complementary to a dynamic dictated by the needs of an independent internal development.' At the same time, if progress were to benefit the few at the expense of the many, 'our economy might grow, but it would not develop'. This rejection of 'growth without development' called among other things, for a programme of economic decentralisation from Bissau, an artificially overgrown urban centre, whose weight should be progressively diminished.

In Cape Verde the accent was placed on improving rural production, with, as on the mainland, an eventual aim of promoting producer co-operatives, and, at the same time as measures to combat drought,[22] with the promotion of appropriate industries, notably in ocean fishing, shipping, and ship repair.

EXTERNAL AFFAIRS

The external policies of the PAIGC have always emphasised its adherence to international non-alignment and its refusal, save in respect of membership of the OAU (and, now, of the Economic Community of West African States), to join any external bloc. During the war decisive military aid was given by the USSR and other communist countries (not including China after about 1965), but non-military aid was regularly sought from the West, and not always without some success. These policies of non-alignment have been repeatedly stressed since independence, and neither country has permitted any foreign base, whether military or otherwise, while both countries have regular diplomatic relations with West and East (including China after 1974). Relations with Portugal greatly improved after the Portuguese, in 1977, abandoned their demand that the independent state of Guinea-Bissau should meet the debts to Portugal of the colonial 'province of Guiné'; and these relations reached a friendly footing in 1978.

This non-alignment is not interpreted as being one of ideological neutrality. On the contrary, again in Pereira's words of November 1977,

When we created our party, we knew very well that the aims of the struggle we were launching could not be confined to a mere liquidation of colonial rule in our countries. For the destruction of colonial rule is impossible without fighting against the imperialism which is the support of colonialism in all its forms. This anti-imperialist factor is a fundamental element in our policy of non-alignment, a policy which for us means that we do not enter blocs or align ourselves with the decisions of others; but it also means that we adhere to an alignment with every cause that works for the dignity, liberty and progress of peoples. . . . Thus, in Africa, there are peoples not yet free and independent. Our party considers that their struggle is its own struggle, and spares no effort in giving the help it can to Africa's fighters for liberty and to their organisations. . . .[23]

BIOGRAPHIES

Amilcar Cabral was born in Báfata, Guinea-Bissau, in 1924, the son of a Cape Verdian schoolteacher and a mainland mother. He was widely judged in his lifetime as among the most remarkable figures of contemporary Africa, whether as a political thinker, a practical revolutionary, or a gifted spokesman of his people. His above all was the vision and intelligence which founded the PAIGC, analysed its prospects, steered its policies, and repeatedly exercised the critical role of leadership. Benefiting from his father's citizenship and living at that time with his father at Santa Caterina on São Tiago island, he was able to attend secondary school in Cape Verde, and from there, thanks to his brains and tenacity, was able to reach university in Lisbon. A poet who was already a man of dour and practical realism, he there chose, and very characteristically, to qualify as an agronomist and hydraulic engineer. At the same time he took part in early nationalist discussions with other Africans from the Portuguese Empire, notably with the Angolans Agostinho Neto and Mario de Andrade.

That was late in the 1940s. From 1952 to 1954 he took employment with the Portuguese administration of Guinea-Bissau, and was able to make the first all-embracing agricultural survey of the country's resources, seeing this work both as a service to his people and as a means of gaining an intimate knowledge of that people. Already politically active, he left the colony in 1954 to escape arrest and took service on sugar plantations in Angola, where, in December 1956, he was among those who founded the Angolan nationalist movement, the MPLA (Movimento Popular de Libertação de Angola). A few months earlier (in September), during a visit to Bissau, he had formed the PAIGC. He returned to Bissau immediately after the massacre of dockers there in August 1959, at once went underground, and from that time forward led the PAIGC in its preparations for insurrection.

From 1960, beginning with a long visit to London, he began to build systematic contacts for the PAIGC in the outside world, and after 1965 achieved a considerable and growing success in this. In that year he formulated the principles of thought and practice of his party in a long series of directives, known as the *Palavras Geráis*,[24] which summarised experience until then and laid down lines for future work. They typify his thinking and incisive style; but at the same time, in a series of international lectures, he both popularised and explained his party's origins and intentions. A penetrating and original thinker, he was also a gifted writer and the master of a clear and vigorous prose. Insistently realist, he none the less looked at wide horizons. Seeing the wood, he never failed to inspect the trees. A wonderfully integrated personality, he conceived of his own country's destiny as part of the movement of the world, but also as a contribution to that movement. It seems unlikely that anyone who knew him could be in any doubt, when he was struck down by traitors in 1973, that he still had much to give his country and his continent. Yet he had worked in such a fashion that the success of the cause to which he devoted his life was already assured.

Aristides Pereira, President of the Cape Verde Republic and Secretary-general of the PAIGC, was born on the island of Boa Vista in 1924. He settled in Bissau when a youth and became a senior official in the post and telegraph service. A founder member of the PAIGC in 1956, he remained the close companion and *alter ego* of Cabral until the latter's death, when he succeeded him as Secretary-general of the PAIGC. In January 1973, at the time of Cabral's murder, he was himself seized by the conspirators and carried in a launch towards Bissau, being rescued only at the last moment by naval craft of the Republic of Guinea. A tireless worker, Pereira then set himself to carry through the liberation that Cabral had initiated, and to follow the plans that Cabral had worked out. After independence he took up headquarters at Praia on São Tiago and became President of the Cape Verde Republic, but he remained the active Secretary-general of the PAIGC as a whole. His reputation is for long vision and great determination.

Luiz Cabral, President of the Republic of Guinea-Bissau and Deputy Secretary-general of the PAIGC, was born in Bissau in 1929. The brother of Amílcar Cabral by the same father but a different mother, Luiz Cabral was another of the six founders of the PAIGC, and has since remained a crucial and often decisive figure in its development. An accountant in a Portuguese trading firm in Bissau, he escaped into clandestinity in 1959 and became the PAIGC's representative in Senegal, with headquarters in Dakar. In 1964 he was among the principal organisers of the critically important First Congress, but, as the armed struggle unfolded, he returned north and became responsible for all operations across the Senegalese frontier. Becoming deputy to Pereira after his brother's murder in 1973, he took up headquarters in Bissau after Portuguese withdrawal in 1974, and was elected President of the Guinea-Bissau Republic. A vivid orator and, like Pereira, another tireless worker, his postwar collaboration with Pereira has produced a team combining many gifts and much experience.

A member of this team was the Prime Minister (or First Commissioner) of Guinea-Bissau, Francisco Mendes, who died in a motor accident in 1978. The team also includes, for Guinea-Bissau, the Commissioner for Defence, Bernardo Vieira; the Chairman of the People's National Assembly, Carmen Pereira (no relation of Aristides Pereira); and the Commissioner for Economic Planning, Vasco Cabral (no relation of Luiz Cabral). Prominent members in the Cape Verdian team have already been mentioned by name.

BASIC FACTS ABOUT GUINEA-BISSAU

Official name: Republic of Guinea-Bissau (Republica de Guiné-Bissau).

Area: 36,125 sq. km. (13,900 sq. miles).

Population (1977 est.): 950,000.

Population density: 26·3 per sq. km.

Population distribution (1975, approx.): 20 per cent urban or semi-urban, 80 per cent rural.

Administrative division: 8 regions, each subdivided into districts, village groupings, etc.

Ethnic nationalities (approx. distribution): Balante, 23 per cent; Mandjak, 14 per cent; Fula, 12 per cent; Mandinka, 10 per cent; about 11 others, 41 per cent.

Major town: Bissau (the capital; 1975 population est. 80,000).

Main natural resources: rice, groundnuts, lesser crops and forest products, cattle, bauxite, timber. Exploration for oil in progress.

Main trading partners: imports – Portugal, USSR, Belgium; exports – Portugal, Cape Verde, FRG.

Road network: 3570 km.

Foreign relations: diplomatic relations with over 33 countries; 13 diplomatic missions residing in Bissau; member of the OAU and UN since 1974.

BASIC FACTS ABOUT CAPE VERDE

Official name: Republic of Cape Verde (Republica de Cabo Verde).

Area: 4033 sq. km. (1550 sq. miles).

Population (1976): 360,000.

Administrative divisions: 14 districts.

Ethnic nationalities: indigenous Cape Verdians 99 per cent; others 1 per cent.

Major towns: Praia (the capital; est. population 50,000), Mindelo, Ribeira Grande.

Main natural resources: fishing, agriculture (with some stock-raising), salt, coffee, castor oil.

Main trading partners: imports – Portugal, Guinea-Bissau, Netherlands; exports – Portugal, Angola, UK, Zaire.

Road network: 1287 km.

382 *Marxist Governments*

Foreign relations: diplomatic relations with over 40 countries; in 1978 one diplomatic mission (Portugal) residing in Praia (the remaining missions reside either in Bissau or in Dakar); member of the OAU and the UN, the latter since 1975.

NOTES

1. A. Carreira, *Migrações nas Ilhas de Cabo Verde* (Lisbon: Univ. Nova de Lisboa, 1977).
2. Derived from the logic of their history, the conviction of the leaders of the PAIGC, from the beginning, was that a successful struggle could only be a joint and common one, followed eventually by unity of the two countries. This conviction was not seen as denying the existence of differences between the two. But, Cabral told a PAIGC seminar in 1969, 'the essential principal of unity resides in the difference between things. If these were not different, there would be no need to unite them, there would be no problem of unity.' For a summary restatement of PAIGC thinking on this matter, see A. Pereira, *Relatório do Conselho Superior da Luta* (Third Congress of PAIGC, Bissau, Nov 1977) ch. 6.
3. A. Teixeira da Mota, *Guiné Portuguesa*, 2 vols (Lisbon: Agéncia Geral do Ultramar, 1954); A. Cabral, *Recenseamento Agricola da Guiné*, Boletim Cultural no. 43 (Bissau, 1956), based on researches made in 1953. Much geographical and ethnographical material may be found in the Boletim Cultural series.
4. See notes and references in E. Tonkin, 'Social Aspects of the Development of Portuguese Pidgin in West Africa' (Seminar paper, School of Oriental and African Studies, University of London, 1971). Guinea creole (*crioulo*) and Cape Verdian creole are, however, considered to be not pidgins, but languages of primary expression.
5. A good introduction to Cape Verdian history is summarised in A. Carreira, *Cabo Verde, Classes Sociais, Estrutura Familiar, Migrações*, Biblioteca Ulmeiro no. 9 (1977), and supplemented in Carreira, *Migrações*, 1977 (see n. 1 above). For Cape Verdian creole, see papers in *Miscelânea Luso-Africana* (Lisbon: Junta de Investigações Cientificas do Ultramar, 1975), especially M. F. Valkhoff, 'A Socio-Linguistic Enquiry into Cabo-verdian Creole'.
6. The historical narrative in this paper is based on (a) a personal observation of the PAIGC beginning in 1960; (b) periodical visits to the country between 1967 and 1977; (c) access to unpublished PAIGC records; and (d) published sources, whether in PAIGC documents or in the writings of A. Cabral. The best available collection of the latter is A. Cabral, *Unité et Lutte*, 2 vols (Paris: Maspero, 1975), largely available also in English as A. Cabral, *Unity and Struggle* (London: Heinemann, 1979). For a review until 1968, see B. Davidson, *The Liberation of Guiné* (Harmondsworth: Penguin, 1969). Records from the side of the colonial government, on the other hand, are sparse or unavailable.

7. See ibid., p. 32.
8. A. Moreira, *As Élites das Províncias Portuguesas de Indigenato (Guiné, Angola e Moçambique)* (Lisbon: Junta de Invest. do Ultramar, 1956).
9. Carreira, *Migrações*.
10. For a detailed treatment of these decisive episodes, See B. Davidson, *Africa in Modern History* (Penguin and Allen Lane, 1978) pp. 341–50.
11. The narrative here is based on sources listed in n. 6 above, but especially on a copious series of communiqués and summaries and corresponding military analyses issued by the PAIGC from 1962 onwards, together with Portuguese official communiqués (Forças Armadas da Guiné) and such other Portuguese materials as have come to hand. There is also much material from newspaper correspondents of at least half a dozen countries, but of varying quality.
12. Quoted in *Afrique–Asie*, LXVI (1974) xxv. For an extended discussion, see also B. Davidson, 'The Politics of Armed Struggle', in B. Davidson, J. Slovo and A. Wilkinson, *Southern Africa* (Harmondsworth: Penguin, 1976).
13. For Spínola's ideas about a 'better Guinea', see his statements to a South African reporter, A. J. Venter, in Venter's *Portugal's War in Africa*, Munger Africana Library Notes (Pasadena: Californian Institute of Technology, 1973), relating to interviews with Spínola during April 1971. For a summary of the history of 1973–4, see Pereira, *Relatório*, ch. 1.
14. The Milan lecture (1964) is 'Brief Analysis of the Social Structure of "Portuguese" Guinea' – add to which a corresponding analysis of the social structure in Cape Verde (published later); and the Havana lecture (1966) is 'Foundations and Aims of National Liberation and Social Structure'. Texts of all three are available in *Unité et Lutte*, and in English in Cabral's collected writings published by Heinemann (London, 1979).
15. For discussion and analysis, see also B. Davidson, 'African Peasants and Revolution', *Journal of Peasant Studies*, I, no. 3 (Apr 1974).
16. See B. Davidson, 'Guinea-Bissau: People's Elections', in *People's Power*, no. 6 (M.A.G.I.C., London, Jan–Feb 1977), drawing on electoral returns published by the newspaper *Nô Pintcha* (Bissau). See also P. Freira, *The Letters from Guinea-Bissau* (London: W & R Pub. Coop, 1978).
17. Pereira, *Relatório*, ch. 2.
18. Ibid., ch. 5.
19. In the measure that the PAIGC were able to develop a new educational system during the armed struggle in their liberated areas, they evolved and published a series of directives, guiding principles, and programmes. For the philosophy behind these, see Cabral at many points (in *Unité et Lutte*); for an example, see *Programa do Ensino* (Bissau: PAIGC, Departamento da Reconstrução Nacional, 1972); and, for a brief summary of achievements and intentions after independence, see Pereira, *Relatório*, ch. 4.
20. For a summary of this and connected points, see L. Rudebeck, 'Conditions of Development and Actual Development Strategy in Guinea-Bissau' (seminar paper, Scandinavian Institute of African Studies, 1977); and, for an extensive treatment of the background, see Rudebeck, *Guinea-Bissau* (Uppsala: Scandinavian Institute of African Studies, 1974).
21. Rudebeck, 'Conditions'.
22. *Aperçu sur la Situation aux Îles du Cap Vert Découlant de la Poursuite de la*

Sécheresse and Programme d'Emergence 1977–78 (both Praia: Sécretariat d'État à la Co-opération et Planification, Oct 1977).
23. Pereira, Relatório, ch. 9.
24. In Cabral, Unity and Struggle (London: Heinemann, 1979).

14 Hungarian People's Republic

GEORGE SCHÖPFLIN

Hungary today is an industrial-agrarian country, with Budapest, the capital, as its single most important urban concentration; its most rapid phase of economic growth has been the period since 1945. However, the modern period in Hungary can be dated from 1867, the year of the Compromise (*Kiegyezés*, *Ausgleich*) between the Hungarian nobility and the Austrian court in Vienna, whereby Hungary achieved internal self-government. This ushered in the last phase of Hungary's long relationship with the Hapsburgs, who had established their ascendancy over the crown of Hungary after the Battle of Mohács (1526), at which the Ottoman Empire finally defeated the Kingdom of Hungary. However, the Hapsburgs only succeeded in liberating Hungary from the Turks in 1701, and then incorporated its entire area into the Hapsburg domains. The emergence of modern nationalism, the so-called 'Reform Era' of the early nineteenth century, led the Hungarian political elite into simultaneous conflict with Vienna and the non-Hungarian (i.e. non-Magyar) nationalities in 1848–9. Hungarian refusal to recognise the rights of the minority nationalities resulted in the eventual disintegration of the Kingdom of Hungary in 1918–20.[1] That proved to be the first of the three caesuras of twentieth-century Hungarian history. The loss of large areas of territory and approximately 3 million ethnic Hungarians to the successor states left Hungary with a 'loss of empire' complex which continues to inform attitudes. At the same time, the collapse of 1918 was associated with the bourgeois radical revolution under Count Mihály Károlyi and the Hungarian Soviet Republic led by Béla Kun. These events made the restoration of a neo-feudal authoritarian regime under Admiral Miklós Horthy much easier to sustain.[2] In the Second World War Hungary found itself allied to Nazi Germany, having under German aegis recovered portions of the territory lost in

385

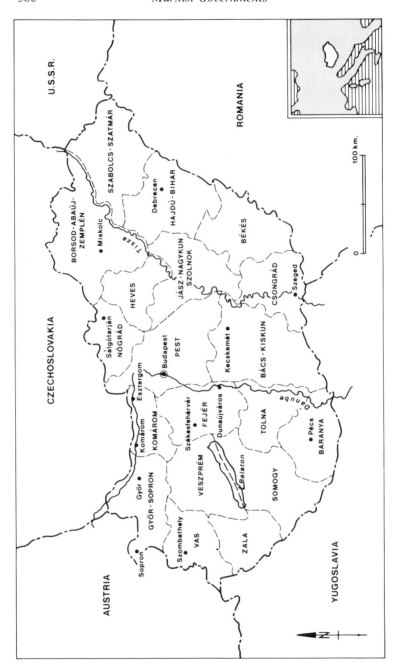

Hungary: county boundaries

1920. In 1944 Horthy was replaced by the Hungarian Nazi Arrow Cross regime of Ferenc Szálasi, which was responsible for an anti-Semitic bloodbath even as the Red Army was advancing steadily westwards across Hungary. Defeat was accompanied by the collapse of institutions and constituted the second caesura. In free elections held in 1945, the Smallholders gained an absolute majority and it took the communists, led by Mátyás Rákosi, the better part of two years to destroy the party and shortly thereafter to establish their political monopoly.[3] This monopoly was shattered by the revolution of 1956, the third caesura, and resulted in the destruction of the Communist Party as an organised body. Communist power was restored under János Kádár, who has exercised it ever since, with considerable skill in the 1960s and 1970s.

COMMUNIST PARTY OF HUNGARY

In the ghetto, 1918–44

The Communist Party of Hungary (CPH), which has had a variety of names, was founded in November 1918. The exact date is unknown, but its founders came from two broadly defined groups. There were the former prisoners of war who had participated in the Russian revolution on the side of the Bolsheviks – the leader of the Party, Béla Kun, fell into this category – and there were radicals and left socialists who had spent the war years in Hungary. Although these two rather loose groupings had comparatively few adherents – the long-established Social Democratic Party was the dominant force on the Left – by January 1919 the CPH counted an estimated 10,000 members, and by March that year the Party was in such a powerful position that, together with the socialists, it was accepted as the only alternative to Count Mihály Károlyi's politically bankrupt government of liberals. Under Béla Kun, a brilliant orator, the CPH capitalised on the turmoil of the immediate aftermath of war (unemployment, large numbers of demobilised soldiers, poverty, food shortages) and on the resentment at the dismemberment of Hungarian national territory. These proved to be a weak foundation and the weakness was exacerbated by the left sectarian policies pursued by the rulers of the newly proclaimed Hungarian Soviet Republic. They alienated the peasantry, which had hoped for land reform instead of land expropriations; nationalisation of all enterprises employing over twenty people, confiscations of bank deposits, control of the professions, and the depredations of the new political police alienated the middle classes, who in any case withdrew their support from Kun once he had failed in his attempts to regain lost territory. After 133 days the Hungarian Soviet Republic collapsed, its leaders took refuge abroad or suffered at the hands of the White Terror, and the country was occupied by interventionist troops mostly from Romania. From that point on until 1944, the CPH was banned and was forced to operate at different levels of illegality.[4]

Support for the communists died away as rapidly as it had grown, and the new regime, led by Admiral Horthy, had little trouble in consolidating itself. By skilful use of the communist failure in 1919, it bolstered its own position, identifying the communists with the dismemberment of Hungary, with the Soviet Union (a disadvantage in a traditionally anti-Russian country) and with the Jews (many of the leaders of the CPH were Jewish), which enabled the regime to exploit anti-Semitism. In consequence, the Horthy system, deploying an efficient political police, had few problems in keeping the CPH in a political ghetto, something to which the Comintern made its own contribution by the sectarian policies it obliged foreign communists to adopt. Thus when, in the 1930s, the communists sought to forge links with other potential allies (the Social Democrats, the Radicals), they were not taken particularly seriously. Communist influence was effectively restricted to a few sections of the working class, notably in the construction industry, and to sections of the intelligentsia, which Party activists did little to encourage. The net result was that in 1944, when the Red Army entered Hungary, the CPH had perhaps 3000 members (a generous maximum) and perhaps an equal number of sympathisers. To that could be added the few hundred communists who had survived the purges in the Soviet Union.

The organisational history of the Party was also rather discouraging. After the shock of 1919, it took several years for the Party to recover and to recommence clandestine activity. It tried to do this at first by launching a front party (the Hungarian Socialist Workers' Party — confusingly, the name it has used since 1956), but this was soon banned by the authorities. The communists restricted their activities thereafter to infiltration of the trade unions and other institutions and to agitprop. Further confusion was created by the Comintern decision to dissolve the few extant organisations of the Party in 1936 (still a mysterious event); attempts were made, with scant success, to relaunch the Party during the war (police surveillance was effective) and in 1943, misinterpreting the dissolution of the Comintern, the CPH dissolved itself as well. It was not reconstituted until September 1944.[5]

The road to monopoly power, 1944–9

In December 1944 a provisional government was set up under the aegis of the Red Army in Debrecen. This was a four-party coalition under a figurehead Prime Minister, a former general, and it operated only on liberated territory. It was not transferred to Budapest until March 1945, and Hungary was fully liberated only on 4 April that year. The members of the coalition were the newly relegalised Communist Party, the Social Democrats, the Smallholders and the National Peasant Party. This four-party system was replicated in the *ad hoc* local committees established in the wake of the Red Army, and the communists, the dominant political force, were frequently obliged to take the initiative to revive other parties. The four-party system remained in being after the November 1945 elections, which the communists had expected to win, and enabled them to use the powers of the State for their own ends. Portfolios were distributed among all four parties, with the Ministry of Interior going to the communists; this proved to be the single most important factor in enabling it to advance on the road to monopoly. The complex story of how this was achieved, the 'salami tactics' (i.e. slicing off opponents one by one) boasted of by Rákosi, involved the destruction of the Smallholders by the summer of 1947, merger with the Social Democrats in 1948 and the creation of a single list in 1949. In this process, several factors played a role, notably the following: (1) the communists gained control of substantial parts of the administrative machinery from a very early stage; (2) they used *ad hoc* institutions – enterprise councils, kangaroo courts (*népitélet*) to further their aims; (3) by using the 'unity document' (*egységokmány*) signed in 1944, which locked the two working-class parties into close collaboration, they prevented the Social Democrats from re-establishing their wartime alliance with the Smallholders; (4) they gained support from sections of the peasantry through the land reform and the National Peasant Party, which was rapidly transformed into a communist branch organisation on the land; (5) they had control of the trade unions; (6) they made occasional but effective use of terror (arrests, internments) and the judicial machinery; and (7) there was the impact of the Red Army as an occupying force. The process of establishing monopoly power was completed with the proclamation of the 1949 constitution, which named the Communist Party as the sole political actor in Hungary. Its authority was specifically stated as having derived from the 'revolutionary struggle'.[6]

High Stalinism, 1949–53

This was a period of high mobilisation and the penetration of society at all levels by the State. All enterprises with ten employees or more were nationalised, and by 1950 81·8 per cent of all employees were working for the State. Income-bearing property – apartments for rent – were likewise nationalised, and agricultural collectivisation extended the power of the State over the land – for the first time in Hungarian history, so far as large proportion of the peasantry was concerned. The State assumed vast powers of coercion and used these against its real or presumed enemies. On the political scene, the most significant development was the extension of police and judicial action against members of the Party regarded as potentially unreliable. This involved the judicial murder of László Rajk, in the largest ritual show trial, and the imprisonment of hundreds of others. The middle classes were subjected to deportations to the countryside, often under the most brutal conditions. The working class was also caught up in the cycle of violence. Heavy penalties were imposed for negligence and damage to State property; direction of labour was made possible; and absenteeism was declared an offence. The system was underpinned by an efficient secret police and a network of informers. This machinery was deployed in a massive effort to create an industrial infrastructure, regardless of the cost, under the five-year plan, which stressed heavy manufacturing rather than light industry, for which Hungary was better suited. Mobilisation was maintained through the constant raising of work norms, and capital accumulation was increased by a massive squeeze on consumption. By 1952 the standard of living had fallen below the 1949 level. At the same time, accelerated industrial growth resulted in a steady rise in imports, as Hungarian productivity remained low and capacity was wastefully employed. By 1953 the Hungarian economy was in serious trouble. Hungarian society was also reacting with hostility to the pressures imposed on it. The widespread use of terror was demonstrated by the fact that between 1952 and 1955 the authorities investigated 1,136,434 individuals, the bulk of them peasants, but also a number of industrial workers. In other words, about 10 per cent of Hungarian society was in some way the subject of police action. However, the bases of communist power and of industrial development had been laid.[7]

Stalinism without Stalin, 1953–56

Following on the death of Stalin, the CPH leadership was summoned to

Moscow. Rákosi was sternly rebuked for his policies and was ordered to accept Imre Nagy as Prime Minister and to introduce the New Course, the essence of which was an easing of pressure. This meant greater concern for the consumer, a diminution of work norms, an end to forced collectivisation and the release of political prisoners. Hence, the New Course in effect offered an alternative set of policies, deriving from a different set of values, to the Party membership: either the development of heavy industry at all cost (Rákosi) or concern for human welfare despite a decline in output (Nagy). This division within the Party leadership was to have a major impact on the cohesiveness and morale of the rank and file. In particular, the communist intelligentsia was acutely caught up in the questioning of what had happened under Rákosi and transmitted these doubts to other sections of the Party. The divisions were intensified by the fact that Rákosi, who had retained control of the Party, sabotaged the New Course wherever he could and in February 1955 forced Nagy to resign. He then attempted to revert to his earlier policies, but by that stage he no longer had a united Party behind him and criticism of his leadership mounted, especially in respect of his role in the Rajk trial. In April 1956, Rákosi reluctantly acknowledged that Rajk had been innocent and in July he finally resigned. He was succeeded by Ernő Gerő, a rigid Stalinist of the same stamp as Rákosi, who obstinately sought to pursue a hard line. This not only failed but culminated in the revolution of October 1956, which in turn totally destroyed communist power in Hungary and forced the Soviet Union to reconstruct it by armed intervention.[8]

Reconstruction, 1956–62

János Kádár, who emerged as the new leader of the Hungarian communists, was no Stalinist, but in the initial phase of his rule he behaved like one, both because he had to destroy the opposition of Hungarian society to the reimposition of communist rule and because he had to rely on old Stalinists to achieve his objectives. Kádár first broke the power of the workers' councils which had arisen after the revolution, particularly in Budapest; then he intimidated the intelligentsia; and finally he re-established the control of the Party over the countryside. He used terror and coercion to reach these goals, albeit not on the same scale as Rákosi had done, and at least 200 people were executed between 1956 and 1958 (a conservative minimum).[9] Collectivisation was re-started in 1958 and concluded by 1960, although here the pressure of the Stalinists forced his hand.[10] At the same time, Kádár made it clear that his policies were to be a break with the past. He proclaimed a policy of 'alliance', namely that Party loyalty was no longer to be the sole criterion of appointment to a wide range of posts, a move which eventually reconciled most of the intelligentsia. He set about raising the standard of living, so that real wages rose by 32 per cent between 1952 and 1957 alone. This gained him the neutrality of the working class. The Party under Kádár was not to be the exclusive elite body that it had been and it was to act in unity with the people. Modernisation by means of developing an industrial base in tune with Hungary's capacity was to be pursued with a measure of consent.[11]

Reconciliation and stability, 1962–73

This decade was undoubtedly one of the most successful in Hungary's history. Under Kádár, society grew substantially more prosperous – for the first time in the country's history, a majority of the population moved above starvation level – and the beginnings of political development could also be discerned. In the wake of the New Economic Mechanism (1968), which abolished compulsory plan targets and transformed the planning mechanism into one where incentives operated, political reforms were launched. The role of Parliament was upgraded and it was encouraged to undertake some genuine scrutiny of legislation, at least in less contentious fields. Multiple candidacies were allowed in national and local elections, giving electors a sense of participation. The press was urged to reflect public opinion through debates and to play a kind of ombudsman role in uncovering abuses. Trade unions were armed with the right to veto decisions of the enterprise management and were entrusted with an element of real interest protection. The government began to act independently of the Party, especially in economic planning. Underlying these changes was the central concept that society was not monolithic, that social conflict was inevitable and even healthy and that the State should establish institutions to mediate between these conflicting interests.[12] In all this, however, the leading role of the Party, its political monopoly, was not undermined, only exercised with greater restraint. A significant proportion of the Party machine, especially at the middle level, merely acquiesced in the Kádár model, showing no great enthusiasm for it. These officials resented the autonomous role played by other institutions, and, probably with some backing from the Soviet Union, launched a counter-offensive in the early 1970s. In a sense, much of the Hungarian reform had been overtaken politically by the invasion of

Czechoslovakia, which had set out a much stricter definition of the leading role of the party than that employed in Hungary, so that the restrictions imposed from the November 1972 Central Committee plenum onwards should be seen as part of this campaign to assert tighter neo-Stalinist norms and to reduce from what had previously been permitted the degree of autonomous action from below.[13]

In uncertain waters, 1973–9

The world economic crisis, coinciding with internal political shifts, affected the Hungarian political constellation most gravely, for it undermined the strategy of the New Economic Mechanism, the modernisation of Hungary through foreign trade. The central authorities were constrained to play an ever-increasing role in the running of the economy, thereby impairing enterprise autonomy. The dogmatists in the Party – a mixture of old Stalinists and younger Soviet-trained cadres – succeeded in excluding the revisionist Marxist group of philosophers and sociologists around András Hegedüs from public life and thus, for the first time in more than a decade, struck a blow against the freedom of manoeuvre of the intelligentsia. This was followed by other restrictive moves. The dogmatists used the dissatisfaction of the industrial workers to curb the autonomy of agricultural collectives and even attempted to cut down on the right of the peasants to produce for the private market, but this last resulted in a dramatic fall in food supplies and was swiftly abandoned. The assault on the autonomy of the government was successful with the March 1974 plenum, at which a number of important figures associated with the reforms were dropped. This signified the re-establishment of full Party control over the ministries. Similarly, the trade unions, which never took their interest-protection role too seriously, fell into line; elections resumed their more overtly ritualistic character; and attempts at parliamentary scrutiny dwindled. But the counter-offensive was not wholly successful, so that elements of the reform were retained and some representatives of the dogmatic wing were excluded from office. Kádár's own position, although apparently never in any serious danger, appeared more secure in the late 1970s than in the middle of the decade. The principal uncertainty, however, was whether the prosperity of the 1960s and early 1970s could be sustained. The late 1970s also saw the emergence of a small opposition, drawing on Polish and Czechoslovak models, which sought first and foremost to break the official monopoly of information and to create a counter public opinion. It had issued a certain amount of *samizdat* by the end of 1978.[14]

THE HUNGARIAN SOCIALIST WORKERS' PARTY

Organisation

The Hungarian Socialist Workers' Party (HSWP – Magyar Szocialista Munkáspárt) is organised on the model of the CPSU. According to data released at the Eleventh Congress (March 1975), the Party had 24,450 primary organisations (*alapszervezet*), each with an average of thirty-two members; in practice urban organisations tend to have more members than rural ones. Next in the hierarchy are the 201 district organisations (*járási pártbizottság* in country areas and *városi* or *kerületi pártbizottság* in towns or Budapest). Above that are the county organisations (*megyei pártbizottság*), including the Budapest Party Committee, which send delegates to the Party Congress (843 in 1975) which meets every five years. The Congress elects the Central Committee (Központi bizottság), and the latter meets around four times a year, occasionally in an enlarged session (i.e. having invited non-members to be present). Day-to-day policy-making is in the hands of the Political Bureau (Politikai bizottság), in practice the highest and most important policy-making body in the country. The Political Bureau meets around twice a month and is assisted by a seven-man Secretariat, the real centre of power, which in turn is backed up by the Party machine. The Secretariat is organised into nine departments (Party and mass organisations; agitprop; science, education and culture; foreign and inter-party affairs; economic policy; regional economic development; Party finances; State administration; and the office of the Central Committee). The Political Bureau has three committees (agitprop, economic policy and youth). The Central Committee is also served by a number of collectives and by three institutes (the Party Academy, the Social Sciences Institute and the Party History Institute); it also publishes a newspaper and two journals. The *nomenklatura* of the HSWP is thought to encompass around 1000 posts.[15]

Membership

The membership of the Party has fluctuated widely since the war, as Table 14.1 shows.[16]

TABLE 14.1 Membership of the CPH/HSWP

Date	Membership
Nov 1944	2,000
Feb 1945	30,000
May 1945	150,000
Oct 1945	500,000
May 1948	884,000
May 1949	1,500,000
Feb 1951	862,114
Oct 1956	900,000
Dec 1956	37,818
Jan 1957	101,806
June 1957	345,733
Nov 1962	512,000
Dec 1966	585,000
Nov 1970	662,000
Dec 1974	754,000

Turnover in the 1970s was relatively low. Between the Tenth and Eleventh Congresses (1970–75), the Party lost 56,332 members through death, resignation, expulsion or non-payment of subscriptions; over the same period 148,288 members were recruited. By 1975, 67 per cent of the membership had joined since 1956 and around 7 per cent of the population was in the Party. The social composition of the Party is shown in Table 14.2.[17]

TABLE 14.2 Social composition of the HSWP, 1967

Social class	Percentage
Industrial workers	34·9
Peasants	7·8
Intellectuals	38·1
Pensioners	9·0
Armed forces	7·9
Students and others	2·3

The most striking aspect of this is the under-representation of the peasants. The percentage of those aged under twenty-six was 44·1. 55·4 per cent had had an education of eight or fewer years, and 33·8 per cent of twelve years, while 10·8 per cent had finished tertiary education. The proportion of manual workers in the Party increased steadily in the 1970s and reached 45·5 per cent by 1975 (or 59·2 per cent according to their original employment). The proportion of women remained rather low – 32 per cent. There were 8212 members who had joined the Party before the liberation (4 April 1945), the bulk of them in Budapest.[18]

GOVERNMENT

The constitution

Hungary's communist constitution was promulgated on 20 August 1949, an act of deliberate syncretism, for this was traditionally observed as St Stephen's Day. It declared Hungary a People's Democracy and established the Communist Party as the leading political power in the State. In many respects this constitution followed the Soviet model. It was extensively revised in 1972, producing in many ways a new constitution, in all but name. It was more explicit on the rights and duties of citizens, was somewhat less programmatic and asserted that Hungary was in a transitional phase on the road to socialism.

The legislature

The unicameral National Assembly (*Országgyűlés*) is elected every five years. There were 352 constituencies in 1975, so each deputy represented around 30,000 voters. Mutliple candidacies occurred in thirty-four constituencies (forty-nine in 1971). Of those elected in 1975, 137 deputies were new, representing a turnover of 38·9 per cent. One deputy had served in every postwar parliament. All candidates and deputies subscribed to the programme of the People's Patriotic Front and voting in Hungary has always been compulsory. Parliament usually meets four times a year, for two to three days at a time. The December session is usually devoted to consideration of the State budget. The other sessions (spring, summer, autumn) debate legislation and pass laws (*törvény*), usually without making significant changes to the submitted drafts. Ministers are questioned in the chamber by interpellations from the floor. But the most important work is carried out by standing committees (eleven in 1972), the work of which is sometimes reported in the press. In practice, a great deal of the current legislation is enacted by the Presidential Council, which has the power to issue decrees (*törvényerejű rendelet*) and these may never be subjected to parliamentary scrutiny.[19]

The Council of Ministers (Minisztertanács) is composed of twenty-four members, including the Prime Minister, five deputy prime ministers and nineteen ministers (who are flanked by a State secretary); in addition, the heads of nine government departments (for instance, the Central Statistical Office, the Office of Church Affairs and the National Bank) have the rank of State secretary.

Local government

Counties are subdivided into districts and at the level below that are towns, villages and small villages. The 1971 local-government reform established a clear chain of hierarchical command and improved the financial conditions of local councils. The 24,000 or so local councils are regarded as independent units of local self-government, with certain powers to levy taxes and with some right of consultation in regional development, communal services, education, housing, health and the like. There has been a steady trend towards the amalgamation of small villages into single larger units. Councils are elected on a basis similar to that of parliament, so that multiple candidacies are permitted.

Party–State relations

In line with other Soviet-type states, the Communist Party dominates policy-making in all institutions, both directly and indirectly. The Party maintains its own departments, which control and supervise ministries and similar institutions, and the *nomenklatura* system ensures that appointments to important posts take place only with the Party's approval. Indirect influence is exercised in a variety of diffuse ways – exhortation, pressure, informal contacts, occasionally intimidation. (See Table 14.3 for Party–State relations in terms of interlocking positions.)[20]

Mass organisations

All public institutions and organisations operate under the umbrella of the People's Patriotic Front (PPF – Hazafias Népfront). The PPF does not have individual members, but mass organisations belong to it as collective or corporate members. It has around 4000 local committees.

TABLE 14.3 Multiple holding of positions in Party, State and mass organisations in Hungary, 1978

Political Bureau	Party	State	Government	Mass organisations	Parliament
János Kádár	First Secretary of the Central Committee	Member of the Presidential Council			
György Aczél			Deputy Prime Minister		Member
Antal Apró					Speaker
Valéria Benke	Editor of *Társadalmi Szemle*				
Béla Biszku					Member
Jenő Fock					Member
Sándor Gáspár		Deputy Chairman of the Presidential Council		Secretary of the National Trade Union Council	Member
István Huszár			Deputy Prime Minister; Chairman of the National Planning Office		Member

Table 14.3 (*cont.*)

Political Bureau	Party	State	Government	Mass organisations	Parliament
György Lázár			Prime Minister		Member
Pál Losonczi		Chairman of the Presidential Council			Member
László Maróthy				First Secretary of the Youth Federation	
Dezső Nemes	Editor of *Népszabadság*				
Károly Németh	Secretary of the Central Committee	Member of the Presidential Council			Member
Miklós Óvári	Secretary of the Central Committee				
István Sarlós				Secretary of the PPF	Member

In addition to the trade unions, the youth and women's movement – the most significant of the mass organisations – the PPF includes the Hungarian Defence Alliance, the Hungarian Federation of Partisans, the Hungarian–Soviet Friendship Society, the unions of craftsmen and retailers, and organisations of the national minorities and of the churches. The PPF is officially described as having the character of a mass movement 'in which the cohesion of all classes and strata of society is manifested with the aim of building socialism'. In other words, it is a transmission belt. Its most important function is probably the organisation of elections, the nomination of official candidates and the arrangement of the count.[21]

The trade unions are probably the most influential mass organisation; the roots of unionism go back to the early years of the century and unions had some power in the interwar period. Since the 1960s, the unions have been formally entrusted with the two functions of defending the workers' interests and communicating Party policy to them. They have the right to veto enterprise management decisions when the union representative believes that this would violate the labour code, but this right has been used rather timidly in practice. In general, the unions are regarded by the workers as an organ of the State. Unions are active in about 7500 industrial and other units and cover virtually the whole of the active labour force, about 4 million people.[22]

The Communist Youth Federation (Kommunista Ifjúsági Szövetség) is rather less successful as a mass organisation. Its functions are hazy in that other mass organisations are also entrusted with the supervision of youth policies, and the Movement itself tends to work in a fairly rigid fashion, so that it attracts little genuine support. It had over 800,000 members in 1975 and has virtually 100 per cent membership among university students.

INTERNAL AFFAIRS

Education

The development of a comprehensive system of education has been somewhat slow in Hungary. Nursery places are available to about three-quarters of those entitled, testifying to considerable efforts in this area. Education is compulsory and free between the ages of six and sixteen. The first eight years are devoted to a general education, and specialisation takes place at the age of fourteen. Thereafter, education is provided at two-year general and vocational schools, whilst preparation for entry to university is at the four-year senior secondary schools, or gymnasia. Eight gymnasia were maintained by the churches. At Hungary's fifty-five universities and other institutions of tertiary education, a small fee is charged; around 5 per cent of the eighteen to twenty-five year old age group entered this level of education in the mid 1970s, and 36·6 per cent of these were the children of manual workers. Education is used as one of the principal instruments of socialisation, both through the curriculum and through extra-curricular activities. Support by the Youth Federation is essential for admission to university, and social origins remain a factor in gaining a place.

Religion

About three-fifths of Hungarians are nominally Roman Catholic, and, of the remainder, Calvinists and Lutherans are divided roughly in a proportion of three-to-one. Although organised religion has weakened since the war, partly by reason of official pressures on the churches and partly because of modernisation, in a survey carried out in the 1970s 48 per cent of the population admitted to having 'religious beliefs'. The Roman Catholic Church, which was locked in a corrosive conflict with the authorities as long as Cardinal Mindszenty was in asylum in the US Embassy in Budapest, has improved its relations with the State under László, Cardinal Lékai, Mindszenty's successor. There is a full bench of bishops and some movement has taken place on religious instruction and the training of priests. The Protestant churches have posed far less of a problem for the authorities and they have been largely transformed into transmission belts. That in turn has given rise to some neo-Protestant activism (Methodists, Baptists, Nazarenes, Jehovah's Witnesses), particularly on the fringes of Hungarian society.[23]

The economy

At the end of the war, Hungary was still a predominantly agrarian country, but it had developed important industrial concentrations, notably in the capital. Wartime industrial growth was a significant factor. War damage was largely made good by 1948, by when prewar levels of production were reached. Thereafter, in the twenty years that followed, industrial production increased at least fourfold, with an annual average growth rate of 6·3 per cent. However, this was markedly slower in the late 1970s than in earlier years. Agricultural output, on the other hand, improved in the 1960s with the stabilisation of agricultural policy. Hungary again became self-sufficient in grain in the late 1960s. In terms of the value of the dollar in 1960, per capita income in 1975 was calculated at $1160. Real incomes rose steadily in the 1960s and early 1970s, but showed a slower growth rate in the latter half of the decade. The economic policies of the early 1950s – concentration on heavy industry – were abandoned, but the distortions of that era continued to be felt, notably in serious lags in infrastructural investment.[24] Hungary's dependence on foreign trade has been very high, and, although it has generally achieved a positive balance in the rouble area, its indebtedness to the West increased in the mid-1970s to reach an estimated $2500 million. The overall strategy pursued by economic policy-makers was to develop a high-technology-based, tertiary processing industry in Hungary, but this policy was negatively affected by the worsening of the terms of trade in the 1970s – above all, the increased costs of energy.

EXTERNAL AFFAIRS

Hungary maintained diplomatic relations with 125 states in the mid 1970s and in general subordinated its foreign policy to that of the Soviet Union and to its own foreign trading interests. Hungary was a founder member of both the Warsaw Pact and Comecon and was bound to its allies by the customary network of bilateral treaties and agreements. Hungarian military units took part in the invasion of Czechoslovakia, and in other areas the Hungarian government has followed Soviet dictates. In the late 1970s Kádár began a series of visits to Western countries, as part of a forward foreign policy (his earlier trips to the West were to the UN in 1960 and to Finland in 1973); significantly, he chose to visit Austria, Italy and West Germany, the successors of Hungary's three wartime allies, first. In 1978 he also visited France. With the return of the Crown of St Stephen in 1978 by the United States, which had held it for safekeeping since 1945, the way was opened for a major improvement in relations between Washington and Budapest. Relations with the EEC were troubled from time to time by EEC restrictions on agrarian imports, which at times gravely prejudiced Hungary's trading position. Hungary also maintained cordial relations with Yugoslavia, despite ideological differences. Kádár paid regular visits to Tito, and the sizable Hungarian minority in Yugoslavia was declared to be a bridge between the two countries. On the other hand, relations with Romania, the country that harboured the largest Hungarian minority (over 2 million), were strained over the issue and the Hungarian government made repeated representations in an effort to improve the minority's position. Hungary maintained trading relations with China and Albania. It also took a relatively moderate line towards Euro-communism, and Kádár refused to condemn it as a form of anti-Sovietism, as some other East European leaders had done, but without accepting its applicability to Hungary. Relations with the Vatican improved in the 1960s and 1970s, and Kádár paid a visit to the Pope in 1977.

BIOGRAPHIES

János Kádár, the First Secretary of the HSWP, was born in Fiume (Rijeka) in 1912, the son of poor and unmarried parents. He was brought up in Somogy county and was apprenticed as a mechanic in Budapest. In the early 1930s he joined the clandestine CPH and subsequently infiltrated himself into the Social Democratic Party. In prison from 1937 to 1940, he returned to illegal work on his release and was elected to the Party's five-man Central Committee in 1942; it was at that point that he assumed the name Kádár. When László Rajk was arrested, Kádár became head of the Party, and it was he who ordered its dissolution in 1943. After the liberation, Kádár played an important role in the Party, albeit subordinate to Rákosi and other Muscovites, and it has been rumoured that he was instrumental in persuading Rajk to go through with the ritual of a show trial. Kádár was himself arrested in 1951, brutally tortured in prison and not released until 1954, when he returned to Party work. By 1956 he was back in the leadership and had apparently been chosen to succeed Gerő even before the revolution. During the revolution he first joined Imre Nagy and supported the aims of the revolution, but he deserted once he concluded that it would lead to the destruction of communist rule. After reconstructing the Party, he established complete and unchallenged control over it, even though he never purged his political opponents. His public image improved vastly once his alliance policy was implemented and his modest personal style won him genuine popularity. For all practical purposes, he runs a reverse personality cult and projects himself in a low-key fashion.[25]

Károly Németh was promoted to the inner sanctum of power in March 1974, when he was appointed Central Committee secretary in charge of economic policy. With the removal of Béla Biszku from the Secretariat in March 1978, Németh emerged as Kádár's first lieutenant and likeliest successor. He was born in 1922, the son of an agricultural labourer, in Zala county, and worked as a butcher until 1945, when he joined the CPH and was given a Party post. He served first locally in Zala, studied at the Party academy, was transferred to Csongrád county as first secretary and was appointed to the Central Committee in June 1956. In 1960 Németh moved up the hierarchical ladder to a position in the Central Committee administration, and in 1965 he was given the important post of first secretary of the Budapest party. He became a full member of the Political Bureau in 1970. Although Németh is disliked by Hungarian intellectuals, who regard him as a hard-liner, the evidence suggests that he is, in fact, more of an adaptable centrist, very much in the Kádár mould. He has shown himself loyal to Kádár and has proved reasonably efficient and flexible in the handling of economic policy, though without any of the political flair of his leader. In all, he is a somewhat grey figure, an apparatchik neither liberal nor conservative.[26]

György Lázár, the Prime Minister, took over this position in 1975 after the sudden resignation of Jenö Fock. Lázár was born in 1924 to a working-class family and attended a technical secondary school before the war. He joined the Party in 1945 and worked as a designer until 1948, when he was transferred to the National Planning Office. He served there until 1960, ending his career there as Deputy Chairman. He was Minister of Labour (1970–73) and then Deputy Prime Minister (1973–75); he has been fairly successful as head of government. He has great experience and specialist knowledge of planning and of the economy and he has a reputation for competence and flexibility.

BASIC FACTS ABOUT HUNGARY

Official name: Hungarian People's Republic (Magyar Népköztársaság).
Area: 93,350 sq. km. (35,900 sq. miles).
Population (1978): 10,671,000.
Population density: 114 per sq. km.
Population distribution (1977 est.): 52 per cent urban, 48 per cent rural.
Membership of the HSWP (Magyar Szocialista Munkáspárt) (1975): 754,353.
Administrative division: Budapest and 19 counties (*megye*).

Hungarian People's Republic 405

Ethnic nationalities other than Magyars (est.): Germans, 250,000; South Slavs, 200,000; Slovaks, 100,000; Romanians, 25,000.

Population of major towns (1978 est.): Budapest, (the capital) 2,090,000; Miskolc, 206,000; Debrecen, 196,000; Szeged, 176,000; Pécs, 169,000; Győr, 125,000; Székesfehérvár, 102,000.

National income by sector (1975 est.): industry, 47·0 per cent; construction, 12·9 per cent; agriculture and forestry, 16·3 per cent; transport, 6·1 per cent; trade, 15·0 per cent; others, 2·7 per cent.

Main natural resources: bauxite, oil, natural gas, coal.

Foreign trade (1977, in milliards of foreign-exchange forints) [US $1 = approx 20·30 forints]: exports, 238·6; imports, 267·3; total, 505·9.

Main trading partners (1977 share of trade): USSR (28·95 per cent), FRG (9·8 per cent), GDR (8·7 per cent), Czechoslovakia (6·35 per cent), Poland (4·65 per cent), Austria (4·15 per cent).

Distribution of foreign trade (1975): socialist countries, 68·9 per cent (USSR, 36·8 per cent); non-socialist countries, 31·2 per cent (developed countries, 23·2 per cent, developing countries, 8·0 per cent).

Rail network (1977): 8336 km.

Road network (1977): 29,895 km.

Universities (student numbers 1976–7): 56 institutions, with 110,528 students (Eötvös Lóránd University of Arts and Sciences, Budapest, 8713 students; Polytechnical University, Budapest [Műegyetem], 10,605 students; Karl Marx Economics University, Budapest, 4175 students; Semmelweis Medical University, Budapest, 3672 students).

Foreign relations (1975): diplomatic relations with 125 states; member of Comecon (since 1949), the WTO (since 1955) and the UN (since 1955).

Sources: *Statisztikai Évkönyv 1976; Statistical Pocketbook of Hungary 1978; A Magyar Szocialista Munkáspárt XI. kongresszusának jegyzőkönyve* (1975).

NOTES

1. C. A. Macartney, *The Habsburg Empire 1790–1918* (1969).
2. C. A. Macartney, *October Fifteenth*, 2 vols (1961).
3. G. Schöpflin, 'Hungary', in M. McCauley (ed.), *Communist Power in Europe 1944–1949* (1977).
4. R. Tőkés, *Béla Kun and the Hungarian Soviet Republic* (1967); T. Hajdu, *Az 1918-as magyarországi polgári demokratikus forradalom* (1968) and *A magyar tanácsköztársaság* (1969).

5. G. Ránki (ed.), *Magyarország Története 1918–1919, 1919–1945* (1976); T. Erényi and S. Rákosi, *Legyőzhetetlen Erő*, 2nd ed. (1974); and H. Vass (ed.), *Studies on the History of the Hungarian Working Class Movement 1867–1966* (1975).

6. S. Balogh, *Parlamenti és Pártharcok Magyarországon 1945–1947* (1975); and I. Vida, *A Független Kisgazdapárt Politikája 1944–1947* (1977).

7. P. Toma and I. Völgyes, *Politics in Hungary* (1977); and B. Lomax, *Budapest 1956* (1976). The figures are from J. Berecz, *Ellenforradalom tollal és fegyverrel 1956* (1969) p. 30.

8. See note 7; also T. Méray, *Nagy Imre élete és halála* (1978), and P. Kende and K. Pomian, *1956 Varsovie–Budapest: La Deuxième Révolution d'Octobre* (1978).

9. Lomax, *Budapest 1956*; I. Kovács (ed.), *Facts about Hungary* (1958); I. Szenes, *A kommunista párt újjászervezése magyarországon 1956–1957* (1976).

10. L. Orbán, *Két agrárforradalom Magyarországon: demokratikus és szocialista agrárátalakulás 1945–1961* (1972); Toma and Völgyes, *Politics in Hungary*, p. 17.

11. W. Robinson, *The Pattern of Reform in Hungary: A Political, Economic and Cultural Analysis* (1973) esp. pp. 232–4.

12. Ibid.; Toma and Völgyes, *Politics in Hungary*, p. 17.

13. M. Rakovski, *Towards an East European Marxism* (1978); G. Schöpflin, 'Opposition and Para-opposition in Hungary', in R. Tőkés (ed.), *Opposition in Eastern Europe* (1979).

14. G. Schöpflin, 'Hungary: An Uneasy Stability', in A. Brown and J. Gray (eds), *Political Culture and Political Change in Communist States* (1977); I. Kemény, 'Hol tart a társadalmi kompromisszum Magyarországon?', *Magyar Füzetek*, I (Paris, 1978).

15. Data from *A Magyar Szocialista Munkáspárt XI. konresszusának jegyzökönyve* (1975) (hereafter cited as *Jegyzökönyv*), and from Toma and Völgyes, *Politics in Hungary*, ch. 3.

16. Table compiled on the basis of information taken from ibid., p. 21, and from Schöpflin, in McCauley, *Communist Power*.

17. Taken from Toma and Völgyes, *Politics in Hungary*, p. 22.

18. *Jegyzökönyv*, p. 9.

19. Robinson, *Pattern of Reform*, pp. 215ff.; Toma and Völgyes, *Politics in Hungary*, p. 71.

20. Compiled on the basis of Radio Free Europe Research, *East European Leadership List*, 3 Aug 1978; and *Hungary 75* (1975).

21. Ibid., p. 24.

22. *Jegyzökönyv*, p. 17.

23. T. Beeson, *Discretion and Valour* (1974); M. Tomka, 'A vallási önbesorolás és a társadalmi rétegződés', *Szociológia*, no. 4, 1977.

24. I. T. Berend and G. Ránki, *Hungary: A Century of Economic Development* (1974).

25. W. Shawcross, *Crime and Compromise: János Kádár and the Politics of Hungary since Revolution* (1974).

26. Radio Free Europe Research, *Károly Németh: A Brief Profile*, 12 June 1975.

BIBLIOGRAPHY

Hungarian-language books were published in Budapest, unless otherwise indicated; London publication of English language books does not preclude prior, simultaneous or subsequent publication elsewhere.

Balogh, Sándor, *Parlamenti-és Pártharcok Magyarországon 1945–1947* (Budapest: Kossuth, 1975).
Beeson, Trevor, *Discretion and Valour* (London, 1974).
Berecz, János, *Ellenforradalom tollal és fegyverrel 1956* (Budapest: Kossuth, 1969).
Berend, Iván T., and Ránki, György, *Hungary: A Century of Economic Development* (Newton Abbot: David and Charles, 1974).
Erényi, Tibor and Rákosi, Sándor, *Legyőzhetetlen Erő*, 2nd ed. (Budapest: Kossuth, 1974).
Hajdu, Tibor, *Az 1918-as magyarországi polgári demokratikus forradalom* (Budapest: Kossuth, 1968).
—— *A magyar tanácsköztársaság* (Budapest: Kossuth, 1969).
Hanák, Tibor, *Die marxistische Philosophie und Soziologie in Ungarn* (Stuttgart: Ferdinand Enke, 1976).
Kemény, István, 'Hol tart a társadalmi kompromisszum Magyarországon?', *Magyar Füzetek*, 1 (Paris, 1978).
Kende, Pierre and Pomian, Krzysztof, *Varsovie–Budapest: La Deuxième Révolution d'Octobre* (Paris: Seuil/Esprit, 1978).
Kovács, Imre, *Facts about Hungary* (New York: Hungarian Committee, 1958).
Lomax, Bill, *Budapest 1956* (London: Allison and Busby, 1976).
Macartney, C. A., *The Habsburg Empire 1790–1918* (London: Weidenfeld & Nicolson, 1969).
——, *October Fifteenth*, 2 vols (Edinburgh: Edinburgh University Press, 1961).
A Magyar Szocialista Munkáspárt XI. kongresszusának jegyzökönyve (Budapest: Kossuth, 1975).
Méray, T. *Nagy Imre élete és halála* (Munich: Újváry 'Griff', 1978).
Molnár, Miklós, *A Short History of the Hungarian Communist Party* (Boulder, Colorado: Westview Press, 1978).
Nógrádi, Sándor, *Történelmi Lecke* (Budapest: Kossuth, 1970).
Orbán László, *Két agrárforradalom Magyarországon: demokratikus és szocialista agrárátalakulás 1945–1961* (Budapest: Akadémiai, 1972).
Radio Free Europe Research, *Károly Nemeth: A Brief Profile*, 12 June 1975.
Rakovski, Marc, *Towards an East European Marxism* (London: Allison and Busby 1978).
Ránki, György (editor-in-chief), *Magyarország Története 1918–1919, 1919–1945* (Budapest: Akadémiai, 1976).
Robinson, William F., *The Pattern of Reform in Hungary: A Political, Economic and Cultural Analysis* (New York and London: Praeger, 1973).
Schöpflin, G., 'Hungary', in Martin McCauley (ed.), *Communist Power in Europe 1944–1949* (London: Macmillan, 1977).
——, 'Hungary: An Uneasy Stability', in Archie Brown and Jack Gray (eds), *Political Culture and Political Change in Communist States* (London: Macmillan, 1977).

408   *Marxist Governments*

——, 'Opposition and Para-opposition in Hungary', in Rudolf Tőkés (ed.), *Opposition in Eastern Europe* (London: Macmillan, 1979).

Shawcross, William, *Crime and Compromise: János Kádár and the Politics of Hungary since Revolution* (London: Weidenfeld & Nicolson, 1974).

Sinor, Denis (ed.), *Modern Hungary: Readings from the 'New Hungarian Quarterly'* (London: Indiana University Press, 1977).

Szenes, Iván, *A kommunista párt újjászervezése Magyarországon 1956–1957* (Budapest: Kossuth, 1976).

Tőkés, Rudolf, *Béla Kun and the Hungarian Soviet Republic* (New York: Praeger – Pall Mall, 1967).

Toma, Peter and Völgyes, Iván, *Politics in Hungary* (San Francisco, Calif.: W. H. Freeman, 1977).

Tomka, Miklós, 'A vallási önbesorolás és a társadalmi rétegződés', *Szociológia*, no. 4, 1977.

Vass, Henrik (ed.), *Studies on the History of the Hungarian Working Class Movement 1867–1966* (Budapest: Akadémiai, 1975).

Vida, István, *A Független Kisgazdapárt Politikája 1944–1947* (Budapest: Akadémiai, 1977).

15 Democratic Kampuchea

LAURA J. SUMMERS

The socialist revolution in Kampuchea (formerly known as Cambodia) is one of the most significant in world history. It issued from a society which was not highly developed in economic terms and from a region where major imperialist powers have fought for decades to force local peoples to support the costs of their international economic and security strategies. It is because Kampuchea is a small and backward country composed mostly of peasants that its revolution must be viewed as an important lesson especially in other small states or backwater regions of the world.[1] Moreover, the victory of the Kampuchean revolutionaries took place in spite of opposition from and without much support from other socialist states. That the revolutionaries now radically reject, in favour of an independent socialism, association with any capitalist or socialist powers who would dominate them is proof of the impossibility of obtaining international socialist unity in the manner envisaged by Karl Marx. For societies lacking a substantial working class, the ideals and requirements of proletarian revolution and internationalism are at their best unobtainable; at their worst, they promote social imperialism or enduring inequalities within the socialist movement. The history of the Kampuchean revolution and the experiences of the Communist Party of Kampuchea bear witness to these realities and suggest an alternative Marxist strategy.

KAMPUCHEAN NATIONALISM AND COMMUNISM: THE INDOCHINA PHASE, 1863–1953

Because of its geographical isolation and unusual pre-colonial history, Kampuchea's revolutionary potential developed slowly. From the ninth to the fourteenth century, the ancient Angkor Empire of Kampuchea ruled most of mainland South-east Asia and its peoples, excluding the

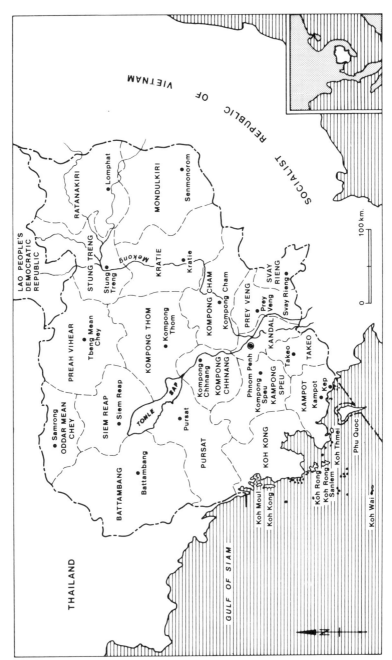

Kampuchea: provincial boundaries

Siamese and Vietnamese civilisations. In the fifteenth century, however, the Empire and its vigorous monarchy succumbed to internal difficulties and foreign conquest. The ruling aristocratic and religious strata had grown too large and too factious. This resulted in neglect of critical administrative tasks and led to the rejection of official religious cults by subject populations, including the dominant Khmer group. Thai and Vietnamese population migrations sealed the fate of the Empire, reducing Kampuchea's territorial domain to its current modest but ethnically homogenous heartland. By the nineteenth century, the Khmer monarch was obliged to pay tribute to both the Thai and Vietnamese courts.

At this moment French missionaries and merchant-explorers moved into the South China Sea in search of river routes to China and strategic positions from which to halt the advance of British imperialism from India and Malaya. Reigning Khmer monarchs of the period believed that French power could be used to prevent Thai or Vietnamese annexation. They encouraged France to extend its protection to the once wholly autonomous state, an act of traditional state nationalism with both ironic and tragic consequences. In asserting a desire for state autonomy, Khmer rulers willingly placed the country in the hands of a greater power, which of course had separate interests. Instead of protecting the existing state and its administration, the French proceeded to dismantle it and to integrate the country into their Indochina federation, which included Laos and Vietnam. This provoked a violent national uprising, but the French consolidated their power by force of arms, in the process gradually denying the Kampuchean monarch all but ceremonial responsibilities.[2]

Continual monarchal collaboration with French colonialism in Kampuchea blocked political initiative and development within the Khmer nation for the next eighty years. Neither the French nor the Khmer aristocracy promoted economic development of the country: the general prospects were brighter in Vietnam, while changes in traditional Khmer agriculture might have led to costly political instability. Limited French efforts to appropriate labour resources and to extract food surpluses from the rural population frequently provoked peasant opposition, but in general the salience of monarchy in Khmer political consciousness shielded the imperial power from normal political reprisals. If peasant traditions of resistance to immoral or unscrupulous kings posed a latent threat to the imperial alliance, peasant beliefs that most kings were just and protective, especially in times of crisis, gave France great political flexibility.[3]

New ideas about the state and the nation emerged in Kampuchea during the world depression of the 1930s and in response to the rise of modern nationalism in Vietnam. The impetus for the movement came from new urban or marginal social strata formed in the course of commercial and administrative expansion of the colonial protectorate. Nationalists such as Son Ngoc Thanh, one of the editors of the first Khmer language newspaper, *Nagaravatta* ('Capitol City'), recognised the necessity of reforming and defeating colonial power on its own legal and administrative terms. Tacitly rejecting restoration of absolute monarchy, the unrealistic dream of traditional state nationalists, *Nagaravatta* accepted the value of European-style administrative and democratic order and defended modern technology as a means of improving the quality of life in Khmer society. The Thanists followed the lead of Vietnamese nationalists in agitating publicly for reforms, especially for expanded public services and civil liberties. Unlike the Vietnamese, however, they had no political parties. Their ideas were spread by word of mouth, especially by sympathetic Buddhist monks, by the alumni of the country's only lycée and by *Nagaravatta*.

In contrast, the nationalist and communist movements in Vietnam had more than a dozen organisations and newspapers and serious efforts were being made to mobilise the mass of the peasantry. The Communist International in Moscow was so impressed with organisational activities in Vietnam that it (mistakenly) assumed the prospects for revolution in the whole of the French federation to be equally high. For this reason, Vietnamese Marxists who asked the Comintern to support the creation of a *Vietnamese* communist party in 1930, were told that they should have an *Indochinese* communist party. This amounted to ordering the Vietnamese comrades to organise communist movements in Laos and Kampuchea, where there was little indigenous Marxist activity.[4] The Vietnamese agreed to the wishes of the Comintern, but do not appear to have made great efforts to spread socialist ideas within the Lao and Khmer ethnic nations. There was only one communist cell in Kampuchea in the 1930s, its members most likely Vietnamese.[5] Some Khmer rubber-plantation workers joined the Vietnamese/Indochinese Communist Party cells in the 1940s,[6] but, on the whole, communist organisation does not appear to have spread from Kampuchea's rubber plantation region until the final years of the decade. At that moment, the myth of colonial protection and the possibilities of independence were widely recognised. Moreover, the role of the monarchy was being questioned.

The colonial *status quo* had been upset by the Japanese occupation in the Second World War. The decade opened with Japan supporting Thai annexation of two Kampuchean provinces and signing an accord with Vichy France. These acts brought into play a seemingly irreversible trend of events. France was immediately concerned to keep Indochina within its colonial sphere after the war and to use existing nationalist sentiment within the protectorates against Japan. This prompted an abrupt change in cultural policy in Kampuchea, where the incipient nationalist movement was, in the view of France, too ethnically centred. Efforts were made to romanise Khmer script and to promote European education. More Khmers received scholarships to French lycées and universities. Son Ngoc Thanh, the country's best known anti-colonialist, was exiled, while several of his associates, including militant Buddhist monks, were imprisoned. Meanwhile, Japan's need for wartime supplies and transport facilities disrupted rural life dramatically, as did cessation of normal trading relations with metropolitan Europe. All sections of the Khmer nation were alienated in the process, including the aristocracy. The loss of the two provinces and the fate of the peasants living under Thai occupation directly affected public perceptions of the power of the dynasty.

A Khmer Issarak (Khmer Independence) movement was founded in Bangkok in 1940; by 1947 it numbered about 5000 guerrillas. These forces were divided into royalist, republican and communist tendencies and included several independent bands whose leaders were more interested in liberating small territorial fiefdoms for themselves than they were in independence for the nation as a whole. Thus, unity in the movement was negatively determined in widespread resistance to foreign domination rather than in a positive strategy for securing independence or democracy.

The rise of the Issarak movement forced the Khmer aristocracy to renegotiate the constitution of the protectorate with the French. By allowing political parties to function freely in a parliamentary order, King Sihanouk hoped to accommodate both royalist and moderate nationalist demands. He would be seen to be loyal to the nation by negotiating these terms with the French and become the guarantor of further freedom. After Japan's defeat, it was also in France's interest to make political concessions in support of their aristocratic ally. The colonial power lacked the military resources required to fight both the Khmer Issarak and the Viet Minh. If the Issarak could be neutralised by political means, colonial military forces could be concentrated in Vietnam.

The Vietnamese revolutionaries were deeply concerned about the rapid reintroduction of French power in Kampuchea (and in Laos) in 1946. Anticipating a long struggle for independence, they sought to block French efforts to secure strong military positions on the length of Vietnam's western frontier, from which its north–south supply lines would be vulnerable. Once the war with France had begun, the Viet Minh contacted Issarak groups in Siem Reap province and in southern Vietnam.[7] Viet Minh influence within the movement in these areas was assured by Khmer-Vietnamese militants who were bilingual and by the conversion of *achars*, former Buddhist monks and lay leaders, to socialism. A Khmer People's Party and a provisional resistance government of Kampuchea headed by Son Ngoc Minh were set up in 1951.[8]

Vietnamese efforts to promote a nationalist-communist synthesis resembling their own met with limited success in Kampuchea. The most important contending forces proved to be the monarchy and traditional state nationalism. King Sihanouk successfully adjusted the colonial alliance in a way that allowed him to take directing control of the modern nationalist movement. Educated urban nationalists were quickly separated from the more radical peasant base of the Issarak movement and absorbed into a rapidly expanding state bureaucracy. Peasants who perceived their monarch actively defending them against the French also rallied to his support. In the remaining more radicalised sections of the peasantry and the Buddhist hierarchy, Vietnamese efforts to promote socialism and to organise the independence struggle were, in the monarchal renaissance of the day, too visible and counterproductive. Meetings with the anti-French, anti-royalist partisans of Son Ngoc Thanh, for example, resulted in acrimony. At a time when success in the Khmer nationalist movement depended upon being seen to resist foreign subjection in all its forms, the Vietnamese antagonised potential allies by insisting upon using the Vietnamese language at international meetings and by subordinating Khmer aspirations to the requirements of their military strategy. The Thanists refused collaboration with the Viet Minh, while those Khmer socialists who did accept Vietnamese tutelage and support were quickly isolated from the mainstream of the Khmer independence struggle. They received the label 'Khmer–Viet Minh', an epithet begging the question of national loyalty.

THE GENEVA COMPROMISE, 1954–9

A settlement of the first Indochina war for independence from France was negotiated at Geneva in 1954. At the conference, the Viet Minh proposed that the resistance government of Son Ngoc Minh be allowed to participate in the armistice and in the political talks. The Vietnamese felt that a lasting political settlement had to involve all the political and military belligerents in the region, as distinct from those parties in dispute in the three French territories in Vietnam. The major powers at the conference, jointly chaired by the United Kingdom and the USSR, did not agree.[9]

The capitalist powers at Geneva wanted to limit the number of revolutionary governments in Indochina and to secure a political settlement which contained communism in Vietnam. The royal governments of Laos and Kampuchea, both of which had seats at the meeting, opposed recognition of their rival delegations, as did the French, British and American delegations. As the talks progressed, it soon became apparent that the Vietnamese, Soviets and Chinese desired a ceasefire urgently and that the minimum interest of the Vietnamese in the settlements in Laos and Kampuchea was one of national security.[10] A compromise was struck. The Vietnamese agreed to drop their proposal for the recognition and seating of Son Ngoc Minh's government, in exchange for informal assurances that foreign military bases would not be established in Kampuchea. There were also assurances of 'protection' for partisans of two unseated resistance governments. They were to be reintegrated into their own national communities without reprisals. On these terms, Vietnam agreed to withdraw its 'volunteer' forces from the two countries. As arrangements for withdrawal were drawn up, the Vietnamese discreetly admitted the presence of regular army units inside Kampuchea, owing to the need to evacuate them *en masse*.[11] Their integrity and goodwill in the matter were not reciprocated. In the final hectic hours of the conference, the royal government of Kampuchea managed to revise the restrictions on the introduction of foreign military power into the country in a way allowing it nearly exclusive discretion in the matter.[12]

The views of the Kampuchean socialist delegation present at the talks were not recorded by historians of the meetings, who tended to concentrate on the strategies of the winners rather than the aspirations of the losers. Years later, a member of Son Ngoc Minh's delegation reported that they accepted the compromise negotiated at Geneva because of their socialist obligation to safeguard the world revolution – in other words, out of faith in proletarian internationalism and the foreign policies of the major socialist powers. Moreover, the Kampuchean socialists opposed the partitioning of their country into regroupment zones. In the radical nationalist context of the time, partition represented institutional escalation of their isolation from the national state, and this would only have been exploited by King Sihanouk.[13] In rejecting partition, the Kampuchean socialists acknowledged their nationalism and awareness of their vulnerability to traditional nationalist assault.

They believed, moreover, that Geneva Conference supervision of the postwar armistice and political arrangements would provide them a measure of protection and that Hanoi would continue to give them support for their national political struggle. Hanoi was in their view obliged to aid them, under the principle of proletarian internationalism, and because of the sacrifice they had made in laying down their resistance government.[14] At the time, Son Ngoc Minh urged his resistance fighters to comply with the Geneva armistice.[15] But, within a year of the compromise, the expectations of the Kampuchean socialists were replaced by a sense of betrayal.

The Geneva agreements for Kampuchea called for a ceasefire and national elections as soon as the French and Vietnamese troop withdrawals had been completed. King Sihanouk immediately grabbed the initiative by ordering the arrest and prosecution of Issarak veterans for 'civil' crimes committed during the war. Other resistance fighters were simply executed. The International Commission for Supervision and Control of the Geneva settlement received many complaints from Kampucheans about official harassment. These were only forwarded to the royal government with requests for information and clarification, as the Commission was internally divided about a more positive response to the situation.[16] Sihanouk, moreover, sought to amend the country's constitution so as to restrict the franchise in the elections, but failing that he abruptly postponed them, abdicated the throne in favour of his father; took the title of Prince and announced the formation of the Sangkum Reastr Niyum (Subjects' Socialist Community, usually designated 'Sangkum'). The Sangkum was said to be a political association for the whole of the nation, not a political party, a concept denoting something less than total national unity. Nearly all existing political parties and groupings immediately rallied to the Sangkum, leaving the socialists and the Thanists (the Democrat Party) to make their separate preparations for the elections in conspicuous isolation from the monarchal *rassemblement*.

The Pracheachon (People's Group) was founded in 1955. It was based on, but should not be confused with, the wartime People's Party, then underground. The Pracheachon described itself as a veteran's association organised for the purpose of taking advantage of Geneva

Conference guarantees of the rights of the resistance to participate in national political life. It nominated a large slate of candidates for the Assembly elections. Initially these were supported in radio broadcasts from Hanoi. As the campaign progressed, however, Radio Hanoi switched its support from the Pracheachon to Prince Sihanouk's Sangkum slate. The shift coincides with a change in North Vietnamese foreign policy following the Bandung Conference and the decision of international socialist powers to support neutralist regimes such as Prince Sihanouk's in the cold war against imperialism. It was also a response to the Prince's complaints to the Geneva Commission about foreign 'interference' in the elections.

Sihanouk's rout of his democratic opposition was confirmed by the elections. When the votes were in, Pracheachon candidates won only 3 per cent (31,000) of the votes cast, while the Democrats, the major party before independence, received only 14 per cent. Prince Sihanouk was the undisputed 'father' of independence. He had succeeded in arresting, executing and exiling his most vocal opponents and had conquered their followers and political organs at the polls. The socialists, in particular, needed to reassess their national strategy as well as relations with international socialist powers who supported the oppressive Sihanouk regime. The need was indeed urgent. The People's Party was losing 90 per cent of its wartime cadres as a result of assassinations and flights abroad.[17]

THE NATIONAL DEMOCRATIC REVOLUTION, 1960–75

The Party decided that counter-revolutionary violence had to be met with revolutionary violence. As its leadership ranks were depleted, a committee to consider the possibility of organising an independent and fully constituted Marxist-Leninist party was set up, in 1957. It included many Marxists who grew up in the radical nationalist days of the 1940s and became socialists in French universities in the 1950s. It was easy for this generation to spot the problems of the earlier socialist resistance and to appreciate the consequences of the Geneva settlement. On the one hand, it had very limited contact with the Vietnamese revolution: it did not share the sense of comradeship which resulted from fighting with the Viet Minh during the war or from tutelage in socialist ideas. On the other hand, and similarly, the strategy of Prince Sihanouk as seen from France was transparently neo-colonial. Successful liberation of the Khmer nation from foreign imperialism thus required alerting the mass of the population to the real meaning of events, thereby deepening the contradiction between the nationalist pose adopted by Sihanouk and his real neo-colonial collaboration. This required revising and modernising peasant nationalism so as to foster a revolt against the new devices of colonialism and imperialism which would have more unity of purpose than the Issarak movement. The lessons of the past thus required an organisation committed to the principles of independence, self-determination and initiative, as well as self-reliance. The result of the intra-Party debate and this analysis was the founding of the Communist Party of Kampuchea (CPK) in 1960.[18]

Party strategy in the 1960s trod a narrow line between its self-determined national and international responsibilities. The two tasks of the national democratic revolution were to struggle against imperialism (which required assisting the Vietnamese revolution when possible) and to struggle against the feudal, landholding regime in Kampuchea, for which no active external support could be expected. For this reason and for its own security, the existence of the Party was to remain a secret.[19]

Three major forms of struggle were adopted by the founding Congress. The first form involved the use of revolutionary violence to protect cadres and supporters in the countryside from the most excessive abuses of the 'enemy'. For this purpose, a clandestine guard or mobile guerrilla force was established in 1961. These forces were the base of the liberation armed forces when the Party entered the civil-war phase of national armed struggle in 1968.[20]

The second and third forms of struggle were open and legal political struggle and clandestine, illegal political struggle. Efforts were concentrated equally in the towns and in the countryside and took the form of work inside the Sangkum government and administration as well as the country's schools, Buddhist hierarchies and factories. The struggle by the workers was thought to be the most difficult, since they were few in number, easily isolated and oppressed by the small capitalist class. Peasants, constituting 85 per cent of the population, were more numerous. This made their struggle more critical and the key to the success of the revolution.[21]

In the city, pro-CPK newspapers openly promoted criticism of American aggression in Vietnam and along the Vietnamese-Kampuchean border. In 1964 and 1965 the CPK also organised demonstrations opposing relations with the United States. In these activities the Party supported the anti-imperialist struggle of the Vietnamese and Prince Sihanouk's traditional anti-capitalism. Such public and legal activities were supplemented by illegal leaflet operations at night. The leaflets contained explicit charges, such as could not be published legally, of corruption, oppression and exploitation on the part of the Sangkum regime. The leaflets urged the public to overthrow the government.[22]

The struggle in the countryside emphasised land reform and active resistance to the feudal landholding regime. The Party analysis of the agrarian problem focused on two different aspects of rural poverty. In some areas of the country, land was scarce and accumulated in large holdings. In others, land was abundant but peasants lacked the capital and the technology to bring it into cultivation. The exploitation of peasant labour through rents and poor prices combined with the suppression of peasant initiative were two distinct features of mass subjection in the Kampuchean countryside. The effects of these forms of oppression were compounded by integration of the agrarian economy into the international market, which kept the national economy in a permanently underdeveloped state. The world market extracted food-stuffs and raw materials in exchange for foreign manufactures, mostly consumer goods desired by the small, wealthy, feudal landowning stratum. As peasants began to understand the different forms and levels of exploitation, they were organised to fight against international imperialism as well as its affiliate, the dependent feudal stratum in Kampuchea.[23]

The rural situation proved more 'volatile' than the Party had anticipated. In 1967, in an area of significant land hunger, peasants revolted against the Royal Army and a Royal Socialist Youth camp in protest against official land-grabbing and rice requisitions. Poor rice harvests in two consecutive years had left several thousand villagers in a close to perilous situation. Approximately 4000 of them are thought to have joined the revolution during the revolt and the repression following it.[24] Official communist histories cite the Samlaut affair as the impetus for the decision to launch a national uprising against the Sihanouk regime in January 1968.[25]

Prince Sihanouk was fearful of the progress made by the revolution and began to denounce 'Vietnamese' intervention in Kampuchea in yet another effort to discredit his opposition as foreign to the nation. At the same time, he moved towards a rapprochement with the United States. At the beginning of 1968, the Americans secured his compliance in military 'hot pursuit' across the Kampuchean–Vietnamese frontier.[26] In 1969, it is thought, Sihanouk agreed to secret B-52 bombing raids on (genuine) Vietnamese base camps inside Kampuchean territory, and at the same time formal diplomatic relations with the United States were resumed. If such moves partly compensated for the domestic political and military decline of the Sihanouk regime, they did nothing to repair its economy. Years of excessive public spending and corruption, neglect of agricultural development and chaos in rural marketing, owing to black-market trade with Vietnam and CPK revolutionary activity, left much of the countryside impoverished; the State was close to bankruptcy. Before the revolution could defeat the regime, however, General Lon Nol and the Royal Army intervened. Prince Sihanouk was deposed in a parliamentary-military coup in 1970. He was left with two clear political options, early retirement or joining the revolution.

The revolutionary war that followed was structured by the invasions of the United States armed forces and Vietnamese liberation forces, a South Vietnamese military occupation of eastern Kampuchea in 1970–1 and saturation bombing on an unprecedented scale by the United States Air Force in 1973. Indeed, the war was extended beyond national political reason, owing to the position of the country in American foreign policy thinking.[27] More than a third of the whole population were made homeless refugees. Most young men and many women fought in Lon Nol's army or the Kampuchean liberation armed forces, nominally led by Prince Sihanouk but increasingly controlled by the CPK. The social and economic devastation confronting the Party when the war finally ended, in April 1975, was nearly total. Its response to the post-war crisis was necessarily radical, but this was not generally appreciated by global public opinion. The Western European media, for example, dwelt on the radical policies of the CPK, giving the impression that most postwar hardships were the result of these policies rather than legacies from the war. The situation will be examined in more detail after a brief look at this controversial party.

THE COMMUNIST PARTY OF KAMPUCHEA

Little is known about the Communist Party of Kampuchea. Documents alleged to be official CPK policy statements, interviews with captured prisoners of war and statements by two double defectors comprise the bulk of available evidence. The two most important studies of the Party were prepared by officials of the United States government, who relied upon translations and interpretations which sometimes contradict known Party views.[28] The following sketch of CPK organisation is an interpretation of the available evidence and the American studies which takes into account information gleaned from official publications of the revolutionary government.

With one exception, Party organisation parallels current administrative divisions within the country. The smallest organ is, of course, the cell, which has a minimum membership of three. Cells function in hamlets (*phum*), townships (*khum*) and in military units. Cells form branches of the Party in each co-operative and in some Army companies. The civilian Party branches nominate representatives to district (*srok*) committees. Beyond the district level, there appear to be some Party committees functioning at the sector (*dambang*) level and some municipal Party committees. The absence of civilian administration from the sector level suggests that those committees represent military branches only or that they are products of earlier, wartime organisation. District, municipal and sector committees appear to merge in the seven regional committees of the Party, which are simply identified by their compass bearing (for instance, the North-eastern Region). The regions amalgamate and replace the royal provinces of pre-revolutionary days, even though provincial boundaries still appear on current maps. (See map accompanying this chapter.) The Party Central Committee is elected by the regional committees.

Elections at all levels are based on the Kampuchean interpretation of democratic centralism. This combines discussion of possible candidates with an informal determination of who has support. Only when agreement is reached on a potential nominee is his name formally put forward for election.

Requirements for Party membership have changed two or three times since 1960. Candidates are supposed to have a 'revolutionary attitude', to have a sound personal background and to be from the 'poor and lower-middle peasant' classes. Since the liberation war, the minimum age has been lowered from eighteen to sixteen years, in accordance with a Party policy to expand membership.[29] During the war, when the Party was concerned about the security of its struggle within the National United Front, candidates had to be supported by two sponsors who were already Party members and be approved by the full branch and full district committees.[30] This careful vetting combined with postwar efforts to expand membership suggest that full Party membership may be small. No membership figures are available.

The Party Congress meets irregularly and appears to ratify important policy decisions drafted by the Central Committee. The four Party congresses held so far met in September 1960 (the founding congress), February 1963, September 1971 and January 1976, each date signalling a crisis or an important transition in Party policy. The number of people attending these meetings has not been made public.

The Party Central Committee is thought to be led by approximately one dozen people but may have as many as ninety-one members.[31] The small number and social cohesiveness of prominent Party personalities (who include several husband-wife teams and other family groupings), the absence of any known political bureau and the Party's emphasis on collective leadership at all levels probably means that the 'Standing' or 'Permanent' Committee of the Central Committee functions as a corporate policy-making and leadership core with few if any permanent specialist Party departments.[32]

THE GOVERNMENT

The royal constitution was formally replaced by a revolutionary constitution in January 1976.[33] The State is described as 'independent, united, peaceful, neutral, non-aligned, sovereign and democratic'. No reference is made to monarchy or to Marxism-Leninism, since the Constitution was promulgated before the Party emerged from secrecy. Nevertheless, all major means of production are nationalised and the State is said to belong to the 'workers, peasants and other labourers' of Kampuchea.[34] The 'other labourers' include intellectual and military workers as well as those who labour in the salt pans and fishing zones.

Legislative power is vested in a 'People's Representative Assembly' elected every five years and comprising 150 peasant representatives, fifty representatives of workers and other labourers, and fifty representatives of the revolutionary armed forces. The special role of the Army in the Assembly reflects its prominence in the worker-peasant alliance during the liberation war. The first national election was held in March 1976. Candidates competed in constituencies for nomination but only a single list of nominees appeared on the ballot. After the election, the Assembly met briefly to select the Cabinet, the members of the State Presidium and its own Standing Committee.

The Cabinet formed in April 1976 had nine portfolios, most of which were received by high-ranking members of the CPK and their spouses. The Party Secretary, Pol Pot, became Prime Minister, while the Deputy Secretary of the Party, Nuon Chea, was elected Chairman of the Assembly's Standing Committee. This body has ten members in all. According to the Constitutin, the Cabinet is the executive organ of the

Assembly and determines national policy guidelines. In the last two years, the Assembly appears not to have met, leaving much responsibility and policy initiative in the hands of its Standing Committee and the Cabinet, both dominated by the CPK. The CPK is also predominant in the Assembly as a whole, as 150 Party members hold seats.[35] No other political parties exist.

The State Presidium is composed of a President and two vice-presidents. Khieu Samphan became President amidst speculation that Prince Sihanouk might have been chosen for the post. The international association of the Prince with the liberation struggle has limited local resonance, however. Moreover, the CPK opposes even partial or ceremonial restoration of monarchal power, which was a vital element in the feudal landowning regime destroyed by the war. Restoration would undercut the Party's efforts to replace any lingering elements of the 'subject' mentality of the population with more modern democratic feelings of individual competence and 'mastery'. The selection of Samphan, a widely admired personality with many traditional, ascetic leadership qualities, shows that the Party is none the less concerned to have a head of State with whom the public can readily identify. Samphan is also among the top-ranking members of the Party Central Committee.

The pattern of Party-State relations emerging from the constitutional design of government and Party staffing of key posts suggests that Democratic Kampuchea is directly governed by the Standing Committee of the CPK Central Committee. It is probably significant that the Central Committee administered the North-east 'special region' during the liberation war. Other regions were administered by specially elected regional committees, which included non-Party members of the National United Front. The prominence of the armed forces in government no doubt reflects Party concern to integrate all productive forces into its collectivist socialist order and especially those militarily wrenched from their traditional way of life during the fighting.

DOMESTIC AFFAIRS

Security and public-health problems have dominated the domestic policy efforts of the CPK since its April 1975 victory over the Americans and the Lon Nol regime. The Americans left the city's population in an undernourished and disease-ridden condition, while the defeated military regime sabotaged public installations and left behind sniper and rear military bases.[36] The revolutionary development model called for full use of available national resources, including unemployed labour, and as much self-sufficiency in production as available national resources would allow. The goal of the national democratic struggle was to break out of the constraints imposed by dependence upon international markets and political forces for the purpose of creating a balanced national economy, an economy producing more basic necessities of life than the old economy, which was hampered by a large import bill and accumulating balance-of-payments deficits.[37] The conjunction of factors – the unavailability of food in the city, the need to control the spread of disease, the fact that victory was achieved at rice-planting time, knowledge of the counter-revolutionary plan to sow panic in occupied urban areas, fears that the Americans would continue bombing, and the impossibility (aside from the undesirability) of reliance upon foreign assistance to feed the population – all underlay the decision to evacuate Phnom Penh and other towns temporarily swollen in size by refugee inflows during the war. The hardship imposed by the evacuation was real but a larger human catastrophe was no doubt avoided.

The refugees and approximately 500,000 genuine urban dwellers were resettled on co-operatives in the pre-victory liberated zone or organised into production teams responsible for repairing or building roads, irrigation ditches, bridges, houses and the railway.[38] By 1978 the co-operative programme was five years old; most people were permanently settled in groups of 700 to 1000 family units, communities of 5000–6000 people. Mobile work units are now described as 'youth' brigades, suggesting that they are made up of young people from nearby co-operatives on an intermittent basis. The 'newcomer' classification identifying refugees and urban dwellers brought into the system in 1975 was suppressed by the CPK in the autumn of 1978. These developments suggest that the period of postwar crisis is over.

Indeed, visitors to the co-operatives have been impressed by the health of the population, the absence of tension or obvious surveillance and efforts by the government and co-operative authorities to construct houses for all families.[39] Everyone in the community is obliged to work an eight- or nine-hour day. Work appears to be done efficiently and cheerfully, but at a slower pace than would be expected in Europe. Most labour is done by hand or with draught animals. Production quotas are set up by the relevant national departments after consultation with co-operative authorities. This is also the procedure in the major industries where trade unions are functioning. A special national committee supervises the progress of the rubber industry, the country's most advanced.

'Wages' of all workers and labourers are paid in kind in the form of food and other rationed commodities, as no currency of exchange exists. In spite of the fact that basic food consumption is closely monitored through mandatory use of central dining halls, the distribution of supplies of clothing and other supplies seems to be arranged locally without great difficulty. Moreover, people are allowed to grow fruit, tobacco, herbs and vegetables on small plots around their houses. Available evidence suggests that the poorest 40 per cent of the peasantry now has more food and social security than it did in the 1960s. This indicates that local self-reliance will soon have to yield to more concerted efforts to diversify and modernise production and exchange between and among co-operatives, to ensure both equity and constantly improving standards of living. The CPK is aiming for agricultural modernisation in the next fifteen to twenty years, but, in the short term, progress is hampered by an acute shortage of transport equipment, poor roads and limited administrative and popular resources at the regional and district levels. So far, intermediary administrative and work efforts have been concentrated in construction and operation of large- and medium-scale irrigation installations, which underwrite co-operative progress in agriculture.

The future of socialist development in Kampuchea thus depends on the way in which the Party and locally elected co-operative committees reconcile the national need to accumulate resources for agricultural and light industrial innovations with continuing local need for improved public services. Children, for example, now have only two hours of classroom instruction in language and arithmetic each day. Otherwise they receive 'on the job' apprentice-style instruction or are assigned menial tasks in cottage industries and agriculture. Thus, children pay for their education by creating some value in the process. The spectre of child labour raised by a Yugoslavian film misses this important point, but the mistaken interpretation illustrates well the gulf between the radical collectivist and egalitarian practice in Kampuchea and socialist practice in advanced industrial societies, where role specialisation and a concern for efficiency have led to a bureaucratic perspective on the socialisation of labour and the production process. The Kampuchean government anticipates expanding the school system and broadening the available range of technical training courses in the future, but it will undoubtedly retain its current emphasis on changing wasteful pre-revolutionary social practice and values even while new skills are imparted.

The Party's mass or auxiliary organisations assist in the effort to revise existing public attitudes. The oldest, most frequently mentioned ones are the Workers' Union, founded in November 1955; the Youth Organisation, founded in February 1961; and the Women's Organisation, founded in July 1961.[40] The extent of their contribution is difficult to evaluate at the present time, partly because the Party to which these organisations are supposed to relate has only recently come into public view.[41] During the Party's formative years of secrecy and wartime resistance, the mass organisations served as a proving arena for potential cadres and as a base for military recruitment.[42] They also played an instrumental part, along with the armed forces, in handling the transfer and resettlement of half of the country's population in 1975 and 1976. The nature of and the impetus for future activities as well as the locus of control within the mass organisations will be critical measures of the popular and administrative development of the revolution.

FOREIGN AFFAIRS

The CPK's stance of independence from foreign powers in pursuit of the revolution was vindicated during the war. In the light of the impossibility of preserving a neutral, Sihanoukist regime, the coup deposing Sihanouk forced China and Vietnam to support the Party's armed struggle, while the USSR openly supported the US client regime in opposition to what it envisaged as China's regional foreign policy.[43] The National United Front of Kampuchea, created under joint Chinese and Vietnamese sponsorship in 1970, and the Indochinese People's Conference, which later in the same year declared the unity of the struggles in Laos, Vietnam and Kampuchea, provided the framework within which Kampucheans could be mobilised on a large scale for their liberation struggle and within which Vietnamese armed forces would support their struggle. Prince Sihanouk's leadership of the Front was deemed vital by the Chinese and Vietnamese for international reasons, but national response to his radio broadcasts was mixed. The initial peasant response was both limited and qualified.[44] The CPK recognised the tactical objectives of the neutralist, socialist Front from above and from abroad and decided to incorporate it into its own struggle from below.[45] In this manner, the terms of co-operation binding the allied parties to the Front were as limited as their objectives were diverse.

The alliance was forcibly divided into its national and international components in 1973, when Vietnam and China signed the Paris agreements with the Americans. The Americans pressed the Vietnamese to bring about a ceasefire in Kampuchea as their forces were withdrawn from the country. A momentary ceasefire may have occurred. Prince Sihanouk announced his readiness to negotiate with the Americans only to be ignored by Henry Kissinger, America's negotiator. While holding the Vietnamese accountable for the settlement which did not occur and which the US obstructed, the USAF began several months of saturation bombings in Kampuchea, using B-52s freed from service in Vietnam as a result of the Paris pledges to remove foreign forces from that country. In the meantime, Vietnam withdrew its forces from Kampuchea under the terms of the Paris agreement, taking their equipment with them and leaving the Kampucheans to fight alone or to capitulate to American pressure to negotiate directly with the Lon Nol regime for a coalition government.[46]

However discreet the Vietnamese may have been, their actions only invoked memories of their earlier sacrifice of the Kampuchean revolution to national self-interest at Geneva. The violent American support of the Lon Nol regime also confirmed the total dependence of the feudal landowners on American imperialism. the CPK's analysis of the dangers attaching to alliance with other socialist revolutions and to the dependence of the nation or any of its classes on foreign economic or military support gained renewed historical cogency. Winning the war against the American client regime, with which it refused to negotiate, subsequently vindicated CPK reliance upon national forces and national resources. The Party then applied its experience in the international arena to its postwar foreign policy.

Kampuchea is among the most militantly non-aligned of Third World states and the most independent of socialist ones. It maintains only pro-forma diplomatic contacts with most of the eighty-eight states with which it has relations. The exceptions to the rule confirm it.

Warm diplomatic support of the struggle of Fretilin in East Timor and token food aid to Laos show that the government is concerned to support forgotten peoples obliged to struggle in history even harder than the Kampucheans. Close relations with China rest upon Chinese Communist Party support of the CPK's break with Comintern communism in the 1960s, but these do not extend to support of China's international strategy, especially in Africa and South America.[47] There are no diplomatic relations between Kampuchea and the USSR. Kampuchea's suspension of diplomatic relations with Vietnam issues from the lack of any strategic rapport with the Vietnamese revolution and the Vietnamese Communist Party, aggravated by Vietnamese insistence on closer co-operation between the two countries (possibly on the model of Lao–Vietnamese relations) and by Vietnamese insistence on the renogotiation of the terrestrial and offshore boundary shared by the two states. Both Vietnamese demands are unreasonable in the Kampuchean view. The autonomy of its economy is believed to be a condition of its historical progress, while absolute sovereignty and independence within the existing frontiers is a measure of Kampuchean freedom from social and political domination by more advanced social and political forces. The confrontation will be long and costly for both revolutions.

The theory and practice of the Kampuchean revolution posits that historical progress of the socialist revolution depends upon an objective appraisal of the conditions of production and liberation within under-developed and unevenly developed societies rather than idealistic commitment to an international strategy for revolution. This strategy is determined by major socialist powers who are themselves divided in history at different stages of economic progress and by different sets of class contradictions. Some peoples are perhaps too poor to wait for capitalist development or liberation in the final stages of an in-ternational proletarian revolution and may even find themselves caught in perilous situations structured by the contradictions within the world socialist movement on the one hand, and by the military assaults of imperial powers, on the other. Even after Marxist-Leninists have taken the political initiative, international support cannot be substituted for self-reliance and self-development. Forcible integration into the global order after a successful liberation struggle may in fact be positively destructive if recently liberated and once-dependent peoples and classes perceive this as the imposition of new fetters upon their productive potential. In rejecting closer association with the revolution in Vietnam, the Kampucheans assert that genuine socialist internationalism can only be supported by comparable levels of economic and individual achievement.

BIOGRAPHIES

Khieu Samphan, President of the State Presidium, a former journalist, lycée teacher and university lecturer, was born in 1931 in Svay Rieng province, the eldest child in a large family. His father was a low-ranking magistrate whose duties obliged the family to move around the country. Samphan studied economics in France from 1954 to 1959, where he was also active in the left-wing Union of Khmer Students and participated in international socialist conferences. After completing his *doctorat es sciences économiques* in 1959, he founded a progressive biweekly newspaper in Phnom Penh. The paper was banned by the Sihanouk regime in 1960. Samphan himself was imprisoned for four weeks. After a momentary retreat from public life, he joined the Prince's Sangkum movement to win election to the National Assembly in 1962 and in 1966. An active parliamentarian, he was Trade Secretary in a Sangkum cabinet in 1962–3 before being forced underground in April 1967. He reappeared in 1970, announcing his support of Sihanouk's National United Front and as a leader of the Communist struggle union within the Front. Sihanouk named him Deputy Prime Minister and Minister of Defence in the wartime resistance cabinet. Samphan was also named Commander-in-chief of the Kampuchean People's National Liberation Armed Forces when the high command was established in March 1972. After the elections in March 1976, he was named Chairman of the State Presidium.

Khieu Samphan is believed to have joined the Communist Party of Kampuchea shortly after it was founded. He is the only communist leader in the current government to have had a national reputation and a large popular following before the liberation war.

Pol Pot, Prime Minister and Party Secretary and formerly known as Saloth Sar, was born in Kompong Thom province in 1925, the son of peasants. He went to a Buddhist school (*wat*) before undertaking technical studies in the State school system in the 1940s. After earning a teaching certificate in industrial arts, he began a radio-technician course in France in 1949, and devoted most of his time to the large anti-colonial movement in Paris. He returned to Kampuchea in 1953 in time to join the 'Khmer Vietminh' revolutionary resistance, and worked underground for the movement in Phnom Penh after the Geneva Conference.

From 1957 to 1959, Pol Pot served on a committee to found a Marxist-Leninist party. At the founding congress in 1960, he was elected to the Central Committee and to its Standing Committee. In 1961, he became Deputy Secretary of the Party; in 1962, following the kidnapping and assassination of the Party Secretary, its acting Secretary. He was elected Secretary in his own right at an emergency Party congress in 1963. Shortly afterwards and amidst new repressive moves on the part of Sihanouk's intelligence agencies, Saloth Sar (Pol Pot), Ieng Sary and Son Sen fled from Phnom Penh. They were not heard from again until 1971.

Between 1963 and 1971, Pol Pot travelled extensively in rural Kampuchea, spent several months in Hanoi and visited China (in mid 1965). In the civil war period (January 1968 to March 1970), he was Secretary of the North-east District CPK, where the revolutionary struggle was fought by minority hill peoples.

Pol Pot was re-elected Party Secretary at the Party congresses held in 1971 and 1976 and became Prime Minister after the March 1976 elections. Ieng Sary and Son Sen were named deputy prime ministers. The ascendance of Pol Pot in the Government signalled the emergence of the CPK into public view. Pol Pot announced the existence of the Party on its seventeenth anniversary, in September 1977.

BASIC FACTS ABOUT DEMOCRATIC KAMPUCHEA

Official name: Democratic Kampuchea (Kampuchea Pracheatipatay).
Area: 181,035 sq. km. (69,630 sq. miles).
Population (1978): 8,000,000.
Population density: 45 per sq. km.
Population distribution (1968, with 1978 in parentheses): urban 12·6 per cent (est. 4 per cent), rural 87·4 per cent (96 per cent); under 14 years 48·0 per cent.
Membership of the CPK (Pak Kommunis Kampuchea): unknown.
Ethnic nationalities (1978): Khmers 99 per cent. [official statement]
Administrative division: 7 regions, 100 districts, 1067 co-operatives, and an unknown number of municipal committees.
Capital: Phnom Penh.
Main natural resources: Fish, timber; limited and generally unexploited mineral wealth includes offshore oil reserves, semi-precious gems, bauxite, limestone and phosphates.
Foreign trade: major exports – rice, dried fish, rubber, kapok; major imports – sheet steel, petroleum products, military equipment, chemicals for processing of agricultural goods, pharmaceutical supplies, insecticides.
Principal trading partners: China, North Korea, Yugoslavia, Japan, Hong Kong and Singapore.

Value of trade with non-socialist states (1977): exports, $680,000; imports, $19,013,000.

Economic infrastructure (1977): railways, 700 km.; major roadways, 5000 km. (approx.); water-conservancy projects, 400,000 hectares irrigated.

Foreign relations: diplomatic relations with 88 countries; eight diplomatic missions established in Phnom Penh (mid 1978); member of the UN since 1955, and of the Conference of Non-aligned Nations since its foundation (1961).

NOTES

1. Cf. S. Amin, *Imperialism and Unequal Development* (Sussex: Harvester Press, 1977) p. 147.
2. See M. Osborne, *The French Presence in Cochinchina and Cambodia* (Ithaca, N.Y.: Cornell University Press, 1969) pp. 206–58.
3. M. Osborne, 'Peasant Politics in Cambodia: The 1916 Affair', *Modern Asian Studies*, XII (1978) 217–43, discusses one important episode illustrating this.
4. W. J. Duiker, *The Comintern and Vietnamese Communism*, Ohio University Center for International Studies, Southeast Asia Series no. 37 (Athens, Ohio, 1975) pp. 17–20.
5. W. J. Duiker, *The Rise of Nationalism in Vietnam, 1900–1941* (Ithaca, N.Y.: Cornell University Press, 1976) p. 216.
6. W. Burchett, *Mekong Upstream* (Hanoi: Red River Publishing House, 1957) pp. 133 and 138.
7. Norodom Sihanouk, 'Le Communisme au Cambodge', *France-Asie*, no. 144 (1958) p. 192.
8. According to captured documents from the period, the Party was not a fully fledged communist organisation, but its formation coincided with the dissolution of the Indochinese Communist Party into national branches. See B. Fall, *The Viet-Minh Regime*, repr. (Westport, Conn.: Greenwood Press, 1975) pp. 62–4.
9. R. F. Randle, *Geneva 1954: The Settlement of the Indochinese War*, (Princeton, N.J.: Princeton University Press, 1969) *passim*. The initial Viet Minh position is discussed on p. 206.
10. See P. Devillers, 'La Fin d'une "Guerre d'Indochine" (1954)', *Revue Française de Science Politique*, XXIV (1974) 295–308.
11. Randle, *Geneva 1954*, pp. 281–82, 305, 320 and 483.
12. R. Smith, *Cambodia's Foreign Policy* (Ithaca, N.Y.: Cornell University Press, 1965) pp. 65–8.
13. Prince Sihanouk goes out of his way to identify 'Red' strongholds in the 1955 and 1958 elections (see Norodom Sihanouk, in *France-Asie*, no. 144, p. 201).
14. Author's interview, 1971.
15. C. Bell, *Survey of International Affairs, 1954* (London: Oxford University Press, 1957) p. 93. Also cited in Randle, *Geneva 1954*, p. 488.

16. The Commission issued two progress reports and five interim reports between December 1954 and December 1958. See, for example, *Fourth Interim Report of the International Commission for Supervision and Control in Cambodia for the Period April 1 to September 30, 1955, Cambodia No. 1 (1956)*, Cmd 9671 (London: Her Majesty's Stationery Office, 1956) *passim*.
17. Pol Pot, *Les Grandioses Victoires de la Revolution du Kampuchea sous la Direction Juste et Clairvoyante du Parti Communiste du Kampuchea* (Phnom Penh: Ministère des Affaires Etrangères du Kampuchea Démocratique, 1978) p. 23. This is the speech read by Pol Pot to commemorate the seventeenth anniversary of the Party.
18. Ibid., pp. 9–20.
19. Sihanouk knew of a major shift in communist policy almost immediately. The first Party Secretary was assassinated in 1962 and much of the urban-based Central Committee narrowly escaped capture or death in 1963. See the introduction to Khieu Samphan, *Cambodia's Economy and Industrial Development*, trans. and introduced by L. Summers (Ithaca, N.Y.: Cornell University Southeast Asia Program, 1979), on the 'affair of the 34'.
20. The transition to armed struggle is described in a speech by Deputy Secretary of the CPK Nuon Chea in *Democratic Kampuchea: A Workers' and Peasants' State in South-East Asia* (East Berlin: Embassy of Democratic Kampuchea, 1977) pp. 27–34. A well researched and perceptive analysis of the period is S. Heder, 'Kampuchea's Armed Struggle: The Origins of an Independent Revolution', *Bulletin of Concerned Asian Scholars*, XI, no. 1 (Jan–Mar 1979) pp. 2–24.
21. Pol Pot, *Les Grandioses Victoires*, pp. 35–6.
22. The leafleteers were often teenagers. Those who were apprehended were imprisoned. See the report in *Cambodge* (Phnom Penh), 24 Aug 1968.
23. Cf. Khieu Samphan, *Cambodia's Economy*, *passim*, and Pol Pot, *Les Grandioses Victoires*, pp. 33–7.
24. B. Kiernan, *The Samlaut Rebellion and its Aftermath, 1967–70*, Monash University, Centre of Southeast Asian Studies, Working Papers nos 4 and 5 (Melbourne, n.d.).
25. Pol Pot, *Les Grandioses Victoires*, p. 56.
26. C. Bowles, *Promises to Keep: My Years in Public Life, 1941–1969* (New York: Harper and Row, 1971) p. 97.
27. See L. Summers, 'Cambodia: Model of the Nixon Doctrine', *Current History*, LXV (1973) 252–6, 276.
28. T. M. Carney, *Communist Party Power in Kampuchea (Cambodia): Documents and Discussion*, Cornell University Southeast Asia Program Data Paper no. 106 (Ithaca, N.Y., Jan 1977); and K. M. Quinn, 'Political Change in Wartime: The Khmer Krahom Revolution in Southern Cambodia, 1970–1974', *Naval War College Review* (1976) 3–31. US government translations sometimes refer to the 1970–5 war as the 'civil war', but communist documents are careful to distinguish the civil war of 1968–70 from the liberation war of 1970–5, in which American and Vietnamese parties were involved.
29. Cf. Carney, *Communist Party Power*, p. 56, and BBC, *Summary of World Broadcasts*, 10 July 1978 and 28 July 1978.
30. Carney, *Communist Party Power*, p. 57.

31. Ibid., pp. 6 and 44. Cf. Forces Armées Nationales Khmères, Deuxième Bureau, 'Evolution de l'Organisation Politico-administrative et Militaire des Khmers Communists depuis Mars 1970' (unpublished typescript, Mar 1975) p. 6.
32. There may be party committees for communications, agriculture and industry.
33. The drafting and promulgation of the constitution are described by L. Summers, 'Defining the Revolutionary State in Cambodia', *Current History*, LXXI, no. 422 (Dec 1973) 213–17, 228.
34. *Constitution du Kampuchea Démocratique* (Paris: Mission du Kampuchea Démocratique, 1976).
35. *Pol Pot Talks with the Delegation of the Association Belgium–Kampuchea* (Phnom Penh: Government of Democratic Kampuchea, 1978) p. 14.
36. G. C. Hildebrand and G. Porter, *Cambodia: Starvation and Revolution* (London: Monthly Review Press, 1976) *passim*. Some details of the counter-revolutionary contingency plans are contained in Long Champa Leap, *How the Official Departure of the Marshal-President from Phnom Penh, Khmer Republic on 1 April 1975 was Decided and Prepared* (Phnom Penh: Ministry of Information, Jan 1977) 16 pp.
37. Khieu Samphan, *Cambodia's Economy*, pt I.
38. More details are contained in L. Summers, 'Consolidating the Cambodian Revolution', *Current History*, LXIX, no. 411 (Dec 1975) 219.
39. These observations are based on reports by Yugoslavian, American and Swedish visitors to the country in 1978.
40. These had different names and affiliates during the liberation war. See the following pamphlets published by the Royaume de Cambodge, Front Uni National du Kampuchea in 1973: *Les Femmes Cambodgiennes dans la Guerre Revolutionnaire de Liberation Nationale et Populaire*, 31 pp. *La Jeunesse Cambodgienne dans la Guerre de Resistance contre l'Aggression US et les Traitres*, 44 pp., and *La Classe Ouvrière et les Travailleurs du Kampuchea dans la Guerre Revolutionnaire de Liberation Nationale et Populaire*, 54 pp.
41. A more pessimistic view is expressed in P. Rousset, 'Cambodia: Background to the Revolution', *Journal of Contemporary Asia*, VII (1977) 519 and 526.
42. This is especially true of the Youth Organisation. See *Nouvelles du Kampuchea Démocratique* (Peking), no. 40 (1977) 7.
43. International socialist perceptions of their stake in the crisis are apparent in Vietnamese and Chinese efforts to negotiate with the Lon Nol coup group before firmly deciding to support or oppose the Sihanouk Front and armed struggle in Kampuchea. The political programme of the National United Front published in Peking in May 1970 also emphasises non-alignment in foreign policy in the Sihanoukist tradition. References to domestic policy reforms are relatively vague.
44. For a description of the response see L. Summers, 'The Civil War in Cambodia', *Current History*, LXIII (1972) 261–2.
45. The struggle front was led by Khieu Samphan. See F. Debré, *Cambodge: La Révolution de la Forêt* (Paris: Flammarion, 1976) p. 145; and the unpublished manuscript 'Des Mouvements Antigovernementaux au Cambodge' (Phnom Penh: Forces Armées Nationales Khmères internal

intelligence document, July 1973) p. 10. Carney's documents (in *Communist Party Power*) discuss aspects of this struggle.

46. The sequence of events is elaborated in a paper by L. Summers and D. G. Porter, 'Cambodia: Was There an Understanding?', *Foreign Military Sales and Assistance Act. Hearings before the Committee on Foreign Relations, United States Senate, on S. 1443*, 93rd Congress, 1st Session (1973) pp. 457–63.

47. Democratic Kampuchea vigorously denounced rumours that it intended to follow China's lead in recognising the military junta in Chile. See *Nouvelles du Kampuchea Démocratique* (Peking), no. 3 (1976) 3.

BIBLIOGRAPHY

See also references in the Notes.

Carney, Timothy M., *Communist Party Power in Kampuchea (Cambodia): Documents and Discussion*, Cornell University Southeast Asia Program Data Paper, no. 106 (Ithaca, N.Y., 1977).

Caldwell, Malcolm and Lek Tan, *Cambodia in the Southeast Asian War* (London: Monthly Review Press, 1973).

Chandler, D. P., Kiernan, Ben and Muy Hong Lim, *The Early Phases of Liberation in Northwestern Cambodia: Conversations with Peang Sophi*, Monash University, Centre of Southeast Asian Studies, Working Paper no. 10 (Melbourne, n.d.) p. 9.

Debré, François, *Cambodge: La Révolution de la Forêt* (Paris: Flammarion, 1976).

Discours Prononcé par le Camarade Pol Pot, Secrétaire du Comité Central du Parti Communiste du Kampuchea au Meeting Commémorant le 17e Anniversaire de la Fondation du Parti Communiste du Kampuchea et à l'Occasion de la Proclamation Solennelle de l'Existence Officielle du Parti Communiste du Kampuchea (Phnom Penh: Département de la Presse et de l'Information du Ministère des Affaires Etrangères du Kampuchea Démocratique, 27 Sep 1977) 77 pp.

Gour, Claude-Gilles, *Institutions Constitutionnelles et Politiques du Cambodge* (Paris: Librairie Dalloz, 1965).

Heder, Steven, 'Kampuchea's Armed Struggle: The Origins of an Independent Revolution', *Bulletin of Concerned Asian Scholars*, XI, no. 1 (Jan–Mar 1979) pp. 2–24.

Hildebrand, George C. and Porter, D. Gareth, *Cambodia: Starvation and Revolution* (New York: Monthly Review Press, 1976).

Interview du Camarade Pol Pot Secrétaire du Comite Central du Parti Communiste du Kampuchea, Premier Ministre du Gouvernement du Kampuchea Démocratique à la Délégation des Journalistes Yougoslaves en Visite au Kampuchea Democratique (Phnom Penh: Département de la Presse et de l'Information du Ministère des Affaires Etrangères du Kampuchea Démocratique, 17 Mar 1978) 23 pp.

Khieu Samphan, *Cambodia's Economy and Industrial Development*, trs and introduced by Laura Summers (Ithaca, N.Y.: Cornell University Southeast Asia Program, 1979).

Kiernan, Ben, 'Cambodia in the News, 1975–6', *Melbourne Journal of Politics*, VIII (1975–6) 6–12.

——, 'Khieu Samphan: Cambodia's Revolutionary Leader', *Dyason House Papers*, I, no. 5 (June 1975) 5–8.

——, *The Samlaut Rebellion and its Aftermath: The Origins of Cambodia's Liberation Movement*, pts 1 and 2, Monash University, Centre of Southeast Asian Studies, Working Papers nos 4 and 5 (Melbourne, n.d.).

Leifer, Michael, *Cambodia: The Search for Security* (New York: Praeger, 1967).

Martel, Gabrielle, *Lovea, Village des Environs d'Angkor* (Paris: École Française d'Extrême-Orient, 1975).

Meyer, Charles, *Derrière le Sourire Khmer* (Paris: Plon, 1971).

Migozzi, Jacques, *Cambodge: Faits et Problèmes de Population* (Paris: Éditions du Centre National de la Recherche Scientifique, 1973).

Norodom Sihanouk, 'Le Communisme au Cambodge', *France-Asie*, nos 144 and 145 (May–June 1958) pp. 192–206, 290–306.

——, *L'Indochine Vue de Pekin: Entretiens avec Jean Lacouture* (Paris: Éditions du Seuil, 1972).

Norodom Sihanouk and Burchett, Wilfred, *My War with the CIA* (Harmondsworth: Penguin, 1973).

Osborne, Milton E., *Politics and Power in Cambodia* (Camberwell, Victoria: Longman Australia, 1973).

Pol Pot, *Les Grandioses Victories de la Revolution du Kampuchea sous la Direction Juste et Clairvoyante du Parti Communiste du Kampuchea* (Phnom Penh: Ministère des Affaires Etrangères du Kampuchea Démocratique, 1978).

Ponchaud, François, *Cambodge: Année Zero* (Paris: Guilliard, 1977).

Poole, Peter, *Expansion of the Vietnam War into Cambodia*, Ohio University Center for International Studies, Southeast Asia Series no. 17 (Athens, Ohio, 1970).

Prud'homme, Rémy, *L'Économie du Cambodge* (Paris: Presses Universitaires de France, 1969).

Reddi, V. M., *A History of the Cambodian Independence Movement 1863–1955* (Tirupati, Andhra Pradesh: Sri Venkateswara University, 1970).

Rousset, Pierre, 'Cambodia: Background to the Revolution', *Journal of Contemporary Asia*, VII, no. 4 (1977) 513–28.

Sarin Chhak, *Les Frontières du Cambodge*, vol. I (Paris: Librairie Dalloz, 1966).

Smith, Roger M., *Cambodia's Foreign Policy* (Ithaca, N.Y.: Cornell University Press, 1965).

Summers, Laura, 'Behind Khmer Smiles: Prospero's Adventures in Cambodia', *Journal of the Siam Society*, LXI, pt 1 (Jan 1973) 310–25.

——, 'Cambodia: Model of the Nixon Doctrine', *Current History*, LXV, no. 388 (Dec 1973) 252–6, 276.

——, 'Consolidating the Cambodian Revolution', *Current History*, LXIX, no. 411 (Dec 1975) 218–23, 245.

——, 'Defining the Revolutionary State in Cambodia', *Current History*, LXXI, no. 422 (Dec 1976) 213–17, 228.

Swedish-Kampuchean Friendship Association and the Norwegian-Kampuchean Friendship Association, *The Revolution in Kampuchea* (Stockholm, 1978).

Willmott, William E., *The Chinese in Cambodia* (Vancouver: University of British Columbia, 1967).

——, *The Political Structure of the Chinese Community in Cambodia* (New York: Humanities Press, 1970).

Zasloff, J. J. and Brown, MacAlister, *Communism in Indochina* (Lexington, Mass.: D. C. Heath, 1975).

Postscriptum: People's Republic of Kampuchea

BOGDAN SZAJKOWSKI

On 7 January 1979, the government of Democratic Kampuchea was dislodged by the forces of an internal opposition group (the National United Front for the Salvation of Kampuchea—NUFSK) acting with the support of the regular army of the Socialist Republic of Vietnam. A new government was established in Phnom Penh by the NUFSK, and the country was renamed the People's Republic of Kampuchea.

The NUFSK, which was formed with the explicit aim of overthrowing the established regime led by Pol Pot, was founded on 2 December 1978 at a congress attended by 'more than 200 representatives of all strata of the Kampuchean patriotic population: workers, peasants, petty bourgeois, intellectuals, Buddhist monks and nuns, young people, women, Kampuchean ethnic minorities and patriotic insurgents who had abandoned the Pol Pot–Ieng Sary administration and army'.[1] (For membership of the NUFSK Central Committee, see Table 15.1.)

The military offensive by the Front, which was backed up not only politically, diplomatically but also by massive military support from neighbouring Vietnam (although this has always been denied by Vietnam[2]), began on 25 December 1978 from areas adjacent to the border of the two countries.

The programme of the NUFSK is contained in an eleven-point statement[3] and apart from a call for the 'overthrow of the reactionary Pol Pot–Ieng Sary gang!', promises general elections, a new constitution, the creation of new mass organisations affiliated to the NUFSK, and the building up of the Kampuchean Revolutionary Army. It stresses that all people have the right to return to their native

TABLE 15.1 Members of the Central Committee of the NUFSK, 1978

Heng Samrin	President; former member of the Executive Committee of the CPK for the Eastern Region and former Political Commissar and Commander of the Fourth Division
Chea Sim	Vice President; former Secretary of the CPK Committee for Sector 20, Eastern Region, and former member of the Kampuchean People's Representative Assembly
Ros Samay	Secretary-general; Assistant Chief of Staff of Unit 10 of the Kampuchean Revolutionary Armed Forces
Mat Ly	Former member of the Standing Committee of the Kampuchean People's Representative Assembly
Bun Mi	Former Deputy Secretary of the CPK Committee for Sector 3, North-eastern Region, representative of the ethnic minorities
Hun Sen	Former Chief of Staff and former Regimental Deputy Commander in Sector 21, representative of the Youth Association for National Salvation
Mrs Mean Saman	Political commissar of a Kampuchean Revolutionary Armed Forces battalion, representative of the Women's Association for National Salvation
Meas Samnang	Representative of the Trade Union for National Salvation
Neou Samon	Representative of the Peasants' Association for National Salvation
Head Monk Long Sim	Representative of the Buddhist clergy
Hem Samin	Engineer, representative of the Intellectuals' Association for National Salvation
Mrs Chey Kanh Nha	Doctor of medicine, member of the Intellectuals' Association for National Salvation
Chan Ven	Professor of physics, member of Intellectuals' Association for National Salvation
Prach Sun	Journalist, member of the Intellectuals' Association for National Salvation

land, to have freedom of residence, movement, association and religion, the right to work, recreation and education.

The programme states that the country's economic development will be based on a planned economy, and promises an eight-hour working day, the establishment of banks, issue of currency and the restoration and development of the circulation of goods. It promises full development of education, equality of the sexes and abolishes compulsory marriage. Furthermore, it undertakes to protect and restore historical relics, pagodas and temples.

In the area of foreign policy, the programme promises to settle all disputes with neighbouring countries through peaceful negotiations and to end the border war with Vietnam.

This latter point was further emphasised by the Front's foreign-policy statement issued on 20 December 1978, which stressed that the Front's aim was 'to restore the time-honoured tradition of solidarity and friendship between the Kampuchean and Vietnamese peoples', meaning the special relationship which the previous regime had tried to avoid, fearing a re-emergence of the Indochinese Federation. This special relationship was strongly emphasised in an editorial in the Vietnamese party newspaper, *Nhan Dan*, on 8 January 1979; this stated that

> The great victory of the Kampuchean revolution brought to a successful conclusion the heroic struggle of the three fraternal nations – Vietnam, Laos and Kampuchea – for independence and freedom. It ushered in a new era in which the three nations on the Indochina peninsula will unite to build a new life in the spirit of absolute respect for one another's independence and sovereignty and equality and of mutual assistance. The tradition of unity of the three nations in fighting against common enemies for common objectives and ideals is precious and worthy of emulation. This tradition has become an invincible strength and will forever constitute an enormous strength for our three nations.[4]

The new regime in Phnom Penh would now inevitably be drawn closely into Hanoi's orbit, since Vietnam with 50 million people has already become the undisputed leader over the entire Indochinese peninsula.

Predictably the new government was recognised, on 9 January 1979, as the 'sole, legitimate government of Kampuchea' by Vietnam, USSR, Laos, Afghanistan and other socialist countries. The only exceptions were Romania, Yugoslavia and the Democratic People's Republic of Korea, which not only refused to recognise the new government but also condemned the military overthrow of the Pol Pot regime as an 'unjustifiable threat to peace' and a 'heavy blow to socialism'.[5]

China, which perhaps together with Yugoslavia and Romania has been the strongest supporter of the Pol Pot regime, promised to do everything possible to provide aid to the dislodged government 'until its final victory'. The Pol Pot regime is still recognised as the legitimate government of Kampuchea by the UN and the vast majority of its members, including the countries of Western Europe. However, whether the accounts of widespread atrocities, mass killings, starvation and brutalities committed under the Pol Pot administration, and which have come into light since its dislodgement, will put pressure on the international community still remains to be seen.

On 8 January 1979, in order to manage the domestic and foreign affairs, the Front set up the People's Revolutionary Council of Kampuchea (for its membership, see Table 15.2). Areas under the Front's control are to be governed by People's Revolutionary Committees. At the time of going to press it is clear that, although the new regime has been able to establish itself in cities and in the eastern part of the country, it does not control large parts of the countryside, which has always been a successful base for guerrilla warfare. In his last message before leaving the capital, Pol Pot appealed to the population to wage a protracted people's war in order to 'seize final victory'. Preparation for such a war started several months before the dislodgement of his administration. The future of Kampuchea seems to be far from certain.

TABLE 15.2 Members of the People's Revolutionary Council of Kampuchea, 1979

Heng Samrin	President
Pen Sovan	Vice President, in charge of the Ministry of National Defence
Hun Sen	In charge of the Ministry of Foreign Affairs
Chea Sim	In charge of the Ministry of Interior
Keo Chanda	In charge of the Ministry of Information, Press and Culture
Professor Chan Ven	In charge of the Ministry of Education
Nu Beng	In charge of the Ministry of Health and Social Affairs
Mok Sakun	In charge of the Ministry of Economy and People's Welfare

One must, however, emphasise the significance of one socialist country, supporting an insurgent organisation against another socialist country. This is without precedent in the history of the international communist and working-class movement and must be seen as undeniable proof of the inadequacy and lack of substance of *proletarian internationalism*, one of the cornerstones of Marxism-Leninism. The seriousness of this precedent has been underlined by Manuel Azcárate, a leading member of the Political Bureau of the Communist Party of Spain:

Without a doubt, the degeneration of the Pol Pot power in Cambodia reached terrifying extremes; without a doubt, popular sectors of that country rose up against that power. But, in our opinion, that cannot justify Vietnam's armed intervention to change the Cambodian government. It is a question of principle. We condemn that method when the capitalist States use it. And we also do so when socialist States use it. Were we to accept that method, socialism would lose one of the characteristics that *must* differentiate it from capitalism.[6]

BIOGRAPHIES

Heng Samrin, President of the Revolutionary Council of Kampuchea and of the Central Committee of the NUFSK was born in 1934 in Kak commune, Phu Hea Reak district, Prey veng province, to a large family of poor peasants. He began his revolutionary activities in 1959 and became commander of a battalion and then of a regiment. Since 1976 he has been Political Commissar and Commandant of the Fourth Division, Assistant Chief of the General Staff of the Kampuchean Revolutionary Army and member of the Executive Committee for the Eastern Zone of CPK. In May 1978 he led an insurrection against the Pol Pot government and began to mobilise the population to take part in the struggle to topple the Pol Pot–Ieng Sary regime.

Chea Sim, member of the People's Revolutionary Council of Kampuchea, with responsibility for the Ministry of Foreign Affairs, and Vice President of the NUFSK, was born in 1932 to a family of poor peasants in Sampil commune, Romeas Hek district, Svay Rieng province. He has been involved in underground revolutionary activities since 1952. In 1971 he was elected Secretary of Ponhea Krek District Committee of the CPK and since 1976 he has been a member of the Kampuchean People's Representative Assembly. In May 1978 he, together with other cadres, began the struggle for the establishment of bases of resistance in order to topple the Pol Pot–Ieng Sary regime.

Pen Sovan, Vice President of the Revolutionary Council of Kampuchea, with responsibility for the Ministry of National Defence, was born in 1936 in Takeo Province. In 1950 he enlisted in the regular forces in south-western Kampuchea. He became assistant to the division and graduated from the military high school. From 1970 to 1973 he was with the editorial staff of the Radio of the National United Front of Kampuchea. In 1973 he joined the anti Pol Pot–Ieng Sary revolutionary organisation.

NOTES

1. Declaration of the NUFSK, in B. Szajkowski (ed.), *Documents in Communist Affairs – 1979* (annual: 1977–9, Cardiff: University College Cardiff Press; 1980– , London: Macmillan). The National United Front for the Salvation of Kampuchea (NUFSK) is variously referred to as the Cambodian National United Front for National Salvation (CNUFNS), the Kampuchean National United Front for National Salvation (KNUFNS) or the Kampuchean United Front for National Salvation (KUFNS). The name used by Kampuchean and Vietnamese sources is that of the National United Front for the Salvation of Kampuchea.
2. See 6 Jan 1979, statement by the Ministry of Foreign Affairs of the Socialist Republic of Vietnam, in B. Szajkowski (ed.), *Documents in Communist Affairs – 1980*.
3. As note 1.
4. 'Heroic Cambodia Has Entered a New Era', in *Nhan Dan*, 8 Jan 1979.
5. *Scinteia*, 10 Jan 1979. See also 'Challenge to National Independence, Socialism and Peace', editorial article of *Nodong Sinmun* in B. Szajkowski (ed.), *Documents in Communist Affairs – 1980*.
6. Manuel Azcárate, 'Notes on Some International Problems', for complete text see B. Szajkowski (ed.), *Documents in Communist Affairs – 1980*.

16 Democratic People's Republic of Korea

BRUCE CUMINGS

The Democratic People's Republic of Korea (DPRK) occupies the northern 55 per cent of the Korean peninsula, bordering on the People's Republic of China and the USSR to the north, the Yellow Sea to the west, the Japan Sea to the east, and the Republic of Korea to the south. The peninsula's position between three great powers has made it a bone of contention in strategic politics in North-east Asia for the past century; great-power rivalry caused the division of the country in the aftermath of the Second World War. Occupied by the Soviet Union in 1945, North Korea maintained a close relationship with Moscow until the Korean War began in 1950. The major Chinese commitment to the war in the autumn of 1950 raised the possibility of securing relative North Korean independence by playing upon Sino-Soviet rivalry; this strategy emerged in full bloom in the early 1960s, with open North Korean-Soviet polemics. Since then, the DPRK has maintained correct relations with both socialist powers, zig-zagging between them, although with a bias toward China.

A land of mountains and valleys, North Korea has a rugged terrain with perhaps one-fifth of the land arable. Korea is one of the oldest and most homogeneous of nations, its history going back some 4000 years, with recorded history beginning in 194 BC. It was a unified political entity in the seventh century, and was ruled by an agrarian-bureaucratic dynasty from 1392 to 1910. Japan annexed Korea as its colony in 1910, after three decades of imperialist rivalry; the Japanese then developed the peninsula in the interests of the colonial power, building railways, ports, and highways that linked Korea tightly with Japan. In the 1930s colonial authorities built a heavy-industrial infrastructure in the north, while retaining the south as a rice bowl. When the colonial sphere abruptly disintegrated in 1945, it thus left the north with a highly

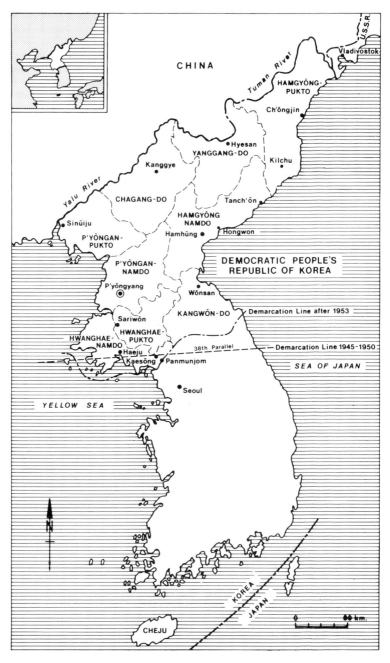

Democratic People's Republic of Korea: State and provincial boundaries

developed but unintegrated economic structure, with much of the transportation and industry skewed toward Japanese needs. North Korea suffered extensive destruction during the Korean War, but the infrastructure remained and, once rebuilt, has enabled the DPRK to remain the most industrialised socialist state in Asia.

The traditional regime after 1392 was a Confucian dynasty, and Confucian family rites continued to dominate Korean customs down to 1945. Stress on the family as the core unit of society continues in the DPRK; this is the only socialist state whose constitution enshrines the family as the basic social unit, and the role of North Korea's leader, Kim Il Sung, bears comparison with this tradition in the emphasis on paternal, benevolent and unitary guidance from the top. Korea's striking homogeneity also biases DPRK practice toward a conception of socialism as one big happy family. A traditional legacy of internal political weakness and factionalism, and external subservience to China and Japan, has also skewed DPRK practice toward strong, hierarchical, disciplined organisation at home and fierce independence abroad. Thus, the DPRK strikes many foreign observers as highly nationalistic for a socialist state. Since the mid 1960s the official State ideology has been 'Juche' (*chuch'e*), a doctrine stressing self-reliance and independence.

THE KOREAN COMMUNIST MOVEMENT, 1918–45

Korea had one of the oldest communist movements in Asia, the first Korean Communist Party predating the establishment of the Chinese Communist Party in 1921.[1] It had an exile life among Koreans in Siberia and China until the mid 1920s, when a party emerged within the Korean colony. The movement had many chiefs and few Indians in the 1920s, with parties and groups calling themselves communist appearing in Siberia, China (especially Shanghai), Manchuria, Korea and Japan. As a movement it was weak and factious, a result primarily of its intellectual leadership and sophisticated Japanese police suppression. Communists succeeded in mounting strikes in factories and agitating students in cities in Korea in the late 1920s and early 1930s, and in the latter period also established peasant organisations within Korea and in the Sino-Korean border region. A number of leaders established themselves during this period and later played important roles in postwar Korea: Pak Hŏn-yŏng, Kim Tu-bong, Yi Yŏng, Hŏ Hŏn, Oki-sŏp, and Yi Kang-guk, among others.

The older leadership elements in the DPRK today, however, trace back to the mid 1930s. Kim Il Sung and his close allies, such as Ch'oe Hyŏn, Kim Il, Kim Ch'aek (d. 1950) and Ch'oe Yŏng-gŏn (d. 1976), are children of the Korean anti-Japanese resistance in the Manchurian border region with Korea. Kim Il Sung began guerrilla activity in 1932 at the age of twenty and continued fighting in a loose alliance with Chinese communist guerrillas such as Yang Ching-yü until the early 1940s. Kim had under his command a partisan force ranging from 100 up to 1000, and became well known in the course of several small but victorious attacks on the Japanese from 1937 to 1940. The resistance tradition is played up daily in the North Korea of today and remains the core of Kim's legitimacy. The unfortunate corollary is that the thousands of Koreans who resisted Japanese rule and were not associated with Kim are little mentioned.

By 1945 there were essentially four aspects to Korean communism: a domestic bunch of groups that were underground or in prison from the early 1930s; a congeries of individuals and groups in the Soviet Union, some of whom were CPSU members; some 300 communists loosely associated with the Yenan-based Chinese Communist movement; and Kim Il Sung's group, which probably numbered about 200 or 300 when Japan capitulated (Kim's whereabouts from 1941 to 1945 remain unknown, although the best evidence suggests that he and his partisan allies retreated across the Manchurian border to the vicinity of Khabarhovsk to wait out the Pacific war). Korean communism never had an effective relationship with the Comintern, although aspects of it were under Comintern discipline in the late 1920s.

SOVIET OCCUPATION AND THE EMERGENCE OF THE DPRK

Kim Il Sung and other Korean communists hoped to liberate their homeland as part of a protracted campaign against the Japanese land armies on the Asian mainland.[2] Japan's rapid collapse in August 1945, however, denied them this opportunity, as the Soviet Red Army engaged and destroyed the Japanese Kwantung Army in a matter of days. On 15 August, Korea was liberated from Japanese rule. The Soviets were already in occupation of much of the North, and at American initiative they accepted a proposal to partition Korea at the 38th parallel. The Americans did not occupy the southern half until 8 September, however, leaving a political vacuum into which moved southern leftists and communists. Very shortly 'people's committees', labour and peasant unions and youth groups dotted the entire peninsula. The committees became the local basis for the northern regime, as the Soviets never set up a military government and instead ruled through the committee structure. Because of the widespread leftist mobilisation in the South, many old-line domestic communists chose to remain there, not realising that the American military government would make their activities impossible within a year or so after liberation.

Kim Il Sung did not make this mistake. Instead he turned up in the North about a month after liberation, in circumstances that remain murky. The scholarly literature differs on whether the Soviets deposited Kim and his partisans in the North or not. In any case, by December 1945 Kim had assumed leadership of the northern branch of the Korean Communist Party, while Pak Hŏn-Yŏng, a senior domestic communist, led the southern branch. Kim and his allies were able to assert central control over the amorphous people's committees in early 1946; Kim emerged as Chairman of the North Korean Interim People's Committee in P'yŏngyang in February 1946, the first central administrative organ to appear after liberation in the North. Shortly thereafter, the northern leadership embarked on a programme of thorough social revolution, the most important aspect of which was a land-reform campaign which began in early March and within two months had destroyed the age-old power of Korea's landed class and had redistributed land to the peasants. Peasants received land titles, but the land was not transferable. No moves toward collectivisation occured until after the Korean War.

The land reform was followed by labour reforms designed to improve working conditions, and laws guaranteeing equality of women and free elections, socialist-style. The cumulative effect of these revolutionary steps was both to strengthen the Kim regime under Soviet guidance, since peasants and workers had much to show for participation in the reform campaigns, and to raise the social question in the South as well. With many dispossessed landlords and other elites fleeing to the South, the relationship between the two halves of Korea took on an aspect of civil war.

The other major leadership grouping in the north consisted of Korean veterans of the exile Yenan-aligned movement in China, with Kim Tu-bong, a scholarly linguist and Marxist, and Mu Chŏng, the highest-ranking Korean in the Chinese Eighth Route Army, at the top. Kim Il Sung and Kim Tu-bong arranged a merger of their two forces in August 1946, establishing the North Korean Workers' Party (Puk Chosŏn nodong-dang). Rudimentary police and military forces also emerged in the first year after liberation, meaning that for all practical purposes the northern socialist regime was in place two years before it was actually proclaimed (the same was true of the anti-communist regime in the South).

The main features that distinguish North Korean socialism also appeared by the end of 1946: (1) emphasis on the critical role of the leader, with a virtual cult of Kim Il Sung already in evidence; (2) much use of so-called 'mass line' procedures, like those in China, to create links between leaders and led; (3) a tremendous emphasis on organisation, so that all aspects of North Korean life and virtually all Koreans of whatever background or age were encompassed in a veritable 'organisation life'; (4) the first murmurings of an independent, self-reliant political and economic line, although this aspect had to be muted as long as the Soviets were in occupation. The concern with having one respected, benevolent leader resonated with Korea's Confucian past, while the mass-line emphasis probably derived from the experience of Kim Il Sung, Kim Tu-bong and others in the Chinese communist movement, as well as from the partisan experience in Manchuria in the 1930s.

The Soviet Twenty-Fifth Army occupied North Korea, of course, and dictated the outer limits of Korean policy: that is, broad guidelines assuring that Korea would be socialist in form and oriented toward the Soviet interest in assuring that the peninsula would not become a base for attack against the Soviet Far East. Within those limits, however, the Soviets showed more flexibility than they did in, most East European countries. Generally Soviet officers retreated to the background, exercising an inauspicious authority, allowing the regime to be for all practical purposes Korean. It is not even clear that Kim Il Sung was their first choice to lead the North, although clearly he was well within the bounds of acceptability. Kim came out on top primarily because among communist leaders he was one of the few with an armed force under his command, and because he had both survived the Japanese period unscathed and achieved a reputation for himself as a resistance fighter. He was never unopposed by other Koreans during this period, and outmanoeuvred them one after another.

THE DPRK AND THE KOREAN WAR

The DPRK was founded on 9 September 1948, about three weeks after the establishment of the Republic of Korea (ROK) in the south. Like its southern counterpart, it claimed to be the legitimate government of all

Korea, and steadfastly refused to recognise the competence of the United Nations in Korean affairs (UN-sponsored elections had created the southern National Assembly, which then chose Syngman Rhee as ROK President). The DPRK's international contacts were as a result limited to the Soviet bloc, and, given the global power and influence of the United States, it started its life as an isolated socialist entity.

In the Korean context the northern regime was quite potent, however, emerging in 1948 as a coalition of the Left; after the merger in 1949 of the North and South Korean Workers' Parties, virtually all the important leftist and communist leaders from the various pre-1945 factions were represented in the top leadership. Kim Il Sung, of course, remained at the top as both Premier of the DPRK and Chairman of the Korean Workers' Party (KWP), and the leadership itself remained an uneasy amalgam of once-disparate factions. The southern communist leader, Pak Hŏn-yŏng, was Vice Premier, and other top posts were held by 'domestic' communists such as Hŏ Hŏn, Yenan-aligned ones such as Kim Tu-bong, and Soviet-aligned ones such as Hŏ Ka-i.

This northern politics also had its southern counterpart. The initially strong Left in the South was forced underground by 1947, after major peasant and worker uprisings in autumn 1946;[3] by early 1948 the civil conflict had moved into a stage of unconventional, guerrilla warfare. For two years the guerrilla campaign in the South went forward, with great strength on the large southern island of Cheju, and numerous pockets of resistance in the mountainous middle regions of the South. The movement was mostly indigenous to the South at the start, but the north became more directly involved as counter-insurgency campaigns took their toll. The North dispatched guerrilla teams by sea and through remote corridors in the eastern mountains along the 38th parallel. It is probable that the southern element in the DPRK leadership, especially Pak Hŏn-yŏng, was particularly interested in supporting and building the base in the South. This effort came to naught, however, in early 1950, with the virtual destruction of the guerrillas. A period of quiet fell on the peninsula as both North and South prepared for the next round, and sought support from their major-power guarantors.

The civil conflict moved into a conventional military phase as the North 'struck like a cobra', in General Douglas MacArthur's phrase, at dawn on 25 June 1950. The assault was a huge success in its first weeks, swallowing nearly the entire peninsula. The dispatch of American air and ground forces destroyed the North Korean calculus, however, and within weeks (September 1950) nearly destroyed the entire DPRK military, State and Party apparatus. North Korea became the only postwar socialist state to have its entire territory occupied by anti-communist forces. The war experience had the following effects on the subsequent development of the DPRK. First, it smashed to bits the coalition leadership, as recriminations over the failures of the war took their toll. Purges in the latter stages of the war and after it was over decimated the southern element in the DPRK leadership; Pak Hŏn-yŏng was purged and executed for treason, along with a number of other southern communist leaders. Kim Il Sung and his anti-Japanese resistance allies then launched an assault on the Yenan-aligned Koreans, purging most of them in the mid 1950s.[4] Secondly, the occupation of the North purged northern society of its older elites and upper classes, as former landlords, teachers, technicians, and experts of various sorts fled to the South. Thus the way was opened to radical socialisation, as collectivisation began (it was finished by 1958); the private commercial sector that had persisted in the late 1940s nearly disappeared; and the DPRK established an inclusive policy toward intellectuals, experts, and technicians in the face of severe shortages of such people. Thus the DPRK, unlike China, has never mounted campaigns against intellectuals and experts, and instead has defined them as part of 'the people'. The diminution of the population in general that the war caused also made for severe labour shortages in all sectors, dictating a rapid mechanisation of agriculture, among other things. Thus, many DPRK policies in the postwar era can be explained in part by the effects of the war on its population and industrial structure. Thirdly, the Chinese involvement in the war gave the DPRK a second guarantor, and the possibility of manoeuvring between the Soviets and the Chinese to carve out an arena of independence and autonomy. The first expression of this was in Kim Il Sung's landmark speech, 'On Eliminating Dogmatism and Formalism and Establishing Juche in Ideological Work', delivered on 28 December 1955. It criticised slavish worship of things Russian, often in remarkably forthright terms, and marked out an independent path for North Korean communism. Although the Chinese under Mao were beginning to say similar things about copying the Soviet model, this speech went further than anything the Chinese had said to that point.

THE CREATION OF A KOREAN PATH TO SOCIALISM, 1953-70

Much of North Korea in 1953 consisted of heaps of bricks and ashes, and simply reconstructing the *status quo* of before the war absorbed the efforts of the DPRK for years afterwards. Still, such destruction implies an opportunity for creation, and it is in this period that the DPRK embarked on a unique path to socialism, what Glenn Paige has called 'socialism in one-half of a country'.[5] DPRK policy toward rich peasants during the collectivisation campaigns departed from previous Soviet experience, in that rich peasants were re-educated and incorporated into the collective arrangements, something of course that reflected as well the small number of kulaks in the DPRK after the war, as compared with the situation in the Soviet Union in the late 1920s. The Koreans also adopted a policy of 'walking on two legs' some four years before the Chinese moved to a similar policy. This was predicated on the simultaneous development of agriculture and industry, although, as in China, heavy industry continued to get more development capital. The policy responded to the skewed and distorted residue of colonial patterns, and was designed to integrate the economy and establish a real basis for self-reliance.

For a brief time in 1958 the North Koreans also flirted with emulating the Chinese Great Leap Forward. Some 13,000 agricultural co-operatives were integrated into about 4000 rural organisations, which approximated the boundaries of the old *ri* or village administrative units. During this period the Koreans spoke highly of the Chinese campaigns, and also experimented with 'backyard' methods of producing iron. The new amalgamated co-operatives, however, did not go as far as the Chinese in instituting a virtual militarisation in rural organisation, with dormitory living, communal mess halls, and so on. Nor did the Koreans suffer as did the Chinese in subsequent years, the worst effects of such pell-mell development.[6]

Mass line policies[7] also emerged full-blown during these years, exemplified by the 'Chŏllima' or Flying Horse Movement, meant to symbolise a rapid leap forward; the 'Ch'ŏngsanni method', an application of mass-line techniques in agriculture; and the 'Taean system', or the mass line as it applies to industry. The point was to find means of integrating leadership with the people, bringing different levels of the society and bureaucracy together, providing participation, and assuring that directives were actually implemented. The DPRK used various means to assure this, including the downward transfer of cadres to village and factory levels; so-called 'on-the-spot guidance' by leaders, with Kim Il Sung doing the lion's share of this (villages and factories record his every visit in plaques and memorials); and requiring students to spend stints at factory or farm to assure 'redness' as well as 'expertise'. Unlike Mao Tse-tung, however, Kim has never denigrated the vanguard role of the Party, nor has he placed peasant above proletarian as the repository of revolutionary consciousness. For Kim it is the Party cadre who is the carrier of such consciousness: it is not latent in the masses but must be brought from without in the first instance, or stimulated from without. Peasants advance by becoming proletarianised.

To the extent that such practice differentiates the DPRK from China, or, more properly, Kim from Mao, the reason probably lies in the different paths to power of the two leaders and the labour shortage in North Korean agriculture. That is, the North Koreans have been less concerned than the Chinese with stimulating commitment to the revolution from masses of peasants, and dignifying their role, since in North Korea the peasantry has been rapidly disappearing as industry and mechanisation advance.

Thus, the DPRK in the 1950s borrowed from the Chinese and continued emulation of certain Soviet practices while beginning to carve out a distinctly Korean path to socialism in the space between its giant socialist neighbours. In the early 1960s the DPRK's separate path became pronounced. The decade began with the public enunciation of the Juche ideology as North Korea's ruling doctrine, and ended with the North Koreans' diverting their trade patterns away from the socialist camp and becoming more involved every year with the Third World and the so-called Non-aligned Movement.

In 1965 Kim Il Sung defined Juche as

> The principle of solving for oneself all problems of the revolution and construction in conformity with the actual conditions of one's country, and mainly by one's own efforts. . . . [We desire] *juche* in ideology, independence in politics, self-sustenance in the economy, and self-defense in national defense.[8]

The DPRK began to present itself as a model of socialist development in a post-colonial, Third World nation. Part and parcel of this was a strident denunciation of past Soviet practice *vis-à-vis* the DPRK. In October 1963 Kim accused the Russians of 'great-power chauvinism', dogged opposition to the DPRK's line of self-reliance, giving aid with strings attached or as 'a precondition for interference in others' internal affairs', and neglecting the class struggle, revolution, and, by implication, the Korean concern with reunification and revolution in the South. Contacts with smaller socialist countries developed on a grand scale during the early 1960s, and the DPRK moved distinctly away from the USSR and toward China.

Problems soon developed with the Chinese, however, as the Cultural Revolution unfolded and Kim found himself the target of red-guard abuse for allegedly being bourgeois and revisionist. There were even reports of shooting incidents along the Sino-Korean border in 1968. A corollary of the emphasis on self-reliance was a programme to develop an independent military posture and a series of provocations in the late 1960s. The DPRK spoke of turning the entire society into a fortress, and spent huge amounts in placing munitions factories and other installations underground. In 1968, apparently without either Soviet or Chinese backing, the North Koreans sent a guerrilla team into Seoul to assassinate the southern leader, Park Chung Hee, and seized the USS *Pueblo*, a reconnaisance ship spying off the coast near Wonsan. DPRK defence spending ran at 30 per cent of the State budget in the late 1960s. An emphasis on reunification of the two Korean states also developed as a major propaganda theme, second only to the Juche ideology.

The emergence of the Juche theme coincided with an enlargement of Kim Il Sung's leadership role, eventually to truly astonishing proportions. Koreans traditionally have venerated their leaders: Syngman Rhee was called the Messiah and the Moses of Korea, and Park Chung Hee's supporters have developed a cult of leadership around him as well. But this all pales before the role of Kim – 'Sun of the world, supreme brain of the nation', in a recent formulation.[9] Since the mid 1960s, but especially since 1972, when Kim turned sixty, (traditionally signifying the completion of a life cycle), Kim has emerged as a God-like figure who is worshipped and revered, and to whom, it would appear, all advances in North Korea are owed. One nation, one leader, one idea, runs the recent theme. Much of Korean history in this century has been rewritten such that the core of it has become Kim's exploits and those of his family; furthermore, both his younger brother, Kim Yong-ju, and his son by a second marriage, Kim Chong-il, have been touted to succeed Kim, raising the possibility of dynastic socialist rule in the DPRK.

The role of the leader, like so much else in the DPRK, is uniquely Korean (although Romania's President Ceauşescu has recently seen fit to emulate it); the basic principle behind this dogged and stubborn independence was stated unequivocally in autumn 1978: 'The Party's solution to all problems has nothing to do with foreign doctrines, whether the issues concern the establishment of a regime, principles for economic development, Socialist economic management, farming, education, or national culture.[10]

THE DPRK IN THE 1970s: A TURN OUTWARD

In the late 1960s a series of events combined to produce the most profound shift in DPRK foreign and economic policies since the end of the Korean War.[11] The North Koreans clearly indicated that Juche did not mean autarky in the world economy, and unification did not mean simply war and revolution. The change in foreign policy came about because of strategic shifts in North-east Asia. For nearly a quarter of a century the North Koreans had been looking south, focusing on improving its position relative to the ROK. Suddenly, however, as a result of the Sino-Soviet split and actual border clashes in 1969, the North Koreans had to peer back over their shoulders to the north, where two whales were doing battle along the Ussuri River. What had perhaps been dimly perceived before was rendered crystal clear: the DPRK could not count on unified backing from its two great allies, and might even be drawn into a war between them. Simultaneously, the North Koreans had to shift their vision eastward. The rapid rise of Japanese economic involvement with the ROK after the normalisation of relations in 1965, combined with the disturbing implications of the Sato–Nixon Communiqué of 1969 (which defined ROK security as essential to that of Japan), seemed to herald a significant Japanese role in ROK defences.

This new situation manifested itself in a spate of joint Sino-North Korean denunciations of Japanese militarism in 1970. Chou En-lai visited P'yongyang in April of that year and issued several denunciations of the Nixon Doctrine and its implications for Japanese rearmament. Kim Il Sung at the same time referred to Japanese militarism and US imperialism (in that order) as 'common enemies' of the Koreans and the Chinese.

Then, in the summer of 1971, a third profound shift occurred in North-east Asia: the Nixon-Kissinger opening to China. Although Sino-American detente was ideologically obnoxious to the DPRK, it had the effect of defusing overnight the pressures generated by the Sino-Soviet split and the Sato-Nixon Communiqué. Now it was *South* Korean security that seemed endangered; with the subsequent American withdrawal from Indochina, the ROK came increasingly to adopt the perspective of the last domino in East Asia.

Thus in 1971 the DPRK embarked on an energetic programme of outreach diplomacy, trying to break its isolation and, perhaps, to defuse the hostile North–South military confrontation and wean the ROK away from dependency on the United States and Japan. The American decision to withdraw 20,000 soldiers from the ROK in 1971 no doubt encouraged the DPRK. Shortly thereafter a series of remarkable policy shifts in both North and South led to joint talks between Red Cross representatives, and then to meetings between Lee Hu-rak, head of the ROK Central Intelligence Agency, and Kim Yong-ju, Kim Il-Sung's younger brother. The North–South Joint Communiqué of 4 July 1972 was the fruit of these shifts, pledging both sides to peaceful unification apart from the influence of 'outside forces', and the creation of a 'great national unity' transcending ideological differences. However, it is clear in retrospect that P'yongyang was more enthusiastic about the mini-detente of 1971–3 than was Seoul. President Park Chung Hee quickly battened down the hatches in the South, with the proclamation of martial law in the autumn of 1972 and the development of a new constitution making him, in effect, President for life. He declared that US troops did not constitute 'outside forces', although the DPRK quickly claimed that this went against their joint understanding. Finally, Park put great pressure on the United States to modernise ROK military forces, so as to negotiate from a 'position of strength'. His assassination on 26 October 1979 has left a considerable political vacuum in the Korean peninsula.

During the same period, the North Koreans invited several American journalists and scholars to visit the DPRK, joined the World Health Organisation and more than doubled the number of nations with which they had diplomatic relations. More important, DPRK defence spending dropped from 15·3 per cent of GNP in 1971 to 9·4 per cent in 1972 (defence spending has been a great burden to the North Koreans, particularly since they usually must pay for the weapons they want). Incidents along the demilitarised zone, amounting to 542 in 1968 with more than 100 deaths, dropped to one incident in 1972 with no deaths. DPRK foreign-policy statements during 1971–3 were, relatively speaking, careful, reasonable, and apparently aimed at a measured *minuet à trois* with the ROK and its US backer, leading to the eventual withdrawal of all American forces.

After 1971 the North Koreans 'discovered' not only diplomacy, but also the virtues of Western and Japanese technology and credits. In the early 1970s the DPRK imported large amounts of advanced technology, including complete plants; machinery imports jumped from $128 million in 1970 to $434 million in 1975 (one item being an entire panty-hose factory from Japan). The DPRK in its actions demonstrated that self-reliance does not mean autarky, and in its quest for foreign help it sharply diversified its trade direction away from socialist nations and developed new links with market-system economies. In its eagerness for advanced technology it ran into credit difficulties with Japan and Western Europe that continued for several years. Kim Il Sung remarked on this in an interview in August 1977 with the editor of *Le Monde*, and also made clear the DPRK's change in orientation toward the world economy. He acknowledged that North Korea had a trade deficit and credit problems, although this was 'a passing phenomenon' which he attributed to troubles in the world economy, meaning the OPEC oil embargo and price rise, which hurt certain raw materials in the world market. Kim said, 'as we live in a world society, we are subject to worldwide influence and can possibly meet with difficulties'. In an interview at about the same time with the Japanese press, he urged that Japan sell the Koreans 'anything we want'.

The 1970s thus saw the DPRK become involved in the world in unprecedented fashion, marking a clear break with its past isolation. A corollary since the Carter administration came in in 1976 has been a variety of attempts by the DPRK to open some form of relationship with the United States.

ECONOMY[12]

North Korea pursues a self-reliant economic policy, making it one of the more autarkic economies in the world, except in respect of items it cannot produce: oil, rubber, coking coal, and certain heavy industrial and machine goods. All the means of production are socialised, except for small private farm plots and 'gardens'.

Basically an agrarian country, North Korea under the communist regime has used its rich mineral resources to promote industry, especially heavy industry. By 1965 the proportions of total value of output deriving from agriculture and industry had reversed the proportions of 1946 (22 and 78 per cent). Since 1965 more emphasis has been placed on agriculture and light industry, the latter because of increasing demand for consumer goods (17 per cent of total industrial investment was targeted for light industry during the 1971–6 six-year plan). In the 1970s industrial investment stood at 49 per cent of total State investment, as compared with 57 per cent during the 1960s.

The Korean War devastated much of the North Korean economy, but growth since the postwar reconstruction has been very rapid. A generally accepted figure puts annual industrial growth in the period 1956–63 at about 25 per cent. The rate slowed in the late 1960s to around 14 per cent; in 1975 the North Koreans officially stated that the average annual rate for 1970–5 was 18·4 per cent, with an increase of 25 per cent in the last year. The official targets for the six-year plan (1971–6) were not met on time; it was only in 1978 that the DPRK embarked on another, extended (seven-year) plan. A State Planning Committee co-ordinates the economy, with corresponding committees at city, county and province levels. Local and regional planning committees have been given greater latitude in planning since 1964.

INDUSTRY

Under Japanese rule, northern Korea was designed mainly as a supplier of raw materials, while manufacturing and processing branches were neglected. In 1944, for example, metal-fabricating industries in northern Korea accounted for only 1·6 per cent of the total value of industrial output, textile industries for 6 per cent and food processing for 7·8 per cent. The Communist regime has emphasised the development of manufacturing industries, and by 1963 the foregoing three industries accounted for 33, 18·6 per cent and 13·7 per cent of industrial output, respectively. At the same time, mining and metallurgy have grown quantitatively but not in terms of percentage of total output (mining down from 15·7 per cent in 1944 to 4 per cent in 1960, and metallurgy from 13·3 per cent in 1944 to 6·8 per cent in 1960). Instead, more sophisticated and consumer-oriented manufacturing industries have accounted for gradually increasing portions of industrial output. Private enterprise in industry declined from 27·6 per cent of total output in 1946 to only 2 per cent in 1956, and the private sector was said to have disappeared by 1959. About 90 per cent of all industry is State-owned and 10 per cent is owned by co-operatives.

North Korea's iron and steel industry produced 3,400,000 tons of pig and granulated iron and 5,850,000 tons of steel (including rolled steel) in 1975, representing increases over the 1970 figures of 70 per cent and 50 per cent, respectively. Major iron and steel works are located at Ch'ŏngjin, Kimch'aek, Kangso and Kangsŏn. New continuous sintering furnaces and coke batteries have recently been added to the Kimch'aek works, while a new steel shop has been added to the Kangsŏn works. The manufacturing industry produced highly sophisticated machinery in 1974, including 50,000-kilowatt generators, 300-horse power bulldozers, 3500-horse power high-speed engines, and 2500-horse power diesel locomotives. Other plants produce aluminium, cement (7·2 million tons in 1974), magnesite, graphite, lead, zinc, machine tools, tractors and lorries. The chemical industry produced 3 million tons of chemical fertiliser in 1974, doubling the 1970 figure, as well as a synthetic fibre, Vinalon, widely used in clothing. The petrochemical industry is centred in the Hungnam area.

AGRICULTURE

The North Koreans stated that total grain production in 1974 reached 7 million tons, thus fulfilling the goals of the six-year plan two years ahead of schedule. Per hectare yields of rice reached a high of 5·9 tons, with a high in maize production of five tons. Total rice yield was put at 3·5 million metric tons, compared with 2·8 in 1972. Kim Il Sung claimed in 1975 that North Korea had achieved 'the world's highest standard in per-unit-area yields of rice'. Gains have been achieved through the use of 'miracle' rice strains, intensive application of fertiliser, and mechanisation. Apparently some four tractors are available for every 100 hectares of arable land, a 350 per cent increase over 1970. With some 30,000 rice-transplanting machines, the claim is that 92 per cent of the rice-transplanting process is now mechanised.

Double-cropping of grains other than rice has been maximised through the use of cold-bed seeding and new seed varieties, so that perhaps half of total cultivated land is now double-cropped. Important crops besides rice include millet, maize, barley, wheat, soyabeans, potatoes, cotton and tobacco.

North Korea seems to have become self-sufficient in grain production. Although it imports certain grain products, it also exports surpluses.

North Korea's farms were collectivised after the Korean War. The movement began late in 1953, and by the end of the following year 32 per cent of the peasants had become members of over 10,000 co-operatives or collectives; 49 per cent at the end of 1955; 81 per cent at the end of 1956; and 95·6 per cent in 16,000 co-operatives at the end of 1957. The process was completed by August 1958, when all of North Korea's 1,055,000 farm families had become members of co-operatives. In order to establish larger and more efficient operating units, the co-operatives were merged in the autumn of 1958 into approximately 3800 units with an average of 300 families each, working 1000 acres each. Produce is delivered to the government, which controls distribution through State stores. Most peasants retain small private plots and can sell produce from them to the State or in regularly scheduled 'peasant markets'.

FOREIGN TRADE

The total value of North Korea's foreign trade in 1975 was $1200 million; the value of exports, $490 million, was nearly twice that of the 1966 level. Foreign trade has diversified substantially in recent years and is no longer so dependent on trade with the communist bloc. Trade with Japan tripled between 1968 to 1973. About 30 per cent of North Korea's exports in 1973 went to non-communist countries, with more than half of it going to Japan. Imports from non-communist countries accounted for about 35 per cent of the total. The Soviet Union remains North Korea's main trading partner, accounting for about 35 per cent of its total trade; China accounted for about 19 per cent. This is a substantial change from 1962, when the Soviet Union accounted for 60 per cent and China for 3 per cent of North Korea's total trade. North Korea has rapidly increased trade with Western European countries in recent years, although defaults on payments hurt its credit rating in 1974.

The commodity structure of North Korea's foreign trade has shifted radically since the immediate post-Korean War era. Mineral exports have given way to metals (the former declined from 82 per cent of trade in 1953 to 7 per cent in 1969), while fuel imports have substantially replaced machinery and equipment as major import items. In 1973 principal exports included rice, fish, iron ore, pig iron, rolled steel, cement, and machinery of various types. Imports included petroleum, coking coal, rubber, wheat, cotton, base metals and manufactures, machinery and transportation equipment.

GOVERNMENT

In the DPRK, State power is under the direction of the communist party, the KWP. The national legislature and constitutionally the highest organ of State power is the unicameral Supreme People's Assembly, elected on the basis of one deputy for every 50,000 persons. The first assembly, elected in August 1948 for a three-year term, actually lasted until 1956, because the Korean War prevented new elections. The second assembly, elected in August 1957 for a term extended to four years by a constitutional amendment, had a membership of 215 deputies. Elections for the third Supreme People's Assembly were held in October 1962, and the new assembly, comprising 383 deputies, held its first session that same month.

The third session of the fifth assembly met in March 1974, with 457 delegates, chosen on the basis of one deputy for every 30,000 people. It decided on a complete abolition of taxation for citizens of the DPRK, which its press hailed as a first for the world. The fourth session, in November 1974, claimed that a record crop of 7 million tons of grain had been reaped during the year.

To handle its functions between regular sessions, the Supreme People's Assembly elects a Presidium consisting of a President (who is the titular head of State), several vice-presidents, a General Secretary, and a number of regular members.

The Supreme People's Assembly also names a Cabinet, consisting of a Premier, several vice-premiers, ministers, and heads of other major government agencies. The executive establishment in 1968 consisted of thirty ministries, five commissions and one committee.

Suffrage extends to all men and women eighteen years of age or older. Elections are on a single slate of communist-approved candidates, on a 'yes' or 'no' basis. In elections it is usually asserted that nearly all those eligible voted, and that their votes were unanimous in favour of the candidates.

North Korea has a relatively unique system of people's assemblies and people's committees at all levels of administration. Members of people's assemblies are elected for four-year terms at the provincial level, two-year terms at county, township and village levels. They are supposed to supervise public, economic, and cultural activities; they meet every three or six months, depending on the administrative level; and they elect and recall people's committees, which are the permanent executive and administrative organs of the State at the local level.

POLITICAL PARTIES

The Korean Workers' (Communist) Party, the ruling party of North Korea, was formed on 10 October 1946 through a merger of the Communist Party and the New Democratic Party. The Party in 1949 further merged with its southern counterpart. Party membership in 1977 was estimated to have risen to about 2·5 million (see Table 16.1). The principal Party organ is the National Party Congress (see Table 16.2 for details of make-up), which met for the fifth time in 1970. The Congress adopts the Party programme and approves the political line set by its Central Committee. To guide the Party between sessions of the National Party Congress, the Congress elects a Central Committee and a Central Auditing Commission, which looks after the Party's financial affairs.

TABLE 16.1 Membership of the KWP

Year	Membership	% of population	Make-up (%)
1946	366,000	4	Workers 23 Peasants 20 Samuwon[a] 48 Others 9
1948	750,000	8	Workers 22 Peasants 26 Samuwon 46 Others 6
1952	1 million[b]	10	Peasants 60 Others n.a.
1956	1,164,945	10	Workers 23 Peasants 61 Samuwon 13 Others 3
1961	1,311,563	12	Workers 57 Peasants 16 Samuwon 27 Others 1
1965	1,600,000[b]	12	n.a.
1975	2 million[b]	12	n.a.

[a] A category including bureaucrats, functionaries, clerks, intellectuals and, in the 1940s, small merchants.
[b] Estimates – no official figures.

The Central Committee (117 regular and fifty-five alternate members) elects a Political Committee (eleven regulars and nine alternates), which itself has a Standing Committee (six members in 1966, later reduced to the current four). (For multiple affiliations of members of the Political Committee see Table 16.3.) North Korea maintains a 'united front' policy with ostensibly non-communist political parties: the Korean Democratic Party, and the Chŏngu or 'Friends' Party for adherents of the Ch'ŏndogyo faith.

BIOGRAPHY

Kim Il Sung is the pre-eminent figure in the DPRK, and, Tito apart, is the world's most senior socialist leader in longevity of tenure, having led

TABLE 16.2 Elections to KWP congresses

Year	No. of delegates	Make-up (%)
1948 (2nd Congress)	1008	Workers 46 Peasants 27 Samuwon[a] 23 Others 4
1956 (3rd Congress)	918	Workers 48 Peasants 21 Samuwon 27 Others 4
1961 (4th Congress)	1660	Workers 57 Peasants 27 Samuwon 12 Others 4
1970 (5th Congress)	1871	n.a.

[a] A category including bureaucrats, functionaries, clerks, intellectuals and, in the 1940s, small merchants.

Note. In the DPRK, election turnouts and votes for KWP candidates are always put at 98–100 per cent of the total eligible population. Data on the make-up of the Fifth Congress (1946) and the Fifth Congress (1970 – the last one) are unavailable.

North Korea since 1946 and having been Premier of the DPRK since its establishment in 1948. Kim was born in a small town near P'yongyang on 12 April 1915, the eldest son of a peasant named Kim Hyŏng-jik. Kim's given name was Sŏng-ju, which he changed to Il Sung in the 1930s. He went with his family to Manchuria in his teens and attended primary and middle school there; his formal education probably ended at about the tenth grade. He was active in the communist youth in the late 1920s, and in 1932 he began organised guerrilla activity against the Japanese in the Sino-Korean border regions. At this time some 160,000 Korean and Chinese guerrillas, partisans and secret-society stalwarts were fighting the Japanese establishment of the puppet state of Manchukuo; Kim was a minor figure in this effort until the late 1930s, when he began to appear regularly in Japanese counter-insurgency reports. By that time he had under his personal command a force of about 400 guerrillas; in 1939 he and a Chinese, Yang Ching-yu, were the main targets of Japanese suppression campaigns in the Sino-Korean border region.

As the Japanese war effort shifted southward and as the Americans

TABLE 16.3 Multiple affiliations of the members of the Political Committee of the KWP, 1976

Members of Political Committee	Member of DPRK Central People's Committee	Other positions
Kim Il Sung	General Secretary	Commander, People's Armed Forces
Kim Il	yes	Vice-President
Pak Song-ch'ol	yes	Vice-President
Ch'oe Hyon	yes	Vice-Chairman, National Defence Commission
Kim Yong-ju	no	
O Chin-u	no	Vice-Chairman, National Defence Commission; Minister of Defence
Kim Tong-gyu[a]	no	
So Ch'ol	yes	Director, Political Bureau of People's Army
Kim Chung-rin[a]	no	
Han Ik-su[a]	no	
Yang Hyong-sop	no	Party functionary (ideology, education)
Yi Kun-mo	no	Industrial expert
Yon Hyong-muk	no	Party functionary
Yi Yong-mu[a]	no	Army General
Ch'oe Yong-gon	yes	(Died 1976)

[a] Members demoted since 1976.

Note. The DPRK Central People's Committee is elected by the Supreme People's Assembly and exercises the following chief functions: directs the work of the government and its agencies; implements the Constitution; establishes and abolishes ministries; appoints and recalls ambassadors and defence personnel; confers titles and decorations; grants general amnesties and declares a state of war. It is assisted by a number of commissions, dealing with internal policy, national defence foreign policy, and other matters.

Sources: Chong-sik Lee, *Korean Workers' Party* (1978) pp. 121–2; *Vantage Point* (Seoul: Naewoe Press) I, no. 1 (May 1978) 22–4, 28–9.

entered the war in the Pacific, Kim and his allies retreated to northernmost Manchuria; according to the best evidence (and there is not much on this dark period in his past), Kim spent the period 1942–5 near Khabarovsk in the USSR, just across the Manchurian border, undergoing training and preparing for coming land campaigns against the Japanese. There are suggestions that he may have become an officer in the Soviet Army, but this has never been proved.

It does not appear that Kim and his allies were part of the Soviet occupation forces in northern Korea after Japan's capitulation on 15 August 1945. Kim's first recorded appearance back in Korea was in early October 1945. By late December he had come to head the northern branch of the Korean Communist Party, and by February 1946 he was the head of the Interim People's Committee, the first central Korean administrative body to appear. It is from this date that we can mark his ascendancy, although in the period 1946–50 he was more first among equals in a coalition leadership than the pre-eminent and dominating figure that he became after the end of the Korean War. The literature differs on Kim's role up to 1950, some viewing him as little more than a Soviet puppet and others arguing that he had a legitimacy of his own as a resistance leader. Kim became Premier of the DPRK at its founding on 9 September 1948, and, after the merger of the southern and northern parties in 1949, he was concurrently Chairman of the Korean Worker's Party. He has maintained the dual position of Party and State head ever since.

In the early and mid 1950s, Kim and his allies, most of them partisans with Kim in the 1930s, progressively purged rival leaders and their followers. At the same time Kim emerged as a figure of great popular adulation; although the cult of Kim waxed and waned during the 1950s and 1960s, it was always there. Since Kim has, by Korean counting, become an elder statesman (that is, past sixty years of age), the degree of adulation has known no bounds.

Little is known about Kim's personal life. His younger brother, Kim Yong-ju, has been an important figure in the regime, and for a time was thought to be a possible successor to Kim Il Sung. The younger brother suffers from an unknown ailment, however, and so Kim's own son, Kim Chong-il, may now be the designated successor. This suggestion of dynastic socialist leadership has provoked much opposition from other elements in the regime; in 1976–7 there was apparently a political struggle over this question, such that in 1978 there was little talk about Kim Chong-il. Kim's first wife died; his second wife, Kim Song-ae, is a member of the Central Committee.

Since the 1972 constitution was implemented, Kim has held the title of President rather than Premier, but he continues to head the government and chair the Central People's Committee, the highest State organ. Concurrently he is Secretary-general of the KWP and chairs the Central Committee and the Political Committee (the equivalent of a political bureau).

Other prominent Koreans in the DPRK stand so much in the shadow of Kim Il Sung that it would be difficult to choose from among them any others for biographical treatment. Those prominent include Kim's brother, Kim Yong-ju; his son, Kim Chong-il; and several close allies from the partisan struggle in Manchuria: Kim Il (Vice President), Pak Song-Ch'ol (Vice President), O Chin-u (Minister of the People's Armed Forces), and Ch'oe Hyon (fourth-ranking member of the Political Committee). The Foreign Minister, Ho Dam, is married to one of Kim Il Sung's cousins.

BASIC FACTS ABOUT THE DEMOCRATIC PEOPLE'S REPUBLIC OF KOREA

Official name: Democratic People's Republic of Korea (Chosŏn min-jujuŭi inmin konghwaguk).
Area: 121,600 sq. km. (46,768 sq. miles).
Population (mid 1978): 17,808,000. (Median age of population 18·6 years; life expectancy 68 years.)
Population density: 146·6 per sq. km.
Membership of the KWP (Chosŏn nodong-dang) (1978 est.): 2·5 million, roughly 14 per cent of population.
Administrative division: nine provinces, three 'special cities', 163 counties.
Major towns: P'yŏngyang (the capital) pop. 1,800,000; Hamhŭng, pop. 750,000; Ch'ŏngjin, pop. 300,000; Kaesŏng, pop. 240,000.
Ethnic nationalities: Koreans make up the entire population except for perhaps 50,000 Chinese.
National income (1976): per capita GNP estimate, $600; industry 78 per cent of GNP; agriculture 22 per cent of GNP.
Natural resources: gold, tungsten, zinc, iron, coal, nickel, timber.
Foreign Trade (1976): exports, $400 million; imports, $575 million; total, $975 million. Major exports: iron, steel, and non-ferrous metals manufactures; machinery and equipment; foodstuffs, principally grain; clothing; raw materials. Major imports: industrial machinery, transport equipment, petroleum and coking coal, grain, textile fibres and edible oils.
Main trading partners: Soviet Union, China, Japan.
Rail network: 11,300 km., of which about 75 per cent electrified.
Road network: 5600 km.
Education: in the 1970s there were 140 colleges and universities, 4980 secondary schools, and 4470 elementary schools; education is compulsory up to and including the twelfth grade, and some 100,000

students attend colleges and universities, of which the principal one is Kim Il Sung University in P'yongyang.

Foreign relations: about 90 nations recognise the DPRK; since 1972 the DPRK has maintained an observer group at the UN and belongs to several UN agencies.

NOTES

1. The following section on the Korean communist movement is drawn from Dae-sook Suh, *The Korean Communist Movement 1918–1948* (1967); and from R. A. Scalapino and Chong-sik Lee, *Communism in Korea*, vol. I (1973) pp. 3–232.
2. This section is drawn from B. Cumings, *The Origins of the Korean War* (forthcoming) vol. I, ch. 11.
3. See B. Cumings, 'American Policy and Korean Liberation', in F. Baldwin (ed.), *Without Parallel: The American-Korean Relationship Since 1945* (1974) pp. 39–108.
4. Koon Woo Nam, *North Korean Communist Leadership*, pp. 71–100.
5. G. Paige, 'North Korea and the Emulation of Russian and Chinese Behaviour', in A. D. Barnett (ed.), *Communist Strategies in Asia* (1964).
6. Ibid.
7. The following section is drawn from B. Cumings, 'Kim's Korean Communism', *Problems of Communism*, Mar–Apr 1974, pp. 27–41.
8. In ibid., p. 34.
9. Korean Central News Agency, *Korean Daily News*, 23 Nov 1978.
10. *Vantage Point* (Seoul: Noewoe Press) I, no. 7 (Nov 1978) 28.
11. The following is drawn from B. Cumings, 'North Korea and American Policy', testimony before Subcommittee on Future Foreign Policy of the US House International Relations Committee, 8 Mar 1976.
12. The following is drawn from B. Cumings, 'Democratic People's Republic of Korea', in *Worldmark Encyclopaedia of Nations* (New York: Wiley, 1976) pp. 184–8; and from Central Intelligence Agency, *Korea: The Economic Race between the North and South* (1978).

BIBLIOGRAPHY

Brun, Ellen and Hersh, Jacques, *Socialist Korea: A Case Study in the Strategy of Economic Development* (New York: Monthly Review Press, 1976).
Byong Sik Kim, *Modern Korea: The Socialist North, Revolutionary Perspectives in the South* (New York: International Publishers, 1970).
Byung Chul Koh, *The Foreign Policy of North Korea* (New York: Praeger, 1969).
Central Intelligence Agency, *Korea: The Economic Race between North and*

South (Washington: National Foreign Assessment Center, 1978).

Chong-sik Lee, *Korean Worker's Party: A Short History* (Stanford, Calif.: Hoover Institution, 1978).

Choson chungang nyongam (Official Yearbook of Korea) (P'yongyang: Korea News Service, intermittent).

Chung, Joseph S., *The North Korean Economy* (Stanford, Calif.: Hoover Institution, 1973).

Cumings, Bruce, 'American Policy and Korean Liberation', in Frank Baldwin (ed.), *Without Parallel: The American-Korean Relationship since 1945* (New York: Pantheon, 1974) pp. 39–108.

——, 'Kim's Korean Communism', *Problems of Communism*, Mar–Apr 1974, pp. 27–41.

——, 'Democratic People's Republic of Korea', in *Worldmark Encyclopaedia of Nations* (New York: Wiley, 1976) pp. 184–8.

——, *The Origins of the Korean War* (forthcoming).

Dae-sook Suh, *The Korean Communist Movement 1918–1948* (Princeton, N.J.: Princeton University Press, 1967).

Kim, Ilpyong J., *Communist Politics in North Korea* (New York: Praeger, 1975).

Kim Il Sung, *Selected Works*, 4 vols (P'yongyang: Foreign Languages Publishing House, 1972).

Koon Woo Nam, *The North Korean Communist Leadership, 1945–1965* (University, Ala.: University of Alabama Press, 1974).

Korean Central News agency, *Korean Daily News* (Tokyo: Korea News Service).

Paige, Glenn D., 'North Korea and the Emulation of Russian and Chinese Behaviour', in A. Doak Barnett (ed.), *Communist Strategies in Asia* (New York: Praeger, 1964).

——, *The Korean People's Democratic Republic* (Stanford, Calif.: Stanford University Press, 1966).

Pukhan Ch'onggam 1945–1968 (General Survey of North Korea) (Seoul: Kongsan munje yonguso, 1968).

Rudolph, Philip, *North Korea's Political and Economic Structure* (New York: Institute of Pacific Relations, 1959).

Scalapino, Robert A. (ed.), *North Korea Today* (New York: Praeger, 1963).

Scalapino, Robert A. and Chong-sik Lee, *Communism in Korea*, 2 vols (Berkeley, Calif.: University of California Press, 1973).

17 Lao People's Democratic Republic

LAURA J. SUMMERS

Throughout history, Lao politics have been dominated by the country's natural and social ecology. Situated in the hinterlands of China and Vietnam, the mountainous regions, plateaux and valley passages of Laos formed a continental divide between the traditional Indianised and Sinicised sections of the South-east Asian region.[1] The divide was by no means neat, especially as populations expanded. Some of the many dozen national groups in Laos, notably those in the highlands, are closely related to the national minorities in the northern regions of Vietnam, while many of the lowland and upland groups belong to or are related to ethnic nationalities in Thailand.[2] The frontiers of the modern state were finally fixed in the nineteenth century by the French and British colonialists who decided to use the Lao corridor as a buffer area separating their spheres of influence; the French shifted and divided some of the local civilisations in the process.[3] Between this ethnic division and diversity and the rugged terrain, a unitary national consciousness and the emergence of a modern society and economy in Laos remain visions attaching to the future rather than realities of contemporary political life. Even an official communist history depicts the country from an external perspective as an 'enclave in the Indochinese peninsula'.[4] It is possible to see in such remarks the joining of the peripheral status of Laos in imperial history with its ancilliary role in what Lao Marxists still defend as a united world socialist revolution.

ORIGINS OF LAO COMMUNISM, 1930–55

Communism and Marxist ideas were introduced into Laos in the 1930s by the Vietnamese and upon instruction from the Comintern. As in

468

CHINA

Phong Saly

PHONG SALY

BURMA

Nam Tha

LUANG
NAM THA   M.Sai

LUANG
PRABANG

HOUA PHAN

Sam Neua

OUDOMSAY

Hanoi

Hai Phong

SAYA BURY   Luang Prabang

XIENG KHOUANG

Saya Bury

M.Phan

SOCIALIST REPUBLIC OF SOUTH VIETNAM

GULF OF
TONKIN

VIENTIANE

Vientiane

Vinh

KHAMMOUANE

Thakheck

Mekong River

SAVANNAKHET

Savannakhet

Hué

THAILAND

Saravane

SARAVANE

Paksé

Champassac

CHAMPASSAC

ATTAPEU

Attapeu

N

DEMOCRATIC KAMPUCHEA

0   200 km.

Laos: provincial boundaries

Kampuchea (see above, Chapter 15), French colonialism did not foster the necessary social and economic conditions allowing for indigenous development and modernisation, especially in the realms of economics and administration. Moreover, and in contrast to the case in Kampuchea, pre-colonial political traditions in Laos were both weak and diverse. If the lowland Thai–Lao peoples defended their traditional monarchal order, it was significant that this section of the Lao peoples was internally divided by loyalty to competing, regionally based dynasties and generally opposed by upland and highland peoples with separate political traditions. Thus, Marxism did not immediately confront a strong indigenous political consensus, as was the case in Kampuchea, and its Vietnamese emissaries were less distinctly viewed as intruders in the ethnically heterogenous society of traditional and colonial Laos. As in Kampuchea, the Vietnamese initially organised their own nationals, most of whom were employed in French-sponsored service or extractive industries.[5]

Lao nationals and individuals of mixed Lao–Vietnamese ancestry became involved in the Indochinese Communist Party (ICP) in the early 1940s. In the case of Kaysone Phomvihane (who is half Vietnamese) and Nouhak Phoumsavanh (who married a Vietnamese), both leading members of several successive Lao communist organisations, it was the elimination of the language barrier and personal contact with leaders of the Vietnamese revolution in Vietnam during the Second World War which led them to Marxist-Leninist commitments.[6] In the colonial crisis, immediately following the war, the Viet Minh organisation and the ICP leadership in their turn brought together several promising young Lao nationalists, including Prince Souphanouvong, in support of movements within Laos for independence from France in an effort to galvanise a genuine Lao resistance to imperialism which would help the Viet Minh defend its northern frontiers from French (and later American) invasions. The Viet Minh were inadvertently aided in their recruitment efforts by French military preparations and exactions in the late 1940s. These took the form of forced-draft conscription into the French expeditionary corps and into labour teams forced to build roads, bridges, air strips and other military installations.[7]

Initial military resistance to the reintroduction of French power in Laos failed. A *Lao Itsala* (Lao Independence) government unilaterally declared the independence of the country on 12 October 1945 in the wake of the Japanese surrender in Asia. Prince Souphanouvong and other Laos in Vietnam immediately returned to the country to assist the government in the organisation of a Lao Itsala army.[8] The French response was rapid and decisive, however: Lao Itsala partisans and their government were evicted from the administrative capital at Vientiane in April 1946. This defeat soon divided the movement into liberal and radical components.

Most of the Lao Itsala government went into exile in Bangkok, where the government of Dr Pridi was actively supporting the efforts of anti-colonial movements in the region, including the Viet Minh. Prince Souphanouvong, Foreign Minister in the exiled independence government, returned to Hanoi after making contact with the Viet Minh's delegate in Bangkok. By the end of the year, he was leading guerrilla raids inside Laos with the support of Viet Minh military advisers. The ICP simultaneously established a Committee of Lao Resistance in the East, with which Kaysone and Nouhak, already members of the Party, were associated. The emergence of a Vietnamese-supported eastern resistance comprised of independent tribal units and ICP-promoted Itsala guerrilla groups separate from the Bangkok-supplied western resistance based in different ethnic communities reinforced emerging liberal-radical tendencies within the Itsala movement.[9] The reinstated pro-French royal government in Vientiane and the French colonialists exploited the situation by gradually co-opting the Bangkok branch into colonial ranks with guarantees of a more liberal constitution within the French union. The prospect of a compromise with the French was made more attractive to the aristocratic and lowland Lao directed Itsala movement as Viet Minh influence grew among the upland and highland Lao tribes, who had always resisted lowland Lao rule as well as French colonialism.[10] Thus, both the French and the Vietnamese successfully exploited existing class and ethnic divisions within the protectorate. When the French union agreement was signed in 1949, Prince Souphanouvong broke with his erstwhile Itsala allies and became more deeply involved in the Viet Minh strategy.

From 1950 until 1954, the Lao resistance confronted its national problem of integration. At a 'Lao National' Assembly in 1950, a new resistance government led by Souphanouvong was created, along with the *Neo Lao Itsala* (Lao Independence Front).[11] Documents distributed at a meeting carried the imprint 'Pathet Lao' (Lao Nation). The Lao nation represented by the resistance government and living within the country comprised *Lao Loum, Lao Theung* and *Lao Soung* peoples, respectively Laos of the generic lowland, upland and highland types – which is to say, all equally Lao, as well as Thai, Alak, Meo, as the accident of birth determined. The implicit attribution of equality of status to the upland and highland peoples reversed centuries of political and cultural discrimination. Explicit guarantees of this were present in the appointment of two prominent tribal leaders, Kommadam and Faydang, to the resistance government.

By 1954, the Pathet Lao movement and government had a clear territorial base and administrative power in North-east Laos, but neither the government nor its armed forces were allowed direct participation in the Geneva Conference decolonisation armistice and settlement. In partial recognition of their military force, the Pathet Lao were allowed to regroup their forces in areas of Phong Saly and Sam Neua, pending more detailed, national negotiations for reunification of the country and its contending governments.[12]

THE NEO LAO HAKSAT AND THE PEOPLE'S PARTY, 1955–72

After the Geneva Conference, Laos became the front line in the cold war between the Americans in southern Vietnam and the Vietnamese in the Democratic Republic of Vietnam. The Americans opposed many of the compromises reached at the Conference and rushed to create the Southeast Asia Treaty Organisation to compensate for what was deemed the 'soft' line taken by the French and the British in the armistice and political talks and to extend military 'protection' to the countries of what had been French Indochina. Translated into concrete policies in Laos, the American view required a 'hard' stand against coalition government in Vientiane, opposition to political negotiations between the Royal Lao Government (RLG) and the Pathet Lao, and subversion of any neutral (i.e. anti-Western) political momentum that might develop there.[13] Thus, the United States openly supported royalists and conservative families in business and military circles who sought to obstruct the pledges made to the Neo Lao Istala resistance at Geneva. American military and economic aid poured into Vientiane in 1955 and the following years to further this purpose. The Lao military aid programme was America's most lavish in the world at the time, on a per capita basis.[14]

American aid served primarily to deepen feudal factionalism and inter-family competition for material goods within the RLG elite and to undermine its political cohesiveness.[15] It also lent support to Pathet Lao claims that American imperialism had replaced French colonialism. American enlargement of the military and political stakes in Laos also ensured continuing and determined North Vietnamese involvement in the frontier regions of the country in defence of their own aspirations for a united Vietnam, on the one hand, and in fraternal support of the Neo Lao Itsala, on the other. The United States' obstruction of a settlement in Vientiane and provocative military policies may have made a critical difference in the evolution of the Lao communist movement, for under sustained foreign pressure it was forced to mature, while its principal foreign ally was obliged to continue its tutelage.[16] For their part, the Vietnamese refused to admit publicly the presence of their troops and supply lines in Lao territory or their support of the Lao revolutionary movement. Their forces were engaged in a combined military and political struggle for the reunification of their own country, which necessarily involved aiding the Pathet Lao, who protected their northern frontier and who represented political leverage in Vientiane. In both Laos and Vietnam, the Americans were in principle, and later in fact, the only foreign invaders in the Vietnamese view. They were made to be seen as invaders as well. The Vietnamese assisted their allies with a view to making them an effective independent revolutionary force, wearing their uniforms and using the national language; the Americans imposed their views, equipment and language on the capital city and its army.[17]

The new political situation created by the Americans after Geneva posed several challenges to the Neo Lao Itsala. An American-sponsored government immediately ordered RLG troops to attack resistance forces regrouped in Phong Saly and Sam Neua. The same government organised elections for a National Assembly which excluded Neo Lao Itsala candidates and regions. Souphanouvong pressed, nevertheless, for the negotiations outlined by the Geneva settlement, which both embodied and protected, however vaguely, the national political rights of his movement. Upon Vietnamese urging, the Lao communists incorporated their cell groups and regionally based proto-party organisations into a communist Lao People's Party in March 1955, in preparation for the long political struggle.[18] The Neo Lao Itsala was then replaced by the *Neo Lao Haksat* (NLH – Lao Patriotic Front) in January 1956. The Patriotic Front formula signalled the movement's continuing radical nationalist stand in the new American-dominated situation in Vientiane. If full independence from colonial rule had been obtained in theory, thus rendering the Independence Front obsolete, genuine national reconciliation and self-determination were yet to be achieved.[19]

In spite of sustained American and right-wing Lao efforts to subvert the agreement, an armistice between the RLG and the Pathet Lao was signed in October 1956, more than two years after the Geneva Conference. It was followed in December by agreements on the peaceful reintegration of the revolutionary resistance veterans into the national community and the national armed forces. A coalition government was established almost a year later, in November 1957, followed by partial elections to the National Assembly in May 1958, to supplement those held in 1955. The NLH captured nine of the twenty-one contested seats, with four other seats going to the Committee for Peace and Neutrality, a party closely associated with the NLH.[20] The Lao revolutionaries viewed the signing of the Vientiane agreements in 1957, achieved after the RLG military strategy had been overturned, and their success in the 1958 by-elections as confirmation of their support and appeal. National legal status for the NLH represented the formal recognition denied to the movement at the Geneva Conference. It was also the key to extending NLH activities beyond the temporary regroupment zones to other ethnic, occupational and class groups.[21]

NLH success provoked from the United States an immediate reaction consistent with its concurrent support of the Diem regime's repression of Viet Minh partisans in South Vietnam. Within two months of the elections, the RLG-NLH coalition was overturned in a cabinet reshuffle forced by an American threat to cut off aid to the country.[22] As more American military advisers arrived, the RLG banned 'Lao Haksat', the NLH newspaper (in March 1959), encircled Pathet Lao battalions then awaiting reintegration into the national armed forces under the terms of the 1957 agreements (in May) and imprisoned NLH members of the National Assembly (in July). One of the Pathet Lao battalions escaped and civil war resumed.

In a rapid sequence of events, a CIA-backed military coup group took power in Vientiane, the NLH deputies and leaders escaped from prison, and a neutralist-inspired, military mutiny took power from the CIA-backed regime. The neutralists established diplomatic relations with China and the USSR, to offset and to neutralise the dependence of the country on the 'free' world. NLH armed forces supported the neutralist coup group, which in turn acknowledged their legal rights under the Vientiane agreements. Meanwhile, the Soviets and Chinese, responding to urgent requests, sent military aid to the neutralist government to support it and the NLH in the continuing civil war. Thus, and even though a CIA-backed force recaptured the administrative capital of Vientiane in December 1960, pro-American forces were completely routed by neutralist, Pathet Lao and Vietnamese forces by mid 1961. Confronted with the possibility of a 'communist' victory instead of a coalition government, with the only possible alternative being direct military intervention by US armed forces, which carried the risk of

Chinese intervention, President Kennedy agreed to return to Geneva. An agreement for a tripartite neutralist-RLG-NLH coalition government was signed in 1961 followed by an international agreement on the neutrality of Laos in 1962. The Americans appeared finally to agree to an open political struggle in Laos, but only after their military policies had proved disastrous.[23]

Appearances were deceiving. Within months the American CIA began a clandestine war in Laos, employing Meo tribesmen to harass NLH and neutralist forces behind the military lines fixed at Geneva. As before, American military policy upset the fragile political balance in Vientiane. Fighting broke out between 'neutralist' armed forces supporting the coalition government's tacit toleration of American activity and 'dissident' or 'patriotic' neutralist forces opposing it. The patriotic dissidents were led by Colonel Deuane. The split in neutralist ranks resulted in the assassination of several prominent neutralist politicians and military leaders in Vientiane. Anticipating another right-wing takeover, Prince Souphanouvong and Phoumi Vongvichit, both ministers in the coalition cabinet, and other NLH officials fled in April 1963, thus suspending the tripartite coalition.[24]

The Americans promoted the 'secret' war in Laos until 1972, maintaining the façade of 'neutralist' government in Vientiane. Systematic aerial bombardment of neutralist- and NLH-occupied areas began in 1964. By 1965, more than 200 airfields had been constructed, to facilitate the supply of CIA-funded mercenary ground operations. By 1971, approximately one-quarter to one-third of the entire Lao population were refugees, their villages and farmlands razed or destroyed by the combined effects of bombing and artillery.[25]

The NLH response to the war was to accelerate both military and political recruitment. In these efforts, it had strong Vietnamese support.[26] Pathet Lao force levels expanded in a sustained and regular manner. At the time of the first neutralist coup, the Pathet Lao forces numbered about 9000. Joined by the neutralists after the CIA countercoup, their forces totalled 16,000 by May 1961, the moment of ceasefire preceding the second set of Geneva agreements. Following the collapse of the 1962 accords, the revolutionary forces numbered 20,000 and grew by several thousands each year until 1970, when approximately 48,000 men and women were engaged in its diverse units. 13,000 were lost by 1972, a measure of the dramatic increase in US bombing in Laos after the cessation of bombing in North Vietnam in 1969.[27]

Throughout the decade, the NLH concentrated on solidifying its political alliance with the Deuanist and other patriotic neutralists, always defending the Geneva agreements of 1962 as the constitutional basis for a settlement of the civil–American war. In 1970, after the Pathet Lao had retaken the strategically critical Plain of Jars in fierce fighting, a personal emissary of Prince Souphanouvong to the neutralist government in Vientiane led by his half-brother Souvanna Phouma reported that the NLH would enter into negotiations if US bombing were halted in northern Laos, the area removed from the Vietnamese supply routes known as the Ho Chi Minh trail. Souvanna Phouma had little leverage in the matter or with the Americans, who appeared to be holding Laos to ransom in negotiations with the Vietnamese in Paris.[28] Negotiations among Lao parties to their civil war commenced only in late 1972, when the United States and the Vietnamese were in the process of concluding their Paris talks on 'ending the war and restoring peace' in Vietnam.

The war in Laos ended on 21 February 1973, with all parties broadly agreeing to return to the tripartite coalition framework of 1962, although it was clear that the balance of political power among the various components had shifted in ten years.[29] The removal of US air power and mercenary forces exposed the narrow political base of the right-wing oligarchs and of the neutralists allied with the RLG. Moreover, Souphanouvong and other NLH leaders took up posts in Vientiane with a vigour, discipline and sense of purpose which elicited the national pride and respect of the city's population. Vientiane's history of factionalism and its years of humiliating fiscal, administrative and political subordination to the Americans contrasted sharply with the cohesiveness, continuity and competence of the Lao revolutionary leadership. And the contrast had significant political consequences.

The focus of the transition from post-war coalition government to the Democratic Republic established in 1975 was the National Political Consultative Council (NPCC), rather than the Provisional Government of National Union. The NPCC was originally conceived as a device for circumventing NLH objections to continuation of the existing National Assembly, elected without its participation after the failure of the 1962 tripartite government; its duties were explicitly advisory and de-liberately less legislative than those attaching to the Assembly, which had been adjourned. The NPCC was to meet infrequently and to present its considered views on general issues of domestic and foreign policy. Under the leadership of Prince Souphanouvong, the NPCC became a forum for discussion of national reconstruction and broad con-stitutional matters. The Prince organised the body of forty-two along the lines of democratic centralism, submerging the Leninist principle under a unanimity rule. The work of the Council was supplemented by deliberations of a number of standing committees. Within weeks, Souphanouvong had secured unanimous agreement on an NLH eighteen-point programme for reconstruction and guarantees of civil liberties in the interim period before general elections.

The NPCC projects then became national blueprints used in political agitation by NLH ministers and their supporters at all levels in the joint administrative and supervisory agencies established by the Vientiane agreements. Students and trade unions took up the cause, using street demonstrations and strikes to pressure recalcitrant rightists into acting to implement the documents. After the revolutionary victories in Kampuchea and Vietnam in April 1975, several prominent anti-communist ministers and generals resigned under explicit public pressure, many of them rushing into exile with their families. This coincided with student occupation of the American AID headquarters, resulting in the termination of the aid programme, and Lao People's Liberation Army moves against the recalcitrant Meo general Vang Pao, commander of the largest of the American-supported irregular forces. With the isolation and exile of Vang Pao, the Liberation Army 'merged' with the RLG forces by means of a rapid sequence of inspired mutinies, local invitations and orders from the Ministry of Defence in Vientiane. Local administrations simultaneously coalesced, paving the way for the triumphal parade of the Liberation Army in 'liberated' Vientiane on 23 August 1975, the thirtieth anniversary of the formation of the Lao Itsala. Local elections for people's councils occurred in November, followed closely by the 'voluntary' abdication of King Savang Vatthana, and the convening of a National Congress of People's Representatives in Vientiane in December 1975. The Congress laid down the Provisional Government of National Union and declared the Lao People's Democratic Republic. The Lao national democratic revolution was thus consummated peacefully.[30]

THE LAO PEOPLE'S REVOLUTIONARY PARTY

The party directing the political struggle of the 1973–5 period was the Lao People's Revolutionary Party (LPRP), the successor to the People's Party formed in 1955. In his description of the struggle in 'conditions of the existence of three different zones (liberated, neutral and enemy-controlled) and three different regimes (revolutionary, coalition and reactionary)', the Party's General Secretary, Kaysone Phomvihane, emphasised its descent from the Comintern's ICP and its growth and transformation 'in the trying conditions of a protracted resistance fight'. The rise of the LPRP out of the confines of the NLH and the People's Party 'was the result of a historic link-up of the patriotic movement of the whole people with Marxism-Leninism (spreading in all of Indochina)', an allusion to the imminent settlements with the Americans in 1972 and the need to prepare organisationally for the peaceful struggle that resulted.[31] Kaysone's remarks plus the Lao decision to rename their party according to the formulation employed by the southern branch of the Vietnamese Communist Party came close to public admission of the Lao party's fundamentally 'Indochinese' or regional, as distinct from national, character. The LPRP's debt to the Vietnamese Communist Party cannot be denied, even if the full significance of the thirty-eight year long collaboration between the two movements cannot yet be determined. The possibility of the integration of the two communist parties in the near future is implicit in the special relationship between the two revolutionary regimes, as well as Vietnam's determined efforts to impose a more 'internationalist' leadership on the Communist Party of Kampuchea.

The LPRP matured in 'semi-secrecy' because of the requirements of its political struggle.[32] From what is known of its organisation, it appears to adhere to the Vietnamese Party model carefully and to have benefited from special advisory missions from Vietnam. In the 1960s, civilian advisers were attached to each NLH provincial and district committee. Vietnamese military missions were also established in each NLH-controlled province during the liberation war and were responsible to Vietnamese military headquarters based in Son La' and Vinh in Vietnam. Lao People's Liberation Army units normally had one Vietnamese military and one Vietnamese political adviser. The most important posts in the NLH committees and military command were thought to be held by members of the People's Party.

The People's Party was organised at the national, regional, provincial, district and canton levels. The National Congress of the Party was the highest governing body and met annually. Members of the Central Committee were elected for six-year terms by secret ballot of all Party members. The statutes of the Party called for a fifteen-person Central Committee, but in the last known election (in 1968) only eleven posts were filled. The statutes of the LPRP have not come to light, but the historical pattern of changing party and front organisations in Laos suggests that its Central Committee would be larger and more diverse in its ethnic, regional and generational composition.

To become a member of the People's Party required a period of probation and training, varying according to the candidate's class background. Candidates were first proposed by a full member of the Party who had the approval of his cell group (minimum membership of three) and the next highest echelon of the Party. The candidate was then observed for three months before being formally asked to apply for membership. Formal application was followed by six to nine months of training and self-criticism, the period being lengthened or shortened depending upon the candidate's family connections and progress. The probation period is known to have been extended for as long as three years in cases where the applicant was a member of the aristocracy or the bourgeoisie.

The Party made concerted efforts to recruit members from among the highland peoples residing in its North-eastern base areas. Special sections for Lao Soung, Lao Theung and Lao Loum peoples existed within the National Membership Committee to ensure sustained recruitment efforts within each community and to deal with some ethnic problems. In late 1967, Party membership was distributed across the three categories as follows: Lao Theung, 60·02 per cent; Lao Loum, 36·7 per cent and Lao Soung, 3·08 per cent. The predominance of the upland, plateau peoples in the Party suggests that the next generation of LPRP leaders will not be dominated by lowland or Lao Loum personalities, as is the case in 1978. Indeed, 'national' reconciliation in 1973 was undoubtedly facilitated by the aging Souvanna Phouma's expectations that his brother and his brother's Lao Loum associates could be dealt with and trusted to mediate some of the interests of the Lao Loum community with the other ethnic sections of the revolution. The official NLH view of the rapprochement of 1973 claims a 'glorious victory of all Lao nationalities'.[33] Party Secretary Kaysone was later explicit about the democratic content of the national democratic revolution requiring justice for 'all peasants irrespective of ethnic origin'.

GOVERNMENT

Laos is currently governed by a cabinet responsible to and part of a Supreme People's Council designated by the National Congress of People's Representatives in December 1975. The Council has forty-six members, headed by President 'Mr' Souphanouvong, who is assisted by three Vice-presidents, representing the three Lao national groupings. The ex-King is, in theory a member of the Council, serving as an adviser to the President, as is the former RLG neutralist Prime Minister Souvanna Phouma. But while Souvanna Phouma has co-operated with the government, the former King has been sent to a 're-education' centre following his alleged involvement in a 1977 coup conspiracy. The Council also includes two well-known patriotic neutralists.

The cabinet component of the Supreme People's Council is dominated by the LPRP leadership and long-serving officials of the NLH. Kaysone Phomvihane, General Secretary of the Party, is Prime Minister. He and all four deputy prime ministers, who include Nouhak Phoumsavanh and Phoumi Vongvichit, are members of the Party's Political Bureau, as is Mr Souphanouvong.

Below the national level, there are three levels of government in Laos, each reflecting the collective organisation at the national level. People's councils exist in each district (*tasseng*), municipality (*meuang*) and province (*quang*). The district councils have fifteen to twenty members, representing five to ten villages. The standing or executive committees of these councils usually have between five and seven members. Municipal councils have twenty to thirty members, with executive committees containing seven to nine members. Provincial councils have thirty to forty members, with executive committees of nine to thirteen members. These councils and committees are supposed to instruct the public in the meaning of democratic freedom in preparation for the writing of a new national constitution by the Supreme People's Council. Public seminars on the meaning of true independence, democracy and public responsibility were common in the period following the declaration of the Democratic Republic.[34] The initial period of revolutionary fervour was cut short by the country's deepening economic crisis.

DOMESTIC AFFAIRS

Laos is among the poorest countries in the world. Even before 800,000 of its total population became refugees, it was not self-sufficient in foodstuffs. The country was, moreover, held back in its development by the consequences of sustained poverty. A 1969 survey reported that 85 per cent of the villagers in RLG zones were illiterate, that only 50 per cent of all infants survived childhood and that average life expectancy was thirty years.[35] In NLH zones, where administration was superior, the health situation may have been better. One refugee from the Plain of Jars fighting in 1970 reported that the revolutionaries 'changed everything, so many things!' Among the changes were the introduction of public health services in the late 1960s and literacy classes for the very young and the very old.[36] Since 1975, however, most of the country's small professional stratum have gone into exile. In 1978 there were only ninety-nine doctors in the country. Public-health programmes accordingly concentrated on the training of para-medical personnel, public hygiene and preventive medicine. The sharp decline in American economic aid after 1975 has resulted in a rising problem with malaria, which is endemic in many parts of the country, and which the Americans controlled by constant use of DDT during the war.[37] A limited amount of assistance is received from the World Health Organisation and other UN agencies.

Food shortages aggravate the general health situation and compromise the best efforts of the Party and the Government to promote economic development. The problem has at least three distinct dimensions: ecological, organisational and political.

Less than 2 per cent of Laos's 800,000 hectares of cultivated land is irrigated, making it impossible to plant more than one rice crop per annum. During the war, large tracts of land were taken out of production owing to the effects of bombing and the quantities of undetonated ordnance laying about. Thus, by 1978 only 385,000 refugees had been resettled or returned to their villages, and these have great difficulty reclaiming the land with the primitive tools available to them. Meanwhile, the country has suffered both drought (in 1977) and severe flooding (in 1978). Food production has fallen to half of the (inadequate) pre-liberation levels, necessitating strict rationing and desperate efforts to secure international relief.[38]

The organisational and political problems in the economy relate to the LPRP's decision to follow the Vietnamese example in post-war reconstruction. Initially, no dramatic nationalisation of private trading or rapid, compulsory resettlement or repair of basic infrastructure was imposed on the population. This was to allow the highly inflated economy in the American-supported zone to wind down at a pace commensurate with the population's capacity to accept the revolutionary order. The gradual transition to socialism was also thought to be insurance against hostile international responses to the communist victory. As in Vietnam, this development strategy was sabotaged first by economic blockades and then by exceptionally unfavourable climatic conditions. Food shortages were then aggravated by currency speculation and black-market trading.

In 1978 Laos took more concerted steps to organise production.

Emphasis on inter-family aid groups and collective work in villages shifted to development of agricultural co-operatives and the collectivisation of the means of production. Thus far, the co-operatives are both small and concentrated in certain regions of the country, especially in the southern province of Champassak. By the end of the year there were approximately 800 co-operatives, incorporating about 10 per cent of the population in units of 50 to 100 families. Concurrent efforts to modernise agricultural practices among the plateau and mountain peoples, who work about half of all cultivated land in the country, have been less successful and have precipitated some armed resistance to the government. One reporter who recently visited Indochina judges internal resistance to the revolution in Laos as much more serious than that in Kampuchea or Vietnam.[39] If the food crisis is as serious as the aggregate indicators suggest, this judgement is not difficult to accept.[40]

The LPRP has been more successful in policy areas which depend mostly on its organisational resources, which are impressive by Third World standards. All the 115 districts in the country now have secondary schools; special institutions for war orphans and drug rehabilitation are functioning; and vocational training schemes produce a few hundred graduates each year. It is perhaps significant that the Party and the government rely heavily on administrative resources rather than mass organisations in these activities. Little is known about the few LPRP mass organisations known to exist, but it appears likely that their development has been neglected over the years, owing to the demands of war.[41] This does not bode well for the development of democratic socialism.

FOREIGN AFFAIRS

Since 1975 the Lao People's Democratic Republic has attempted to pursue an active foreign policy of neutrality maintaining a delicate balance in its close relations with the Soviet Union and its allies, major suppliers of foreign aid, and with China, its neighbour to the north. Its close relationship with Vietnam threatens to disrupt this balance in the near future.

A special twenty-five year Treaty of Friendship and Co-operation was signed with Vietnam in July 1977. The agreements included promies of bilateral aid and technical assistance from Vietnam over the coming three years, as well as an agreement on the delimitation of the national frontiers of the two countries. Details of these agreements were not published, but Vietnamese officials let it be known that the border agreement centred on an area of 1000 square km. that had been disputed.[42] In the current circumstances of Laos's dire economic need, the delimitation of the frontier was probably not as significant as Vietnamese pledges to allow Laos to use the Vietnamese port of Danang as a duty-free international harbour. The Vietnamese are also assisting Laos in repairing National Roads 7 and 9 for the necessary overland transport to Danang. The special economic relationship between the two countries has also taken the form of trading agreements between a Lao and a Vietnamese co-operative without the apparent mediation of either national government. The risks of the special relationship with Vietnam involve disruption of amicable relations with China. The Chinese have already withdrawn some of their technical assistance, in response to tacit Lao support of Vietnam in its conflict with China, but neither the Chinese nor the Laos appear to favour an open break in relations: the Lao government does not favour membership of Comecon and is conscious of Chinese leverage in local politics in its northern provinces.

The most serious foreign-policy challenges to the revolutionary regime have come from the United States and Thailand. After the occupation of its aid offices, the United States terminated its economic assistance to the country, because of the 'illegal' damage done to American property. Ignoring the damage it had done to Laos, the United States refused to assist in post-war reconstruction, because no peace agreement had been signed by the two governments. Later it made the possibility of aid contingent upon information about the more than 500 American military personnel said to be missing in action in Laos. The American refusal to grant aid when much of the country's limited industrial infrastructure is tied to the American economy has greatly retarded Lao Government hopes of attaining higher levels of national self-sufficiency by 1980. Laos has made efforts to find the remains of Americans missing in action, but satisfaction of the American demand is next to impossible in the rugged and sparsely populated terrain of most of the country.

The self-interested American effort to leave obstacles in the path of revolutionary development in Laos (and in Indochina generally) is locally supported by Thailand. Taking advantage of landlocked Laos's dependence upon trade, the military governments in Bangkok have regularly imposed trade embargoes on the country, charging the LPRP and the Lao government with supporting the Communist Party of Thailand in its guerrilla war. Negotiations between the two governments in August 1976 resolved some mutual concerns, but the Thais did not cease their periodic embargoes until early in 1978. By this time, the Vietnamese had reduced Laos's dependence on the economic outlet in Thailand, and the UN-sponsored Nam Ngum dam project was giving Laos some economic leverage with Bangkok; Laos will soon be selling electricity to northern Thailand.

Lao relations with its smallest neighbour, Kampuchea, have been friendly and sympathetic, if lacking in the intimacy and official affection lavished on the Vietnamese. Kampuchea has sent small shipments of rice, salt and dried fish to Laos and maintains in Vientiane one of its few foreign embassies. President Souphanouvong led a high-ranking delegation to Phnom Penh in December 1977 just before the Kampuchean-Vietnamese war became public. Laos has assiduously strived to stay out of the conflict.

The Vietnamese have not fully co-operated in Lao efforts, for the remarks of LPRP Party Secretary Kaysone at the Fourth National Congress of the Vietnamese Lao Dong Party in December 1976 featured prominently in Vietnam's *Kampuchea Dossier*. Clearly using Laos as an object lesson for the Communist Party of Kampuchea, Kaysone is quoted as saying,

In the history of the world revolution, there are many brilliant examples of proletarian internationalism but never before has there been such a lasting and comprehensive special militant unity and alliance anywhere; over 30 years have elapsed, but it remains as pure as ever. Such a solid unity and alliance *has greatly enhanced the spirit of independence and sovereignty and all subjective factors of each nation and the two nations have combined their strength, fought together, and won victory together, fulfilling their lofty historic mission and duty towards their respective peoples and towards the world's revolutionary movement.* Relations between Vietnam and Laos have become a pure, faithful, exemplary and rare example of a special relationship, and are being constantly consolidated and developed.[43]

The contrast between Lao and Kampuchean definitions of independence and sovereignty could not be made more clear. Lao perceptions of the unity of the world socialist movement reflect the age and socialist experience of its own movement and the experience of its communist leaders, as well as the absence of objective conditions which would support a more radical definition of independence. Laos is dependent upon the socialist world, especially the Soviet bloc.

Moreover, the belief of Kaysone and other Lao leaders in the unity of this socialist world appears genuine. It is difficult not to conclude that this perception is out of step with the realities of the 1980s and may well have serious consequences for the future of Lao socialism.

BIOGRAPHIES

Souphanouvong, President of the Lao People's Democratic Republic and President of the Lao People's Supreme Council, is among the oldest and longest-serving of the founder members of the Lao Patriotic Front. Born a prince in Luang Prabang in July 1909, he was a brilliant student at the Lycée Albert Sarrault in Hanoi, where he mastered eight languages, including Latin, Russian and English. Subsequently he graduated from the prestigious École de Ponts et Chaussées in Paris and returned to Hanoi in 1938 to work in the French colonial administration as a civil engineer. His work quickly brought him into contact with the ICP and the Viet Minh.

In 1945 Ho Chi Minh personally encouraged Souphanouvong to return to Laos to support the Lao Itsala movement. Accompanied by a guard of sixteen Viet Minh military advisers, the Prince made his way to Souvannakhet, where contact was made with the Lao Itsala, and then to Vientiane, where he became Foreign Minister in its newly proclaimed independence government. Lao Itsala partisans were quickly defeated by the French Army in early 1946, however, and Souphanouvong was seriously wounded in battle. After his recovery he visited Hanoi, and returned to Laos to direct guerrilla activities. Meanwhile the Lao Itsala government-in-exile in Bangkok negotiated for independence within the framework of the French union. When the neo-colonial agreement was reached in 1949, Souphanouvong, still supported by the Viet Minh, broke with his erstwhile Itsala allies. He became Prime Minister and Foreign Minister of the Neo Lao Itsala provisional independence government in 1950.

By the time of the first Geneva conference, Souphanouvong had several thousand men under arms. His resistance government was not recognised by the Conference, but his supporters were allowed to regroup in Phong Saly and Sam Neua provinces pending further negotiations for national integration. As these negotiations proceeded, Pathet Lao forces administered the zones; the People's Party of Laos was founded there in 1955.

Between 1957 and 1963, Prince Souphanouvong served in two

coalition governments in Vientiane. Each of these was sabotaged by American-backed, anti-communist personalities before reunification of the country and the two rival armies could be achieved. Souphanouvong was among the NLH candidates elected to the National Assembly in 1958 and among the leaders of the resistance to be imprisoned in Vientiane in 1959. When the 1962 Geneva agreements collapsed in their turn, he realised that resolution of the 'Lao problem' depended upon a political settlement in Vietnam. Forced to retreat to Sam Neua from 1964 until 1973, Souphanouvong received many foreign visitors and tributes from the leaders of international socialist states and movements. He made a statement in 1967 announcing that he was a Marxist-Leninist.

Souphanouvong returned to Vientiane in the spring of 1974, shortly after the Paris agreements on ending the hostilities in Vietnam had allowed an armistice to be worked out between national belligerents in the Lao War. Souphanouvong quickly demonstrated that years of isolation and advancing age had not diminished his political abilities. He wrote and skilfully promoted the eighteen-point programme through the NPCC. Under his adept leadership, the NPCC paved the way for the 1975 elections and the transition to a People's Republic. At the December 1975 meeting of the National Congress of People's Representatives, Souphanouvong was named President of the new People's Supreme Council and Head of State. As President of the Council, he holds major responsibility for preparing the country's new constitution.

Souphanouvong is a member of the Political Bureau of the LPRP. He is thought to have joined the Party only in the 1960s. In spite of his recent membership and out of respect for his personal gifts and service to the revolutionary cause, Souphanouvong appears to enjoy as much influence in the Party as former members of the ICP.

Kaysone Phomvihane, Prime Minister of the Lao People's Democratic Republic and General Secretary of the LPRP, was born in Savannakhet in 1925, is the youngest of the major revolutionary leaders in Laos, and is also the one most closely associated with the Vietnamese Communist movement. His father, a Vietnamese who married a Lao woman, was a minor official in the French colonial administration in southern Laos. It is perhaps because the young Kaysone spoke Vietnamese as his first language that he attended school in Vietnam. At lycée, he was taught by Vo Nguyen Giap. Later he befriended Ho Chi Minh. He was among the first Lao nationals to join the ICP (in 1946) and may also have joined its successor Vietnamese party, the Lao Dong Party (in 1951). In the same period, Kaysone entered the Faculty of Medicine in Hanoi, but he soon left university to support the Lao Itsala and Neo Lao Itsala resistance movements. He was a prominent member of the Committee of Lao Resistance in the East, an ICP-sponsored organisation, was among the eighteen founding members of the Neo Lao Itsala Central Committee, and served as Defence Minister in Souphanouvong's 1950–4 resistance government.

As Defence Minister, Kaysone Phomvihane had major responsibility for creating the Pathet Lao army. This work, coupled with his continuing friendship with General Giap and sustained logistical co-ordination of the Neo Lao Itsala–Viet Minh military effort against France served to reinforce and to deepen Kaysone's loyalty to the Vietnamese revolution and its socialist tradition. As a former member of the ICP, he also appears to have been entrusted with special re-sponsibilities for political organisation in Laos following the dissolution of the Party and prior to the official foundation of its Lao national successor, the People's Party, in 1955.

Kaysone attended the Geneva Conference in 1954 as a member of Souphanouvong's unseated delegation and participated in negotiations with the Royal Lao Government throughout the 1950s. He was an unsuccessful NLH candidate in the 1958 elections, but this meant he was not among the leading members of the NLH who were imprisoned in Vientiane in 1959. From that time until 1975, Phomvihane rarely left NLH-People's Party base areas in Sam Neua, where he directed Party and some military affairs as the American war escalated. He was first publicly acknowledged to be General Secretary of the Central Committee of the People's Party of Laos by Vietnamese radio in the summer of 1967.

During the final stages of the local elections for popular assemblies in November 1975, and in anticipation of the All-Laos Congress of People's Representatives meeting of 2 December 1975, Kaysone and his staff quietly moved into suburban Vientiane to observe the monarch's abdication and to take up their posts in the revolutionary government. He formally announced the existence of the LPRP and the successful conclusion of the National Democratic Revolution in a speech in March 1976.

BASIC FACTS ABOUT LAOS

Official name: Lao People's Democratic Republic (Sathalanalat Pasathipatay Pasasonh Lao).

Area: 236,800 sq. km. (91,100 sq. miles).

Population (1978 est.): 3,500,000. 50 per cent less than 20 years old.

Population distribution: 15 per cent urban, 85 per cent rural.

Population of major towns (1973): Vientiane (the capital), 176,637; Savannakhet, 50,690; Paksé, 44,860; Luang Prabang, 44,244.

Membership of the LPRP (1968 est.): 14,000.

Administrative divisions: 14 provinces; 115 districts; cantons and municipalities.

Ethnic nationalities (1972 est.): Lao Loum (lowland Lao) – Lao, Thai, Lu, Phouan and Phou-thai (approximately two-thirds of total population); Lao Theung (upland Lao) – Alak, Ta, Oi, Phou, Noi and other tribes of 'Indonesian' descent; Lao Soung (highland Lao) – Meo, Yao, Ho, Lolo, Mouseu and Lanten peoples; plus 60,000 Chinese, 30,000 Vietnamese, 5000 Thais and 5000 Khmers.

Main natural resources: tin, timber and (largely unexploited) iron, lead, copper, gold, silver, sulphur, antimony and coal.

Foreign trade (1974) [US $1 = approx. 600 kips.]: exports, 6780 million kip; imports, 38,880 million kip; total 45,660 million kip.

Main trading partners: Thailand, Japan, USSR (since 1976) and Vietnam (since 1976).

Economic infrastructure: railways, nil; roadways, 8500 km. (1977); Mekong waterways, 714 km. for 250-ton ships; rice paddy in cultivation, 800,000 hectares (1978); agricultural co-operatives, 800 (Nov 1978).

Foreign relations: diplomatic relations with 52 countries; 23 diplomatic missions established in Vientiane; member of the UN (since 1955) and of the Conference of Non-aligned Nations.

NOTES

1. H. J. Benda, 'The Structure of Southeast Asian History: Some Preliminary Observations', *Journal of South-east Asian History*, III (1962) 103–38.
2. Cf. Nguyen Khac Vien (ed.), *Mountain Regions and National Minorities in the Democratic Republic of Vietnam*, Vietnamese Studies, no. 15 (Hanoi, 1968); C. F. Keyes, *ISAN: Regionalism in Northeastern Thailand*, Cornell University Southeast Asia Program Data Paper, no. 65 (Ithaca, N.Y. 1967); and Phoumi Vongvichit, *Laos and the Victorious Struggle of the Lao People against US Neo-colonialism* (Sam Neua: NLH, 1969) ch. 1.

18. Zasloff, *Pathet Lao*, p. 14.
19. It is significant that the formation of the Marxist-Leninist party preceded organisation of the NLH. The Vietnamese interpretation of the united-front tactic in political struggle emphasises prior mass organisation and mobilisation followed by careful party direction of the front's expansion. See the perceptive remarks of P. Rousset in his *Le Parti Communiste Vietnamien* (Paris: Maspero, 1975) pp. 292–3.
20. The Vientiane negotiations were long and intricate. Owing in part to a secret agreement on the part of the United States, France and the United Kingdom to protect the position of the regime serving as their military 'bridgehead' in the region, many Western histories of the Lao revolution have not given them the attention they warrant. See M. Thee, 'Background Notes on the 1954 Geneva Agreements on Laos and the Vientiane Agreements of 1956–1957', in Adams and McCoy, *Laos: War and Revolution*, pp. 122–38. A succinct chronology of events was published by the NLH on the twenty-fifth anniversary of the Lao Itsala proclamation of independence. See NLH, *Un Quart de Siècle de Lutte Opiniâtre et Victorieuse* (Sam Neua, n.d. [1970] pp. 61–76.
21. Vongvichit, *Laos and the Victorious Struggle*, pp. 116–17.
22. Thee, in Adams and McCoy, *Laos: War and Revolution*, p. 137.
23. An authoritative account of the neutralisation of Laos written from the perspective of the Kennedy administration in Washington is R. Hilsman, *To Move a Nation* (New York: Doubleday, 1967) ch. 9.
24. D. G. Porter, 'After Geneva: Subverting Laotian Neutrality', in Adams and McCoy, *Laos: War and Revolution*, pp. 197–212.
25. R. Littauer and N. Uphoff (eds), *The Air War in Indochina* (Boston, Mass.: Beacon Press, 1972) pp. 81–2.
26. Zasloff, *Pathet Lao*, p. 15, identifies 'an active North Vietnamese military phase in Laos' from May 1959, the height of the crisis in Vientiane and the moment when the Vietnamese Communist Party Central Committee decided to support the reactivated insurgency in South Vietnam. He discounts as 'exaggerated' earlier American and right-wing charges of Vietnamese aggression.
27. Ibid., p. 70. Zasloff's estimates are based on US intelligence estimates. In 1971, US State Department officials in Phnom Penh informed the author that Pathet Lao forces numbered 40,000 and were opposed by 50,000 regular RLG armed forces personnel and 20,000 'irregulars' or CIA-funded mercenary forces. See L. Summers, 'Laos', *Collier's Encyclopedia Yearbook: 1971* (1972) p. 324.
28. One of Hanoi's principal military strategists acknowledged this indirectly at the time. See Douglas Mile's interview with Hoang Tung, 'Laos' Role in the Indochina War', in Adams and McCoy, *Laos: War and Revolution*, p. 461.
29. Negotiations on constitutional matters continued into 1974. A detailed description is M. Brown and J. J. Zasloff, 'The Pathet Lao and the Politics of Reconciliation in Laos, 1973–74', in J. J. Zasloff and M. Brown (eds), *Communism in Indochina* (Lexington, Mass.: D. C. Heath, 1975) pp. 259–67.
30. M. Brown and J. J. Zasloff, 'New Stages of Revolution in Laos', *Current History*, LXXI, no. 422 (1976) 219–20.

31. Kaysone Phomvihane, 'The Victory of Creative Marxism-Leninism in Laos', *Journal of Contemporary Asia*, VII (1977) 393–401.
32. The term is Zasloff's. Most of the information on Party organisation in the following paragraphs is extracted from his 1973 study. Other sources will be cited. Zasloff's analysis is based on interviews with a limited number of prisoners of war and political defectors. The LPRP has revealed little about its internal organisation in its publications and radio broadcasts.
33. NLH, *Victoire Glorieuse de Toutes les Nationalités Lao* (Sam Neua, 1973).
34. This was reported by American missionaries in service in Laos. See 'Laos: A New Beginning', *Indochina Chronicle*, no. 46 (1976) 12.
35. G. F. Breakey and E. Voulgaropoulos, *Laos Health Survey: Mekong Valley 1968–1969* (Honolulu: University of Hawaii Press, 1976), cited by J. McMichael in a review by the same title, *Journal of Contemporary Asia*, VII (1977) 382.
36. N. Chomsky, 'The Pathet Lao and the People of Laos', in Adams and McCoy, *Laos: War and Revolution*, p. 456.
37. L. and H. Hiebert, 'No One Should Die of Malaria', *Indochina Chronicle*, no. 61 (1978) 15.
38. Currently, rice rations are 12 kg per capita per month; 15 kg is considered to be the subsistence level. International relief has made up approximately only one-third of the shortfall between current production and current subsistence need. Food shortages account in part for the large refugee flow into Thailand (totalling more than 200,000 by October 1978).
39. B. Albons, 'A Reporter Looks at Laos' (unpublished manuscript, 1978).
40. Available evidence from radio broadcasts confirms the impression of widespread unrest and local armed resistance. The Government recently claimed a military victory over Meo 'counter-revolutionaries'. French journalists who have visited the maquis in Laos report that opponents of the Government ,resent the taxation (requisition) of rice produce and the dependence of the Party on the Vietnamese. See *L'Express*, 25 Sep–1 Oct 1978, pp. 118–19.
41. Zasloff (*Pathet Lao*, pp 143–4) merely lists references to them.
42. Albons, 'A Reporter Looks at Laos'. The Vietnamese also estimated that the frontier area in dispute between Kampuchea and Vietnam amounted to 65–70 sq. km.
43. Socialist Republic of Vietnam, Foreign Ministry, *Kampuchea Dossier*, vol. I, (Hanoi: Vietnam Courier, 1978) pp. 110–11. Emphasis in original.

BIBLIOGRAPHY

See also references in the Notes.

Adams, Nina S. and McCoy, Alfred W. (eds), *Laos: War and Revolution* (London: Harper Colophon Books, 1970).
Brown, MacAlister and Zasloff, Joseph J., 'Laos in 1975: People's Democratic Revolution Lao Style', *Asian Survey*, XVI, no. 2 (1976) 193–9.
——, 'New Stages of Revolution in Laos', *Current History*, LXXI, no. 422 (1976) 218–21, 228.

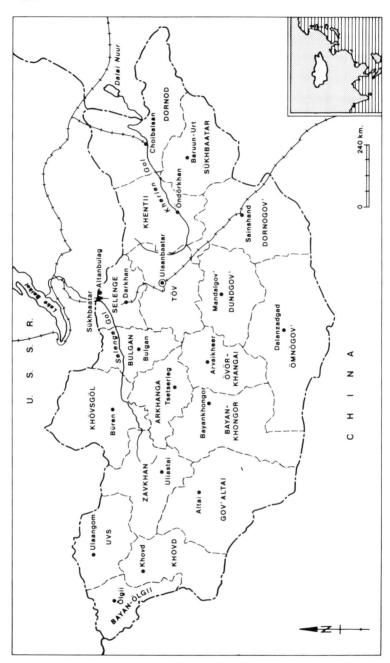

Mongolia: provincial boundaries

this period that the administrative division between Inner and Outer Mongolia begins.

The Mongols found themselves suffering increasing economic hardship under Manchu rule. Nevertheless, the Mongols of Outer Mongolia (roughly the area of the present Mongolian People's Republic) and those of Inner Mongolia were still able to maintain some degree of political independence.

At the end of the nineteenth century Manchu power had declined and the Manchu government was forced to adopt drastic policies in order to forestall Tsarist Russian expansionism in northern Mongolia and Japan's aggressive policy towards Korea and southern Mongolia. In 1906 it introduced the so-called 'New Policy' (implemented between 1909 and 1910), which was intended not only to reduce the power of what modern-day Mongol historians call feudal lords,[4] but also to move huge numbers of Chinese farmers into Mongolia in order to undermine traditional nomadic life there. This provoked the Mongols of Outer Mongolia in 1911, the year before China itself established a republic, to declare independence from Manchu rule for all the Mongols. Under Manchu rule the Mongols had retained their national identity, and, although the declaration of independence in 1911 was the work of feudal lords, it undoubtedly restored the self-confidence of the Mongol common people and created the conditions for the emergence of the leadership of the 1921 revolution.

THE ESTABLISHMENT OF THE MONGOLIAN PEOPLE'S REPUBLIC

The Mongolian People's Republic was established on 25 November 1924, and as such was the first people's republic and the first socialist country to emerge in the world after the Soviet Union, predating the people's democracies of Eastern Europe and the Chinese People's Republic.

In October 1919, while the great powers in Europe were recovering from the war, the Government of the Chinese Republic sent an army and imposed Chinese authority over the Mongolian feudal lords. Chinese traders virtually took control of the Mongolian economy, and the Mongols, already impoverished by mounting debts to Chinese traders and moneylenders,[5] also faced crippling taxes from their own feudal lords and severe taxation levied to pay for the upkeep of the army. Some of the common people also served their feudal lords as personal serfs.

The liberation of Khiagt

Many thousands of Chinese soldiers had fled northwards after their defeat by the White Guards in Khüree, and they gathered in the vicinity of Khiagt. The People's Government, with Sükhbaatar as Commander-in-chief of the Army, issued an ultimatum to the Chinese military authorities in Khiagt on 15 March 1921, demanding that they unconditionally surrender or face severe consequences. The Chinese authorities ignored this ultimatum, and the four regiments of the Mongolian Partisan Army, about 400 strong, moved on Khiagt on the evening of 17 March. After twenty-four hours of heavy fighting, the Chinese withdrew, and Khiagt was liberated at midnight on 18 March. During the battle Sükhbaatar showed his military genius by defeating many thousands of Chinese soldiers with only a few hundred Partisans.

Although the main Chinese forces had been defeated by Ungern's White Guards in Niislel Khüree and by the Partisans in Khiagt, there were still small groups of Chinese soldiers roaming about the country. Baron Ungern's main forces, with some Mongol support , about 8000 troops in all,[16] moved towards Khiagt from Niislel Khüree with the aim of crushing the Partisans and then attacking the Red Army across the Mongolian-Russian frontier.

On 10 April 1921, the Mongolian People's Provisional Government officially requested the Government of the Russian Soviet Federative Socialist Republic (RSFSR)[17] to provide military aid against the forces of Baron Ungern. The Russians complied, and during May and June major battles took place in the area between Niislel Khüree and Khiagt, with minor skirmishes in the western provinces. The combined Mongolian-Soviet forces occupied Niislel Khüree early in July, but the war against the White Guards went on until January 1922, when Magsarjav captured the White Guard general, Bakich, in the Khovd area.

The proclamation of the Mongolian People's Central Government in 1921 and the People's Republic in 1924

When the Mongolian-Soviet forces reached Niislel Khüree, they received a warm welcome from the people of the town, who offered the troops milk and tea, a traditional gesture of welcome.

The Lamaist church still had considerable support among the people, and as a first step, therefore, the revolutionaries created a People's

Central Government in the form of a limited (constitutional) monarchy, with the Bogd as the titular head. The senior ministers were appointed, with Bodoo as Premier and Foreign Minister and Sükhbaatar as Minister of War. The Bogd was enthroned as Khaan but with restricted powers as a constitutional monarch, and he had no authority whatsoever in the government. In August 1921 the Mongolian Revolutionary Youth League was established. This was to be a most important force, organised by Choibalsan and used during the subsequent power struggle.

Since the White Guards were now almost completely defeated and internal peace was gradually being restored, the People's Government was able to direct its attention to foreign policy. In September 1921 it asked the Soviet government to mediate in establishment of relations with China but there does not appear to have been any response from the Chinese government. In November 1921 the Mongols and Russians signed a treaty in Moscow, and Lenin himself attended the ceremony. The Mongolian Government was represented by Sükhbaatar (Commander-in-chief) and Tserendorj (Deputy Foreign Minister). In the treaty the two sides recognised each other as sole legal governments of their respective countries.

Since the period of the signing of the treaty, Mongolia has been officially described by Mongolian historians as being in transition from feudalism to socialism. This analysis is based on Lenin's report to the Second Comintern Congress in 1920, when he said, '. . . with the aid of the proletariat of the advanced countries, backward countries can go over to the Soviet System and, through certain stages of development, to communism, without having to pass through the capitalist stage'.[18]

Other moves made by the new government were to limit the privileges of the feudal lords, by a March 1922 ordinance prohibiting them from using the services of personal serfs, and to establish the Mongolian Consumers' Central Co-operative in April of the same year.

With the death of the Bogd Khaan on 20 May 1924, the opportunity arose to establish a republic, and the government called a Congress of the National Great Khural,[19] which opened on 6 November 1924. On 25 November the First People's Great Khural proclaimed the establishment of the Mongolian People's Republic (MPR) and approved the new constitution. Niislel Khüree was renamed Ulaanbaatar (Red Hero) and the reign title 'Elevated by All',[20] which had been used in the traditional way since the 1911 declaration of independence to enumerate calendar years, was abandoned, so that 1924, for example, was now known simply as the fourteenth year of the Mongolian State.

products of their own household units. This was also the period in which Choibalsan consolidated his domination of the Party and government. The years 1937 to 1939 in particular are characterised by Mongol historians as a period in which a personality cult grew up around Choibalsan, who was accused after his death of various violations of socialist legality, although his overall achievement was still seen as positive.

The battle of Khalkhyn Gol

A new threat appeared from the east in 1931–2, when the Japanese occupied Manchuria. The frontier remained quiet until 1936, but from then on border incidents began to occur. The Soviets had made a verbal declaration of military aid in 1934 and a Protocol Treaty for Mutual Military Assistance was concluded on 12 March 1936. In accordance with this treaty, Red Army units entered Mongolian territory in 1937.

The Japanese Army attacked eastern Mongolia on 11 May 1939 and was engaged by the joint forces of Mongolia and the USSR at Khalkhyn Gol. The fighting went on until the end of August, when the Japanese Army was driven out.

The war with Japan

The external situation of Mongolia became even more tense after the outbreak of the Second World War. The Japanese Army threatened Mongolia from Manchuria to the east and from Inner Mongolia to the south, areas it had occupied since the 1930s. This threat persisted right through to Japan's unconditional surrender in 1945.

Although the Mongolian People's Republic did not take part in fighting the Germans on the Russian fronts, it organised its national economy on a war footing, not only strengthening its own army but also giving aid to the Red Army in 1942 and 1943 with clothing, horses and so on. Within the Soviet Army there was a so-called 'Revolutionary Mongol' tank brigade and a squadron of aircraft with the name 'The Mongolian People', which were financed by the Mongolian government and people. Three months and two days after the German surrender in Europe, on 10 August 1945, the Mongolian Government declared war on Japan. The Mongolian Army, with 8000 men under Marshal Choibalsan, together with the Red Army under the command of Marshal Malinovskii, attacked the Japanese Army in Manchuria and in Inner Mongolia, and forced it to withdraw. This resulted in the occupation of Inner Mongolia by Mongolian forces and of Manchuria by Soviet troops.

THE GOVERNMENT AND PARTY

The constitution

The first constitution of the Mongolian People's Republic was approved by the National Great Khural in November 1924. A second constitution was introduced in 1940, and the present (third) constitution in 1960. The present constitution[23] states that the Republic is a socialist state of workers, of herdsmen and farmers, who are organised into co-operatives, and of intellectuals. Socialist property takes two forms, State property (belonging to the entire population) and co-operative property – belonging, for example, to agricultural co-operatives. There is universal suffrage from the age of eighteen, irrespective of sex, religion or race. Women are accorded the same rights as men. Religion is separated from State organisations, including schools, but there is freedom of worship. The Constitution is destined to be abolished when the State is replaced by a communist association of working people.

The People's Great Khural

According to the Constitution this is the highest legislative organ of State power in the Republic. As a parliament it has, for example, jurisdiction over the passing of laws, the Supreme Court, the formation of the Council of Ministers and general administrative bodies, and its own Presidium. The members, or deputies, of the Great Khural are elected every three years. There is one deputy for approximately every 4000 voters. The sessions of the Great Khural are held annually, and when the Khural is not in session the Presidium operates as its standing committee. The Presidium usually consists of a Chairman, Vice-chairman, Secretary and six members.

Local khurals are organised at all levels – *aimag* (province), *khoroo* (town or subdistrict or *raion* of Ulaanbaatar), *raion* (urban district) and *sum* (rural district or county) – and they are the legislative organs in their particular administrative units. The number of deputies per administrative unit is decided by the Presidium of the Great Khural. The province and town khurals convene at least twice a year, and the rural and urban-district khurals at least three times a year. Each local khural has an executive board of between five and nine deputies.

Table 18.1 (*cont.*)

	Ch. Süren (Light Industry and Transport) (1979)
	Ts. Molom (1979)
Minister of Agriculture	L. Rinchin
Minister of Fuel and Power	P. Ochirbat
Minister of Geology and Mining	Ch. Khurts
Minister of Light and Food Industries	J. Dulmaa (1979)
Minister of Culture	S. Sosorbaram
Minister of Construction and Building Materials	O. Tleikhan
Minister of Forestry	D. Tseden
Minister of Transport	B. Enebish
Minister of Water Economy	B. Bars
Minister of Communications	I. Norovjav (1979)
Minister of Trade and Procurement	D. Dorjgotov
Minister of Foreign Trade	Yo. Ochir
Minister of Finance	E. Byambajav (1979)
Minister of Foreign Affairs	M. Dügersüren
Minister of Defence	Gen. G. Avkhia (1979)
Minister of Public Security	Lt Gen. B. Dejid
Minister of Education	R. Sanjaasüren
Minister of Health	D. Nyam Osor
Minister of Communal Economy and Services	O. Nyamaa
Minister of Justice	B. Chimid (1979)
Chairman, People's Control Committee	Ts. Molon (1979)
Chairman, State Bank	D. Danzan
Chairman, State Committee for Labour and Wages	M. Lkhamsüren
Chairman, State Committee for Information, Radio and Television	S. Pürevjav
Chairman, (Chief Justice), Supreme Court	G. Ish (1979)
Chairman, Central Council of Trade Unions	G. Ochirbat

Table 18.1 (*cont.*)

Chairman, State Committee for Economic Co-operation	D. Saldan
Chairman, State Committee for Prices and Standards	D. Byambasüren
Chairman, State Directorate for Insurance	J. Pürevdorj
First Deputy Chairman, State Planning Commission	B. Rinchinpiljee
Director of Administration	B. Badarch
President of Academy of Sciences	B. Shirendev
Head of State Central Statistical Directorate	D. Zagasbaldan
Chairman Mongolian Revolutionary Youth League	L. Tüdev

Special State committees and commissions are also organised by the Council of Ministers. These include the State Planning Commission, dealing with economic planning, the State Construction Committee and the State Publishing Committee.

Local government

There are altogether 290 rural districts or counties in the eighteen provinces. Within the districts the smallest administrative units are the brigades. The negdels or agricultural and production co-operatives, which have been established since the 1930s, function at the same level as the districts and are, in fact, sometimes fused with them and called *sum-negdels*.

The Mongolian People's Revolutionary Party

The origins of a Mongolian People's Party go back to 1919 and the formation of the two patriotic groups. The First Party Congress was held in March 1921, four months before the declaration of inde-pendence. Because of the particular historical circumstances of Mongolia, political life has taken place entirely within this one party and no other parties have emerged. The First Congress was concerned mainly with organising the political party and carrying out the revolution. The Party became the MPRP in 1925. Many of the early members were private (non-collectivised) herdsmen. In 1922 the membership was 770, and by 1931 it had risen to 30,600. Following the so-called leftist deviation and the subsequent purges, the membership fell to under 8000 in 1934. Since then the numbers have increased, until today there are over 60,000 Party members.[25] Party congresses were held annually in the 1920s, but they became less frequent and shorter in the 1930s and more work was performed by the Political Bureau. In recent years, Party congresses have been held at the beginning of each five-year economic period.

The Party is based on a system of committees. The Party committees of the Sums (small rural districts) are headed by secretaries. Towns have their own urban Party committees. The highest executive Party body between congresses is the Central Committee, based in Ulaanbaatar. In June 1976 it had ninety-one members and sixty-one candidate members. The Central Committee appoints the Political Bureau, which has eight members (Yu. Tsedenbal, the First Secretary of the MPRP, and D. Maidar, D. Molomjamts, N. Jagvaral, S. Jalan-Aajav, N. Luvsanravdan, T. Ragchaa and J. Batmönkh) and two candidate members (B. Altangerel and D. Gombojav). The Political Bureau deals with major decisions and policies in Party work.

The Party ultimately guides and directs the country on political, economic and cultural matters. It thus works closely with the Council of Ministers. The Party organises departments to deal with policies and decisions concerning agriculture, industry, trade, culture, construction and so on.

At the Seventeenth Party Congress, in June 1976, there were 813 delegates, representing a total Party membership of 66,933. Of these delegates, 248 were industrial workers and 243 agricultural workers. There were 189 women among the delegates.

Mass organisations

In 1925 the General Committee of Trade Unions[26] was founded, to protect the interests of industrial workers, civil servants and workers in the co-operatives and service industries. The First Congress of Mongolian Trade Unions took place in August 1927. Trade-union membership at that time was only about 2500, reflecting the small size of the industrial work force. The main function of the trade unions was to co-ordinate Party policies in the factories and work places. In October 1927 the Mongolian unions joined the Trade Union International or Profintern (Profsoyuzniy Internatsional).

In more recent times the unions have taken responsibility for the fulfilment of economic plans. They also attempt to improve labour safety regulations, and the wages and living standards of members. Between trade-union congresses, the Central Council of the Mongolian Trade Unions directs union activities.

Trade Union membership rose from 12,000 in 1935 to 42,000 in 1954, 128,000 in 1962, 163,000 in 1966, 270,000 in 1976 and 318,000 in 1978. Figure 18.1 shows this in the form of a graph. The Chairman of the Central Council of the Mongolian Trade Unions is G. Ochirbat.

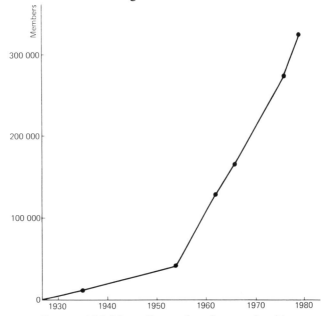

FIGURE 18.1 Mongolian trade union membership

The Mongolian Revolutionary Youth League was organised in August 1921 and developed considerably in the rural areas. Initially the Youth League was independent of the Party and under Choibalsan's influence exercised considerable power. However, in later years its membership was drawn largely (i.e. about two-thirds) from the Party. By 1930 the membership had risen to 23,000, but in 1934, following the Party purges, it was dissolved and reorganised, with a smaller membership and reduced power. Thereafter it was in effect a subsidiary of the Party, but the membership has risen from the low figure of 6000 in 1935 to a current level of about 165,000. Nowadays it is primarily concerned with assisting the development of the economy. Students (aged fifteen to twenty-eight) are regularly organised to work on State farms, building sites, and so on, in response to Party appeals. The Youth League is affiliated to the Young Communist International, the World Federation of Democratic Youth, the International Students' Union, and so forth. The present First Secretary of the Central Committee of the Mongolian Revolutionary Youth League is L. Tüdev.

The Sükhbaatar Mongolian Pioneer Organisation[27] was founded on 8 May 1925 with 200 members. At present there are over 200,000 school children of Young Pioneer and Junior Pioneer status. The Pioneer organisation works closely with the Mongolian Revolutionary Youth League in schools, as many Pioneers go on to enter the Youth League and the Party. Pioneer activities include rallies, spartakiads (sports competitions), olympiads (language and mathematics competitions) and so forth. Pioneer camps are organised in summer, and exchange visits with pioneer organisations in other communist countries are frequent.

Women have traditionally played an important role in life in Mongolia, owing to the chronic labour shortage in the country. This contribution has increased in modern times, and in 1970 43 per cent of industrial workers and 51 per cent of agricultural workers were women. In 1976 women made up 54 per cent of doctors, 46 per cent of teachers and 30 per cent of research workers. In 1970 there were 3000 women's committees in the Mongolian Women's Organisation.

INTERNAL AFFAIRS

Education

There was traditionally no education provided in Mongolia outside the lamaist church, and, between 1913 and 1917, when a secular school was opened for the first time in the history of the country, it was strenuously opposed by the lamas. The population was almost entirely illiterate, and it is generally accepted that in 1921 only about 1 per cent of the adult population could read. The situation has since improved dramatically: in 1947 the literacy level was 47 per cent and nearly 100 per cent literacy is now said to have been achieved. The widespread illiteracy of the past was partly owing to the difficulty of the traditional Mongolian script. A Latin alphabet was experimentally introduced in 1931, but in 1941 a modified form of the Cyrillic alphabet was officially introduced, and this has been used ever since.

A primary school was opened in Niislel Khüree in November 1921 and a seven-year secondary school in 1923. By 1934 there were fifty-nine primary schools and five secondary schools. A training college (*technikum*) for teachers was established in 1924. Many of the early schools taught only Mongolian language and arithmetic, since there was a shortage of trained teachers. From 1935 to 1937 schools to instruct former lamas were built. In 1938 an industrial technical college (*technikum*) was established, to educate specialist cadres. There were as yet no institutes of higher education, and some Mongols went abroad, mainly to secondary schools, higher schools, rabfaks (workers' faculties) and universities in the Soviet Union, but also occasionally to Germany and France (1926).

The Mongolian State University was opened in Ulaanbaatar in 1942, with veterinary, medical and teacher-training courses. The University now has fourteen faculties, with over 600 teaching staff and about 8000 students. It is concerned with research and teaching academic courses, and research work is also organised through the Academy of Sciences. The Mongolian Academy of Sciences[28] consists of institutes of physics and mathematics, chemistry, biology, geography, geology, language, literature, economics and agriculture. It also runs experimental farms, a library with over 3 million books, and a publishing house. In addition to research the Academy offers scientific and cultural help for the development of the economy. Other institutes of higher education include the Institute of medicine (1961), agriculture (1958), and teacher-training (1940). There is also a polytechnic institute (1969). In addition, specialist technical schools at the secondary level teach a wide range of handicraft and other subjects. Apart from a few agricultural and teacher training colleges, most of the institutes of higher education are in Ulaanbaatar except for a teacher-training college in Khovd (1979).

At present, eight-year schooling is compulsory in rural areas, while provincial centres and other major towns have compulsory ten-year schools. Education begins at eight and is free at primary and secondary levels. Higher education is free and the State pays a grant to students. Students usually spend some time in the summer and autumn working on State farms. In 1978 there were 573 schools with 350,000 students in all – that is, 251 per 1000 of the population.

In 1978 a student grant for higher education could be anything from 240 to 375 tögrögs a month (i.e. £36–56), depending on the stage the student had reached in his studies. Some students may receive as much as 450 tögrögs (£68), if they hold a scholarship (for example, the Sükhbaatar scholarship).

Religion

Until recently the prevalent religion was a Mongolian form of Tibetan lamaism. In 1921 there were 747 lamaseries and almost half the male population[29] were lamas. After the proclamation of the Mongolian People's Republic in 1924, the separation of State and church was clearly defined in the Constitution. In the 1930s State opposition to religion was responsible for a great reduction in the number of lamas, who took up nomadic herding or factory work. In 1937 the Office in Charge of Religious Affairs was set up, and in 1969 it was replaced by a Council of Religious Affairs, under the direction of the Council of Ministers. It supervises the operation of religious affairs in the country, ensuring that the laws and regulations relating to religious affairs are carried out.

There is also now a Higher School of Religious Affairs (established in 1970), where some forty lama novices receive instruction. These must all have previously completed ten years of education in a normal State school. Only one lamasery remains in operation in Mongolia, the Gandan in Ulaanbaatar, and daily religious services are held there. About 100 lamas live in the lamasery under the leadership of the Most Rev. S. Gombojav. From time to time lamas from the lamasery go abroad to take part in world religious conferences. This Gandan lamasery appears to be the only religious institution tolerated by the government, and it relies on private donations from its followers for financial support. The lamasery is the headquarters of the Asian Buddhist Conference for Peace of which the Most Rev. S. Gombojar is president (since 1970).

Health service

According to 1976 figures, there were 120 hospitals in the Republic, serving a population of 1·5 million. An official calculation in 1974 stated that there were nineteen doctors and ninety-nine hospital beds for every 10,000 people.

Medical care and treatment are free of charge, and, with the official drive to increase the population, particular emphasis is placed on maternal and child welfare. Women are entitled to forty-five days pre-natal and fifty-six days post-natal paid leave. Mothers with over four children are given cash allowances – for example 4000 tögrögs per annum for mothers with ten children – and in 1969 50 million tögrögs were spent on birth allowances. Pregnant women or women with young children cannot be dismissed from jobs, and mothers of large families are also granted extra holidays and early retirement.

Pensions

Pensions are paid to all men who have worked at least twenty-five years and are aged sixty or over, and to all women who have worked twenty years and are fifty-five or over. People working in hazardous conditions can retire fifteen years earlier in the case of men and ten years earlier in that of women. Housing and rent is cheap and on a scale related to income.

THE ECONOMY

Agriculture

The most important part of Mongolian agriculture is the live-stock sector. At the time of the revolution it was the basis of the whole national economy. The bulk of livestock was privately owned and remained so until the 1950s, but as early as the mid 1920s plans were made to introduce co-operative veterinary services, hay storage and livestock shelters on a limited scale. The lamaseries and remaining nobles owned over 3 million head of livestock out of a total of nearly 24 million in 1930, and a campaign was organised by the MPRP to transfer the livestock to collectives and ordinary herdsmen. The left deviationists forced the herdsmen into collectives, allegedly against the advice of the MPRP. By the end of 1931 33 per cent of the *ard* (ordinary herdsmen) households were collectivised. This caused great losses of livestock, since many herdsmen opposed to collectivisation saw no advantage in tending the collective's animals. In 1932 the collectives were disbanded by the Council of Ministers, but in 1935 voluntary production negdels were founded as substitutes for the collectives, and these allowed livestock to be privately owned.[30]

During the late 1930s grain was supplied to the towns by private growers, but after 1936 the newly established State farms also began to provide grain and meat. Crop-farming increased during the Second World War, but the number of livestock fell, partly as a result of increased exports to the Soviet Union. The first five-year plan (1948–52) saw increasing collectivisation of agriculture, and the number of livestock owned by collectives increased sixfold. There followed a period of voluntary collectivisation, and by the end of the second five-year plan (1953–7) nearly every *sum* had a negdel. By the end of the three-year plan (1958–60) only 800 individual families remained outside the collectivised system and in 1970 there were reported to be only forty. During the three-year plan efforts were made to increase State-farm grain production, and for the first time Mongolia was in a position to export grain. Over this whole period between 1947 and 1957 the Soviet Union provided over 2000 million roubles' worth of credit to Mongolian agriculture.[31]

At present the negdels are operated rather like the Soviet kolkhozes. The members tend communal herds in addition to their own private livestock. They are paid in both money and livestock, and the average salary is approximately 500–600 tögrögs per month. At present the 259 negdels own 17·2 million head of livestock, 73 per cent of the national total, and three quarters of the negdels have between 40,000 and 90,000 head of stock each. The negdels also produce grain, vegetables and, in particular, silage crops. In 1969 the negdels had an average income of 2–3 million tögrögs.

The State farms specialise in, among other things, arable farming, vegetables and fruit, dairy products, pigs and poultry, and timber-processing. The majority of the thirty-six State farms are in northern Mongolia and they own 4·6 per cent of the livestock and farm 78 per cent of the cultivated land. Their workers are paid in money.

The machinery and livestock stations which were established in 1937 were mainly concerned with servicing farm machinery, storing fodder and giving assistance during severe weather conditions. They were phased out between 1960 and 1970, and their work was taken over by the negdels and State farms. During the period 1960 to 1965, fodder-production units were organised to help the negdels. Also seventeen inter-negdel production organisations were formed in various provinces, to do work with which individual negdels would find it too difficult to cope (for example, major construction projects, transport and health services).

During the fifth five-year plan (1971–5) 1900 million tögrögs were invested in agriculture and as a result crop output has been increasing overall. However, livestock numbers remain almost static, although the quality of the stock inproves. There are a number of reasons for this: natural calamities; a severe shortage of labour in the rural areas as urbanisation increases; heavy internal consumption, in addition to exports; and efforts to increase the proportion of cattle and sheep at the expense of goats and camels. The sixth five-year plan (1976–80) envisages a 31 per cent growth in capital investment. (See Table 18.2 for data on Mongolian agriculture.)

TABLE 18.2 Mongolian agriculture – selected data

	Livestock	Grain production (thousand tons)	Number of workers (thousands)	Proportion of national income from agriculture (%)	Income from livestock (%)	Income from crop-farming (%)
1940	26·2	–	1·0	n.a.	99·6	0·4
1960	23·0	227·4	20·4	22·9	71·8	28·2
1970	22·6	284·8	19·5	25·3	81·6	18·4
1975	24·4	482·4	24·9	22·4	76·1	23·9
1976	23·7	376·3	25·8	21·3	78·7	21·3

Industry

Before the revolution of 1921 there was scarcely any industry in Mongolia, apart from some foreign-owned gold mines, a small colliery at Nalaikh, some handicraft businesses and a small electricity-generating plant in Niislel Khüree. In November 1921 the First National Great Khural established guidelines for the development of industry. This was to be based on the livestock economy (leather, meat, wool, and so on), the establishment of handicraft co-operatives (based on carpentry, clothing, and so on) and the exploitation of mineral resources. After the nationalisation of foreign enterprises, between 1926 and 1928, a number of new industrial concerns were developed, including iron workings, brick kilns, timber processing, distilleries and coarse-cloth production; the Nalaikh colliery was expanded and the artisans' co-operative (*artel*, producing leather goods, furniture, and so on) was set up; and various building co-operatives were established. The transport system began to be expanded, and in the late 1930s the first railways were built. From 1921 to 1939 Mongolian industry received substantial technical and financial help from the Soviet Union. The Tenth Congress of the MPRP, in 1940, formally proposed a plan to transform Mongolia from an agrarian into a combined agrarian-industrial socialist economy.

Within this programme the first five-year plan (1948–52) concentrated on improving the livestock economy and food industry. The second five-year plan and the three-year plan (1953–60) saw much greater investment in capital construction and greater industrial diversification. Soviet loans and grants, together with various forms of aid, including manpower from China, were important factors in industrialisation in the 1950s. Other East European countries also gave assistance, particularly after 1962. Until 1962 industry was mostly concentrated in Ulaanbaatar, but, after that year, when the Republic joined Comecon, it began to spread to new development regions. In particular, the regions along the rail link between Ulaanbaatar and the Soviet border saw a major expansion in industrial activity. Existing towns were developed and new towns established, of which Darkhan, founded in 1962, was the largest. The towns of Choibalsan in eastern Mongolia and Uliastai and Ölgii in the western region were developed as light-industrial centres. During the third five-year plan (1961–5) over ninety new factories were set up and over 2400 million tögrögs invested in construction; in the fifth five-year plan (1971–5) industrial investment rose to 4500 million tögrögs. A growth rate of 55 per cent was achieved over this period, and the national income in 1975 was 6·8 times that of 1940.

TABLE 18.3 Mongolian industry – selected data

	Industrial production (million tögrögs)	*Number of industrial workers (thousands)*	*Percentage of national income from industry*	*Number of industrial enterprises*
1940	124·7	13·7	n.a.	n.a.
1960	676·8	35·3	14·6	93
1970	1733·2	46·2	22·6	160
1975	2689·6	53·7	24·7	214
1976	2889·0	55·1	25·1	215

Production figures in 1976 for selected industries:

Coal (million tons)	2·92
Electricity (million kWh)	936·9
Fluorspar (thousand tons)	322·3
Washed wool (thousand tons)	11·4
Bricks (millions)	89·3
Processed meat (thousand tons)	58·6
Industrial alcohol (million litres)	2·2
Matches (million boxes)	6·7
Flour (thousand tons)	131·2
Felt (thousand metres)	587·8
Paper (million printers' sheets)	275·8
Commercial timber (thousand cubic meters)	1066·8

The present five-year plan (1976–80) envisages an industrial growth of 60–65 per cent. The emphasis will be on improving the efficiency and productivity of existing enterprises rather than widespread construction of new factories, although some new factories will be built in industries such as food processing and clothing.[32] The Erdenet copper–molybdenum ore-dressing complex, to be completed during the present plan, will be one of the ten largest in the world.[33] As copper reserves in Mongolia are equal those of the rest of Asia, this sector is found to be significant in the future economic development of the country.

Table 18.3 presents selected data on Mongolian industry, and Figure 18.2 is a graph of the value of industrial production in Mongolia.

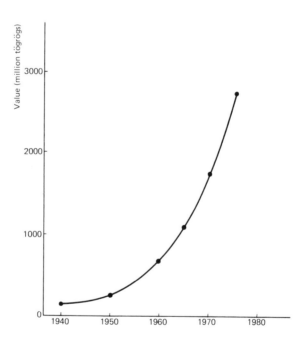

FIGURE 18.2 Industrial production in Mongolia (value in tögrögs at 1967 prices)

Mongolia and Comecon

Mongolia was officially admitted to Comecon[34] in June 1962, although there had already been economic co-operation with the other countries, including China, for several years. Ulaanbaatar's industrial complex was rebuilt in 1959–60 with aid from the Soviet Union, Czechoslovakia, the GDR and Hungary. Czechoslovakia also helped to construct a tannery, and the GDR built a meat-canning plant. As had been the case in the prewar and postwar periods, the Soviet Union supplied most aid. Joint Soviet and Mongolian companies such as Sovmongolmetal (non-ferrous metallurgy), Sovmongolneft (petroleum extraction and refining), Sovmongolbank and the airline and shipping system were formed to accelerate industrialisation.

After 1962 the Comecon countries helped to construct Darkhan and other industrial centres. The Soviet Union supplied capital, technicians, workers and troops to help in the construction, whilst the other Comecon countries sent mainly technical assistance. Projects completed during this period include meat-processing plants, carpet factories, and building-material enterprises. From 1966 to 1970 the Comecon countries supplied over 700 million roubles' worth of aid. Mongolian workers and students have throughout been sent for industrial training in Comecon countries.

Trade

Before the establishment this century of a modern transport system, Mongolia's foreign trading was largely by means of camel and ox-cart caravans to China and Russia. Most of the trade at that time was with China, but companies from other countries, in particular Britain, bought wool, hides and horse tails, and did some mining of gold deposits. Mongolia's trading position changed completely after the revolution, and up to the end of the Second World War virtually all trade was with the USSR. In the postwar period, Mongolia began to develop trading links with East European countries, and with China, Cuba, and so on. In 1976, 95 per cent of foreign trade was with other communist countries (80 per cent with the USSR). In 1974 the value of the Republic's trade with China was 10 million yüan and with Japan $1 million. In 1975 exports to the United Kingdom totalled £118,000, as against imports of £38,000. According to the 1977 figures, the Republic also had a significant trade imbalance with the USSR, imports being

550·4 million roubles (including 375·9 million for machinery, equipment and transport facilities) and exports to the USSR 126·1 million. Exports to the Soviet Union include livestock (over 1 million sheep and goats in 1975), wool, meat, skins and furs, grain and non-ferrous ores.[35]

Just over half of the total imports in 1976 were consumer goods, and the rest were machinery and industrial raw materials. Some trading contacts have also been established outside the communist bloc, with the FRG, Finland, France, Austria, Switzerland, and Japan.

Finance

Table 18.4 presents details of the State budget of Mongolia in 1976.

TABLE 18.4 Mongolian State budget, 1976

Income	Million tögrögs
Turnover taxes	2151·8
Deductions from profits	660·4
Income from forestry and hunting	35·8
Tax levied on agricultural co-operatives	13·2
Social-insurance contributions	128·5
Individual taxation	41·2
Local dues	11·3
Others	200·2
TOTAL	3242·4

Expenditure	Million tögrögs
Economic investment	1243·0
Social and cultural services	1249·5
Administrative expenses, etc.	528·7
TOTAL	3021·2

Structure of national income	%
Industry	25·1
Agriculture	21·3
Construction	5·7
Transport and communications	10·4
Commodity circulation	35·1
Others	2·4
TOTAL	100·0

EXTERNAL AFFAIRS

Foreign relations

Mongolia and Soviet Russia established diplomatic relations and exchanged representatives in 1922. As mentioned earlier, the Mongolian government as early as 1921 tried to persuade China to recognise Mongolia's independence. However, the Chinese Nationalist government refused to accept this until 5 January 1946, and even then the two sides did not exchange diplomatic representatives until after the establishment of the Chinese People's Republic in 1949.

A Mongolian delegation consisting of Tsedenbal[36] and Jargalsaikhan took part in a meeting of the UN Security Council in August 1946 to apply for Mongolian membership of the UN. In February 1946 the Mongolian government formally applied to join the UN, but membership was not granted until 27 October 1961.

In 1978 the Mongolian People's Republic had diplomatic relations with eighty-four countries. A significant recent addition to the list is Japan, with which relations were established in 1972. Prior to that Mongolia already had formal diplomatic relations with a number of West European countries, such as the United Kingdom, France, Sweden and Switzerland. There have been indications for some time that Mongolia and the United States have been considering establishing relations with each other, but no formal steps in this direction have been reported. Mongolia maintains close co-operation with the Soviet Union, and this relationship clearly has an influence on foreign policy.

Defence[37]

Mongolia's armed forces are about 28,000 strong, and of these about 2000 are flying personnel. 13·7 per cent of the annual State budget (407 million tögrögs) is spent on defence. Military service lasts for two years. In addition to military training, many servicemen are involved in civil transport and instruction work.

Outside the standard forces, there is also a para-military security force, with a strength of about 18,000. It is known too that a number of Soviet troops (how many is not known) are stationed in Mongolia for defence and construction purposes.

BIOGRAPHIES[38]

Yumjaagiin Tsedenbal, First Secretary of the Central Committee of the MPRP and Chairman of the Presidium of the People's Great Khural, was born on 17 September 1916 in Davst Sum, Uvs Aimag, north-western Mongolia. He became a member of the Mongolian Revolutionary Youth League in 1931 and a Party member in 1939. He completed his higher education in economics and also lectured in that subject. In 1939 he became Deputy Minister of Finance and later Minister of Finance and Chairman of the State Bank. In 1940 he was elected Secretary-general of the Central Committee of the Party. During the Second World War he held the posts of Deputy Commander-in-chief of the Armed Forces and head of the Department of Political Affairs of the Army. From 1946 to 1947 he was Chairman of the State Planning Commission and Deputy Prime Minister. He became Chairman of the Council of Ministers in May 1952 and remained so until June 1974. In 1958 he became First Secretary of the Central Committee of the MPRP, a post which he has retained continuously since then. In 1974 he was elected Chairman of the Presidium of the Great Khural, and his position as Prime Minister was taken by Dr J. Batmönkh. He is an honorary member of the Academy of Sciences, and has received the honorary title of Hero of Labour of the Mongolian People's Republic (in 1961). Hero of the Mongolian People's Republic (in 1966), the Order of Lenin, the Order of Kutuzov First Class, the F. Juliot-Curie Gold Medal for Peace, and other decorations. In August 1979 he was appointed Marshal of the MPR.

Dr Jambyn Batmönkh, Chairman of the Council of Ministers, was born on 10 March 1926 in Uvs Aimag. After graduating from the State University in 1951, where he obtained an MSc. degree, he held positions in many academic establishments, including the State University, the Pedagogical Institute and the Party Higher School. He has been Deputy Director of the Institute of Economics and was Vice-chancellor of the University from 1967 to 1973. In the Central Committee of the MPRP, to which he was elected in 1971, he was head of the Department of Science and Education. Prior to his appointment, in June 1974, as Chairman of the Council of Ministers, he was Deputy Chairman.

BASIC FACTS ABOUT MONGOLIA

Official name: Mongolian People's Republic (Bügd Nairamdakh Mongol Ard Uls).

Area: 1,565,000 sq. km. (600,000 sq. miles). [Inner Mongolia, 1968: 1,170,000 sq. km., 450,000 sq. miles.]

Length of borders: 7678 km. (3005 with the USSR and 4673 with China).

Terrain and vegetation zones as a proportion of the total land area: forests, 10 per cent; mountain steppe, 20 per cent; plains steppe, 30 per cent; semi-desert (Gov', or Gobi) and desert, 40 per cent; pasture, 83 per cent; unusable land, 3 per cent.

Population (Jan 1978): 1,555,000. [There are also some 1·5 million Mongols in Inner Mongolia, and other areas of China.]

Population density: 1 per sq. km.

Population distribution (1977): urban 47.5 per cent, rural 52·5 per cent.

Birth and death rates (1968): birth rate 42 per 1000, death rate 10 per 1000.

Administrative division: 18 provinces, containing 290 rural districts and twenty-one towns and cities.

Membership of the Mongolian People's Revolutionary Party (Mongol Ardyn Khuv'sgalt Nam) (1976 est.) – MPRP 66,933.

Ethnic nationalities (1969): Khalkh Mongols, 75 per cent; other Mongols, 13 per cent; Kazakhs, 5·2 per cent.

Population of major towns (1977): Ulaanbaatar (the capital), 345,000; Darkhan, 32,900; Erdenet, 27,000 (1976).

Livestock (1976): 23,684,000.

Main natural resources: copper, coal, tungsten, phosphorite, fluorspar, gold and iron ore.

Rail network (1977): 1589 km.

Road network: 1500 km. surfaced roads.

Education (1977): 6 institutions of higher education; 17,000 students.

Foreign trade (in million tögrögs) (1975 est.) (US$1 = 2·91 tögrögs (1979)): exports, 828; imports, 1847.

Main trading partners: 95 per cent of foreign trade with communist countries; 80 per cent with USSR.

Foreign relations: diplomatic relations with 86 countries; 14 diplomatic missions residing in Ulaanbaatar; member of Comecon since 1962; member of UN since 1961.

NOTES

The author would like to express his gratitude to Harvard University for allowing him to use the map in this section, first printed in *History of the*

522   *Marxist Governments*

Mongolian People's Republic, trans. W. A. Brown and U. Onon. Copyright 1976 by the President and Fellows of Harvard College.

1. The word 'Mongol' derives from two words: *mönkh* means 'eternal' and *gol* means 'river'. But some Mongols suggest that there was a river in Mongolia called Mon.
2. Temüjin is derived from the word *temürchin* (*tömörchin*), meaning 'blacksmith'.
3. Chingis derives from the word *tengis* which means a large gulf or ocean.
4. Ecclesiastical (high-ranking lamas) and secular lords (descendants of Chingis Khaan).
5. The total debt amounted to 30 million tael; see U. Onon (trs. and ed.), *Manchu-Chinese Colonial Rule in Northern Mongolia* (forthcoming).
6. The capital city was called Ikh Khüree (Capital, or the Great Lamasery or Big Enclosure). It was renamed Niislel Khüree in 1911 after the proclamation of independence, and Ulaanbaatar (Red Hero) in 1924. It was at one time known as Urga in the West, owing to mispronunciation of Örgöö, which means the residence of a prince.
7. For D. Sükhbaatar and Kh. Choibalsan, see U. Onon (trs. and ed.), *Mongolian Heroes of the 20th Century* (1976) pp. 143–92, 193–216.
8. Ibid.
9. The Party officially became known as the MPRP in March 1925. See W. A. Brown and U. Onon (trs.), *History of the Mongolian People's Republic* (1976) p. 796, note 36.
10. The Bogd (Holy One) was commonly known as the Living Buddha of Urga. He was the eighth reincarnation (1869–1924). The first, Javzundamba Khutagt, lived from 1635 to 1723.
11. The Bogd agreed to the request of the revolutionaries only after he had affixed his seal to similar documents seeking aid from America and Japan. For details see L. Bat-Ochir and D. Dashjamts, *D. Sükhbaatar Namtar* (1967) p. 59.
12. He was captured by the Mongols on 22 August 1921, and executed in Novosibirsk by the Red Army on 16 September 1921.
13. Khiagt is the modern Altan Bulag (see map accompanying this chapter).
14. Deed Shivee is the Russian town of Troitskosavsk, a few miles north of Altan Bulag.
15. For details of this document, see Brown and Onon, *History*, pp. 106–9.
16. The antagonism of some Mongols to the Chinese militarists was deep enough for them to give their support to Baron Ungern.
17. The RSFSR and other republics of what is now the Soviet Union became the USSR in December 1922.
18. See V. I. Lenin, *Collected Works*, vol. XXXI, p. 219; Eng. trs. of the 4th ed. (London: Lawrence and Wishart; Progress Publishers, Moscow, 1966) p. 244. For the text see Brown and Onon, *History*, p. 195. Also see B. Shirendev, *By-passing Capitalism* (1968).
19. *Khural* means an assembly or congress.
20. The idea of 'Elevated by All' is derived from the Sanskrit name of Maha Samadi, who was supposedly the founder of India and (in the ecclesiastical version) the ancestor of the Mongols.

21. For this passage, see Brown and Onon, *History*, p. 209.
22. For example, the ultra-leftists were said to have attacked a lay family of the 'wealthy' class (it had 100 head of livestock) and to have confiscated its property in the same way as that of the feudal families.
23. See Constitution of the Mongolian People's Republic (1960).
24. See *Zaluuchuudyn Ünen* ('Youth Truth'), 29 June 1977.
25. See R. Rupen, *Mongols of the 20th Century* (1964) p. 232.
26. For details see *Mongolia* (London, 1976).
27. See T. Puntsagnorov (ed.), *50 Years of People's Mongolia* (1971) p. 35.
28. In 1921 the Committee of Philology was founded, becoming the Committee of Sciences in 1931. It became the Mongolian Academy of Sciences in 1961.
29. The male population numbered 334,000 in 1922. See *BNMAU-yn Uls Ardyn Aj Akhui, 1976* (1977) p. 35.
30. For a further account of this period see O. Lattimore, *Nomads and Commissars* (1962) pp. 122–47.
31. See A. J. K. Sanders, *The People's Republic of Mongolia* (1968) p. 115. In 1979 currency exchange rates were: $1 = 2·9 tögrögs; 1 rouble = 4·18 tögrögs.
32. See Montsame, *News from Mongolia*, no. 24 (June 1976).
33. See *Mongolia* (Ulaanbaatar) no. 6 (1976).
34. See Puntsagnorov, *50 Years*, pp. 48–50; I. Kh. Ovdiyenko, *Economic-Geographical Sketch of the Mongolian People's Republic* (1965) pp. 80–2.
35. See *Vnyeshnyaya Torgovlya SSSR, 1977* (1978) pp. 223–31.
36. See the brief biography of him near the end of this chapter.
37. See *Europa Year Book 1977: A World Survey*, vol. II (1977) pp. 1113–24; J. Paxton (ed.) *The Statesman's Yearbook 1977/78* (1977) pp. 1166–9.
38. See *Mongolia* (London, 1976) pp. 1, 7.

BIBLIOGRAPHY

Bat-Ochir, L. and Dashjamts, D., *D. Sükhbaatar Namtar* ('Biography of D. Sükhbaatar') (Ulaanbaatar, 1967).
BNMAU-yn Uls Ardyn Aj Akhui, 1976 ('The National Economy of the MPR, 1976') (Ulaanbaatar: Central Statistical Office, 1977).
Brown, W. A. and Onon, U. (trs.), *History of the Mongolian People's Republic* (Cambridge, Mass., and London: Harvard University Press, 1976). (Original published in Ulaanbaatar, 1969.)
Constitution of the Mongolian People's Republic (Ulaanbaatar, 1960).
Europa Year Book 1977, A World Survey, vol. II (London: Europa, 1977).
50 Years of Trade Unions in the People's Republic of Mongolia (Ulaanbaatar, 1976).
Lattimore, O., *Nomads and Commissars* (New York: Oxford University Press, 1962).
Mongolia (London: Diplomatist Publications, 1976).
Mongolia (magazine) (Ulaanbaatar: State Committee for Information. Radio and Television, 1971–8).
Montsame, *News from Mongolia* (information bulletin) (Ulaanbaatar, 1976–8).

Onon, U. (trs. and ed.), *Mongolian Heroes of the 20th Century* (New York: AMS Press, 1976).

——, *Manchu-Chinese Colonial Rule in Northern Mongolia* (London: C. Hurst, forthcoming).

Ovdiyenko, I. Kh., *Economic-Geographical Sketch of the Mongolian People's Republic*, Eng. trs. (Indiana: Mongolian Society, 1965).

Paxton, John (ed.), *The Statesman's Year Book 1977/78* (London: Macmillan, 1977).

Puntsagnorov, T. (ed.), *50 Years of People's Mongolia* (Ulaanbaatar, 1971).

Rupen, R., *Mongols of the 20th Century* (Indiana: Indiana University Press, 1964; The Hague: Mouton, 1964).

Sanders, A. J. K., *The People's Republic of Mongolia* (London: Oxford University Press, 1968).

Shirendev, B., *By-passing Capitalism* (Ulaanbaatar, 1968). (Russian ed., Ulaanbaatar, 1967.)

Vnyeshnyaya Torgovlya SSSR, 1977 ('USSR Foreign Trade, 1977') (Izdatyel'stvo 'Statistika', 1978).

Zaluuchuudyn Ünen ('Youth Truth' – newspaper) (Ulaanbaatar).

Glossary

abgrenzung	sealing off (Germany)
achar	Buddhist leader (Kampuchea)
aimag	province (Mongolia)
apparatchik	government official
chollima	Flying Horse Movement (Korea)
ch'ongsammi	mass line technique in agriculture (Korea)
dambang	sector (Kampuchea)
Dergue	Military Co-ordinating Committee (Ethiopia)
Freier Deutscher Gewerk-schaftsbund	Confederation of Free German Trade Unions (GDR)
indigenato	indigenous
Juche (*chuch'e*)	North Korean State ideology
kebelle	urban dwellers' association (Ethiopia)
Khmer Issarak	Khmer Independence (Kampuchea)
Kommunistischer jungendrerein Deutschlands	Young Communist League of Germany (GDR)
khoroo	town district (Mongolia)
khorshoolol	cooperative (Mongolia)
khum	township (Kampuchea)
khural	assembly (Mongolia)
kiegyezes	compromise (Hungary 1867)
kip	Lao currency unit
kolkhoz	collective farm (USSR)
krajské	regions (Czechoslovakia)
kulak	rich peasant
Lao Itsala	Lao Independence
Lao Loum	lowland Lao
Lao Soung	highland Lao
Lao Theung	upland Lao
líder maximo	commander-in-chief (Cuba)

mestiço	person of mixed European and negro ancestry
městské	cities as administrative units (Czechoslovakia)
meuang	municipality (Laos)
Ministerrat	Council of Ministers (GDR)
negdel	agricultural/production co-operative (Mongolia)
Neo Lao Haksat	Lao Patriotic Front
Neo Lao Itsala	Lao Independence Front
nomenklatura	appointment list controlled directly or indirectly by the Party
okrensí	districts (Czechoslovakia)
Országgyülés	National Assembly (Hungary)
Pathet Lao	Lao nation
phum	hamlet (Kampuchea)
Pracheachon	People's Group (Kampuchea)
quang	province (Kampuchea)
raion	urban district (Mongolia)
ri	village (Korea)
Samizdat	underground publication (USSR)
Sangkum Reastr Niyum	Subjects' Socialist Community (Kampuchea)
Saporanean Kampuchea	Kampuchean National United Front News Agency
sjezd	congress (Czechoslovakia)
srok	district (Kampuchea)
sum	rural district, county (Mongolia)
taean	mass line technique in industry (Korea)
tasseng	district (Laos)
tögrög	unit of currency (Mongolia)
Volkskammer	Parliament (GDR)
wat	Buddhist school (Kampuchea)
zemecha	campaign (Ethiopia)

Index

Paris Agreements (1973), 427
Parliament, *see under*: Cuba, National
    Assembly of People's Power;
    Czechoslovakia, Federal As-
    sembly; German Democratic
    Republic, People's Chamber;
    Guinea-Bissau and Cape
    Verde, People's National As-
    sembly; Hungary, National
    Assembly; Kampuchea,
    Democratic, People's Rep-
    resentative Assembly; Korea,
    DPR, Supreme People's
    Assembly; Laos, National
    Congress of People's Rep-
    resentatives; Mongolia,
    People's Great Khural
Partido Africano de Independência de
    Guiné e Cabo Verde, 367–8,
    370, 371, 372–5
    see also: Guinea-Bissau and Cape
    Verde, Partido Africano de
    Independência de Guiné e
    Cabo Verde
Partition, of Korea, at 38th parallel,
    446
Party–State relations:
    Cuba, 249
    Czechoslovakia, 276–7
    German Democratic Republic, 326
    Guinea-Bissau and Cape Verde,
        372–5
    Hungarian Socialist Workers'
        Party, 397
    Kampuchea, 421, 422, 423
    Korea, DPR, 459–60
    Laos, 480
    Mongolia, 507
Pathet Lao (Lao Nation):
    formation, 471
    forces, 475
    and Royal Lao Government, 472,
        473, 474
    territorial base, 471–2
    see also Lao Itsala; Neo Lao Itsala
Patocka, Jan, 270
Peaceful coexistence, 352–3
Peasant associations (Ethiopia), for-
    mation and role, 301–2

Pen Sovan, biography, 442
People's Central Government
    (Mongolia), 499
People's Chamber (German Demo-
    cratic Republic), 334–6, 338
    membership, 334–5
    powers, 336
    role in constitution, 334
    and State Council, 336
    see also Parliament
People's Committees (Korea, DPR),
    460
People's Great Khural (Mongolia),
    499, 500, 503, 504
    composition, 503
    Presidium, 503, 504
    see also Parliament
People's Group, *see* Pracheachon
People's Militia (Czechoslovakia),
    272
People's National Assembly
    (Guinea-Bissau and Cape
    Verde), 372
    see also Parliament
People's Party (Czechoslovakia), 277
People's Patriotic Front (Hungary),
    396, 397
People's Republic of Kampuchea,
    437–42
    foundation of, 437
    see also Kampuchea [since 7
    January 1979]
People's Representative Assembly
    (Kampuchea), 422–3
    and Standing Committee, 422–3
    see also Parliament
People's Revolutionary Committees,
    440
People's Revolutionary Council of
    Kampuchea, membership of,
    440
Pereira, Aristides, 372
    biography, 380
Pereira, Carlina, 366
Permanent Commission, Partido
    Africano de Independência de
    Guiné e Cabo Verde, 373
Phoumi Vongvichit, 475
Pieck, Wilhelm, 336

DATE DUE

GAYLORD			PRINTED IN U.S.A.